CAMBRIDGE

Grammar for
PET

with answers

Self-study grammar
reference and practice

LOUISE HASHEMI and
BARBARA THOMAS

WITHDRAWN

PUBLISHED BY THE PRESS SYNDICATE OF THE UNIVERSITY OF CAMBRIDGE
Cambridge, New York, Melbourne, Madrid, Cape Town, Singapore, São Paulo

CAMBRIDGE UNIVERSITY PRESS
The Edinburgh Building, Cambridge CB2 2RU, UK

www.cambridge.org
Information on this title: www.cambridge.org/9780521608848

First published 2006

Printed in the United Kingdom at the University Press, Cambridge

A catalogue record for this book is available from the British Library

Library of Congress Cataloguing in Publication data

ISBN-13: 978-0-521-601207 (with answers) and Audio CD
ISBN-10: 0-521-601207 (with answers) and Audio CD

ISBN-13: 978-0-521-601214 (without answers) Paperback
ISBN-10: 0-521-601215 (without answers) Paperback

Designed and produced by Kamae Design, Oxford.

Contents

Exam practice

1 Adjectives

2 Adverbs

3 Comparisons

4 Present tenses

5 Past tenses

6 Present perfect and past simple

7 Past perfect

8 Nouns

9 Determiners and pronouns 1

10 Determiners and pronouns 2

11 Determiners and pronouns 3

12 The future

13 Modals 1

14 Modals 2

Acknowledgements

The authors would like to thank their editors, Alison Sharpe, Jamie Smith and Geraldine Mark, and all the other people who have contributed comments and advice.

The authors and publishers are grateful to the following for permission to reproduce copyright material. It has not always been possible to identify the sources of all the material used and in such cases the publishers would welcome information from the copyright owners:

Photographs: Action Plus: p. 103 All/Neil Tingle; Alamy: p. 22 Todd Bannor, p. 28 PCL, p. 43(c) Mark Sykes, p. 43(r) Justin Kase, p. 87(c) Ian Dagnall, p. 97(cl) Stephen Shepherd, p. 97(cl) David Hoffman Photo Library, p. 109 Robert W. Ginn, p. 125 Charles Bowman; The Bridgeman Art Gallery: p. 101 Van Gogh, Bedroom at Arles, 1888 (oil on canvas), Rijksmuseum Vincent Van Gogh, Amsterdam, The Netherlands; Getty Images: p. 5 (1) Bob Thomas, (2) Catherine Ledner, (3) Manfred Rutz, (4) Charles Gullung, p. 10 Michael Najjar, p. 34(l) Adrian Weinbrecht, p. 43(l) Melissa McManus, p. 46 Taxi, p. 47 Tony Anderson, p. 87(l) John Beatty, p. 87(r) Will & Deni McIntyre, p. 91 Greg Ceo, p. 95 Roberto Espinosa, p. 97(cr) Ghislain & Marie David de Lossy, p. 103 (C) Southern Stock, (F) Jerry Kobalenko, p. 106 Pierre Bourrier, p. 133(l) China Tourism Press, p. 133(r) Mark Scott, p. 142 Britt Erlanson, p. 143 (1) Stephen Derr, (2) Paul Costello, (3) John Sann, (4) Jason Todd, (5) giantstep inc, p. 149 Tim Mosenfelder, p. 160 David Leahy, p. 161 (2) John Sann, (3) Leland Bobbe; Photolibrary.com p. 115(cr) Mark Jones, p. 115(br) Ben Osborne, p. 161 (1) Botanica; Rex Features: p. 97(l) Clive Dixon, p. 103 (G) GPU; Science Photo Library p. 85(l) Ralph Eagle, p. 85(r) Astrid & Hanns-Frieder Michler

Illustrations: Kamae Design: pp. 56b, 57, 62, 77b; Mark Duffin pp. 1, 13, 14, 51, 65, 77t, 97, 99t, 121, 175; Stephane Gamain pp. 7, 22, 49, 55, 61, 67, 73, 75, 79, 127, 157; Ben Hasler pp. 17, 19, 25, 31, 37, 39, 58, 63, 69, 99b, 129, 163; Jo Taylor pp. 56t, 77m, 78, 94, 118, 130, 139, 140, 145, 146, 147, 156, 178; Ian West pp. 33, 112, 135, 165, 169.

(top = t, bottom = b, middle = m, left = l, right = r, centre = c)

To the student

Who this book is for?

This book is for students preparing for the Cambridge Preliminary English Test. It covers the grammar you need for the exam. You can use it with a general English language course for extra grammar practice or with practice tests as part of a revision programme. You can use it in class or for self-study.

What is in the units?

This book contains thirty units. Each unit is in four parts:

A Context listening This introduces the grammar of the unit in context. It helps you to understand the grammar more easily when you study section B. It also gives you useful listening practice. Play the recording and answer the questions. Then check your answers in the key before you read the grammar section.

B Grammar Read through this section before you do the exercises. For each grammar point there are explanations with examples. At the end of each section, there is a note to tell you which exercises in C practise this grammar. You can also check in this section again when you are doing the exercises.

C Grammar exercises Write your answers to each exercise and then check them in the Key.

D Exam practice Each unit has an exam task. These help you practise the different parts of the exam. The exam task is followed by a grammar focus task. This gives you extra practice in the grammar for that unit.

What is in the key?

The key contains:

- answers for all the exercises. Check your answers at the end of each exercise. The key tells you which part of the Grammar section you need to look at again if you have any problems.
- sample answers to help you check your work for exercises where you use your own ideas.
- sample answers for all the writing tasks in the exam practice section. Read these after you have written your own answer. Study the language used and the way the ideas are organised.

Recording scripts

There are scripts for the context listening for each unit, and for the exam practice listening tasks. Look at the script after you answer the questions. It is a good idea to play the recording again while you read the script.

Note on contractions

This book generally uses contractions, for example *I'm* for *I am*, *wasn't* for *was not*, because these are always used in speech and are common in written English. The full forms are used in formal written English.

Irregular verbs

Verb	Past simple	Past participle
be	was were	been
beat	beat	beaten
become	became	become
begin	began	begun
bend	bent	bent
bite	bit	bitten
bleed	bled	bled
blow	blew	blown
break	broke	broken
bring	brought	brought
build	built	built
burn	burnt	burnt
buy	bought	bought
catch	caught	caught
choose	chose	chosen
come	came	come
cost	cost	cost
cut	cut	cut
dig	dug	dug
do	did	done
draw	drew	drawn
drink	drank	drunk
drive	drove	driven
eat	ate	eaten
fall	fell	fallen
feed	fed	fed
feel	felt	felt
fight	fought	fought
find	found	found
fly	flew	flown
forbid	forbade	forbidden
forget	forgot	forgotten
forgive	forgave	forgiven
freeze	froze	frozen
get	got	got
give	gave	given
go	went	gone
grow	grew	grown
hang	hung	hung
have	had	had
hear	heard	heard
hide	hid	hidden
hit	hit	hit
hold	held	held
hurt	hurt	hurt
keep	kept	kept
kneel	knelt	knelt
know	knew	known
lay	laid	laid
lead	led	led
learn	learnt	learnt
leave	left	left
lend	lent	lent

Verb	Past simple	Past participle
let	let	let
lie	lay	lain
light	lit	lit
lose	lost	lost
make	made	made
mean	meant	meant
meet	met	met
pay	paid	paid
put	put	put
read	read	read
ride	rode	ridden
ring	rang	rung
rise	rose	risen
run	ran	run
say	said	said
see	saw	seen
sell	sold	sold
send	sent	sent
set	set	set
sew	sewed	sewn
shake	shook	shaken
shine	shone	shone
shoot	shot	shot
show	showed	shown
shut	shut	shut
sing	sang	sung
sink	sank	sunk
sit	sat	sat
sleep	slept	slept
smell	smelt	smelt
speak	spoke	spoken
spend	spent	spent
spill	spilt	spilt
spoil	spoilt	spoilt
stand	stood	stood
steal	stole	stolen
stick	stuck	stuck
sting	stung	stung
strike	struck	struck
sweep	swept	swept
swim	swam	swum
swing	swung	swung
take	took	taken
teach	taught	taught
tear	tore	torn
tell	told	told
think	thought	thought
throw	threw	thrown
understand	understood	understood
wake	woke	woken
wear	wore	worn
win	won	won
write	wrote	written

A Context listening

A1 Look at the things in the pictures. Which of the adjectives in the box can you use to describe them? You can use some more than once.

| beautiful | long | short | black | grey | white | cotton | leather | silk | wool |

A ...*long black*... B .... C .... D .... E ....

A2 🎧 **1** You are going to hear a conversation between Callum and Emily.
What are they doing? Which of the things in A1 do they talk about?

A3 **1◄◄** Listen to the first part of the recording again and answer these questions.

1 Who is tired? ....*Callum*........
2 Who is excited? ....
3 What is tiring? ....
4 Who isn't really interested in clothes? ....

5 Who is bored? ....
6 What is interesting? ....
7 What is exciting? ....

What is the difference between adjectives ending in *-ed* and *-ing*? Finish the sentences.
We use adjectives ending in .... to describe people.
We use adjectives ending in .... to describe things and people.

A4 **1◄◄** Listen to the second part of the recording again and fill in the gaps.

1 a , ...*lovely*....... .... skirt
2 my .... boots
3 those .... trainers

Look at the adjectives you've written.
Which describe:
someone's opinion? ....
size or shape? ....

colour? ....
the material? ....

What kind of adjectives usually go first? ....
What kind of adjectives usually go last? ....

1

B Grammar

B1 Adjective position

Adjectives usually go before nouns:

I bought a white T-shirt. (**not** *a T-shirt white*)

⚠ Adjectives don't change. (**not** *some whites T-shirts*)

Adjectives go after some verbs (e.g. *be, get, become, look, seem, appear, sound, taste, smell, feel*):

*They're **comfortable** and they'll **look good** with the skirt.*
*The material felt really **soft**.*

⚠ A few adjectives (e.g. *afraid, alone, asleep, awake*) cannot go before a noun:

The cat was asleep on the bed. (**not** *The asleep cat was on the bed.*)

➡ C1

B2 Adjective order

When there are two or more adjectives, they go in this order:

	opinion	size/age/shape	colour	materials	
a	lovely	short	black	wool	skirt
a	beautiful		grey	leather	bag
my	favourite	long	black		boots
some		old	blue		jeans

We put *and*

◆ between two colour adjectives: *a black and white belt*
◆ between two adjectives after a verb: *Clothes shops are always boring and crowded.*

⚠ We don't say *my favourite and long and black boots*

➡ C2

B3 Adjectives ending in *-ing* and *-ed*

Some adjectives have two forms: *-ing* and *-ed*. The adjectives have different meanings:

-ing adjectives describe people and things	*-ed* adjectives describe feelings
Clothes shops are boring.	*I'm bored.*
That's surprising news.	*We're surprised.*
Computer shops are interesting.	*You're not interested in clothes.*

➡ C3

B4 Nouns used as adjectives

When we put two nouns together, the first one works like an adjective, e.g. a *birthday party*:
birthday tells us what kind of party it is.

*a **birthday** party, a **clothes** shop, a **computer** game, a **language** school, a **student** card*

➡ C4, C5

C Grammar exercises

C1 Match the halves of these sentences.

1 My boyfriend sounded ....d.....   a tired because I got up too early.

2 The school was ....g.....   b bad so we didn't drink it.

3 My boss seemed ....e.....   c wonderful because it was home-made.

4 We got ....f.....   d sad on the phone.

5 The bread tasted ....c.....   e angry but she was just in a hurry.

6 I was feeling ....a.....   f wet because we didn't have our raincoats.

7 The milk smelled ....b.....   g unusual because it had no rules.

C2 Rewrite these sentences adding the adjectives in brackets.

1 My friend gave me a ring for my birthday. (*silver/antique*)

    My friend gave me an antique silver ring for my birthday.

2 I wore my jeans when I painted the ceiling. (*old/blue/dirty*)

    I wore my dirty old blue jeans when I painted

3 I borrowed my sister's dress to wear to the party. (*silk/lovely/long*)

    I borrowed my sister's lovely long silk dress

4 I was surprised that Mike wore that jacket. (*white/cotton*)

    I was surprised that mike wore that white cotton jacket.

5 He bought some shoes yesterday. (*expensive/new*)

    He bought some expensive new shoes yesterday -

6 Jenny's father gave her a necklace for her 18th birthday. (*long/gold/beautiful*)

    Jenny's father gave her a beautiful long gold a necklace for her

C3 <u>Underline</u> the correct adjective in each sentence.

1 That was an <u>*interesting*</u>/*interested* lesson.

2 My parents were *tiring*/<u>*tired*</u> after the long flight.

3 We were *boring*/<u>*bored*</u> so we went to the cinema.

4 I enjoy my job but it's very <u>*tiring*</u>/*tired*.

5 You'll be *surprising*/<u>*surprised*</u> when I tell you what happened.

6 We were *exciting*/<u>*excited*</u> about seeing Michael again.

7 All the programmes on TV tonight look <u>*boring*</u>/*bored*.

8 I'm staying in an <u>*amazing*</u>/*amazed* hotel.

9 My friend was *annoying*/<u>*annoyed*</u> with me because I was late.

10 Hans is *interesting*/<u>*interested*</u> in art so I took him to the Picasso exhibition.

C4 Match a noun in A with each noun in B then complete the sentences below.

A

address	alarm	bus	city	credit
football	evening	film	fire
police	traffic	wedding

B

book	boots	car	card	centre
clock	engine	invitation	jam
performance	star	stop

.... address book .... alarm clock ....

.... bus stop ....

....

....

1 I bought a new ....alarm clock........ because I couldn't wake up in the morning.

2 Everyone was looking at the .... as she came into the hotel.

3 The café wouldn't accept my .... so I paid cash.

4 I usually clean my .... when I get home from a match.

5 We couldn't get tickets for the .... so we went in the afternoon.

6 Our teacher was late because there was a big .... on the motorway.

C5 Read this email and look at the adjectives. There are eight mistakes. Correct them.

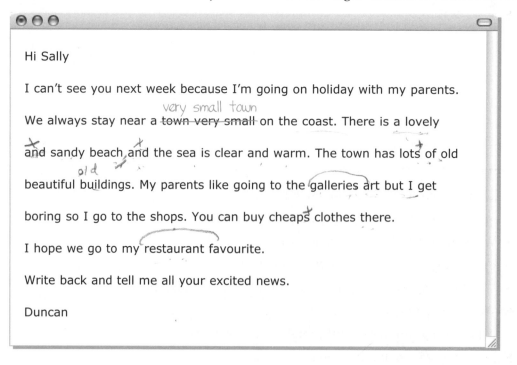

Hi Sally

I can't see you next week because I'm going on holiday with my parents.

                        very small town
We always stay near a ~~town very small~~ on the coast. There is a lovely

and sandy beach, and the sea is clear and warm. The town has lots of old

                old
beautiful buildings. My parents like going to the galleries art but I get

boring so I go to the shops. You can buy cheaps clothes there.

I hope we go to my restaurant favourite.

Write back and tell me all your excited news.

Duncan

D Exam practice

Reading Part 2

The people below all want to hire bikes for short trips.
On the next page there are eight cycle trips in a tourist information brochure.
Decide which trip would be the most suitable for the following people.
For questions **1–5**, mark the correct letter (**A–H**).

1

David is an experienced cyclist. He has a couple of days to spend on his hobby of bird-watching. He has a small tent and wants to get away from the crowds.

2

Ian and his daughters Kim and Kylie would like an easy bike ride with time to play on the beach and have a swim in the sea. They have a picnic with them.

3

Nadine and Lee are interested in old buildings. They don't mind a few hills, but don't want to go to the mountains. They'd like to go to a restaurant for lunch.

4

Elizabeth enjoys cycling to keep fit, but she must be at home in the evening. She enjoys drawing and taking photographs of unusual natural scenery.

5

Zoe and Bea don't want to cycle very far and they can't start early in the morning. They're interested in art and would like to have lunch somewhere near the sea.

RECOMMENDED CYCLE RIDES FROM AILSEA

A Seaview Gallery (less than an hour's ride along the coast road) shows paintings and photographs by local artists in attractive rooms on the cliffs. Open 2pm–5pm. There's a teashop next door which serves delicious lunches and teas.

B An excellent destination for families is Ailsham, where there is a campsite. The route includes only one tiny hill and the views of woods and farmland are lovely. Stop for a picnic under the trees. When you arrive, enjoy a swim in the river, then spend a night in one of the tents provided.

C Picnic at Ailmouth Castle after a two-hour cycle ride along the coast. For five hundred years it has stood on the cliffs, looking down on the dangerous black rocks and waves far below. Now it's a beautiful old ruin. Remember your camera, because you'll want to photograph it at sunset.

D If you enjoy really brilliant scenery and don't mind starting early, go to the mountains for the day. You'll want to bring your camera with you for the amazing rocks, quiet pools and exciting waterfalls. The return journey is all downhill, so you can get back quickly in the afternoon.

E This pleasant flat route uses the pretty little lanes which follow the coast to an excellent sandy beach, less than an hour away. There's plenty of room for ball games and it's very safe to swim. A pleasant day out for anyone who can ride a bike.

F A good day's bike ride through attractive countryside away from the coast brings you to Otterbourne Hall, a historic house open to the public. You can enjoy a surprisingly cheap but delicious lunch in the cosy restaurant, and then you'll be pleased to discover that there are no steep hills on the return route.

G Perfect for active young cyclists who enjoy being alone in beautiful scenery. Leave in the afternoon to catch the wonderful sunset from high in the mountains. Camping is permitted for up to two nights. See wild birds and animals among the rocks and trees.

H Only half an hour's ride away at Fendwich, is a popular new restaurant with amazing views across the beach. Eat a delicious lunch and watch the birds on the cliffs, then look round the souvenir shops before cycling back along the coast. An excellent trip if you don't have a whole day available.

Grammar focus task

Put the two adjectives in each sentence into the correct order. Check your answers by finding them in the text.

1 He told us about the *black/dangerous* snakes in the jungle. dangerous black
2 There was a *beautiful/old* tree in the middle of the field. ....
3 We followed a *flat/pleasant* path beside the river. ....
4 The model wore a *little/pretty* hat which matched her coat. ....
5 The old couple employed two *active/young* students to tidy their garden. ....
6 We went to a concert by a *new/popular* band. ....

A Context listening

A1 Josh lives in Manchester. The rest of his family live in London. What are they all doing on Friday morning?

A2 🎧 2 You are going to hear three conversations Josh has later on Friday.
Conversation 1: Where is Josh? .... Why is he going home? ....
Conversation 2: Where is Josh? .... Why is his sister unhappy? ....
Conversation 3: Where is Josh? .... Where is his sister? .... Why? ....

A3 2◀◀ Listen to conversation 1 again and fill in the gaps with adverbs.

1 I cycle very ....   3 I know I'm .... late for everything.
2 Oh, but ride .... won't you?   4 You've arranged everything ....

How do we usually make an adverb from an adjective? What are the adjectives for these four adverbs?

A4 2◀◀ Listen to conversation 2 again and fill in the gaps.

1 It's going to be .... boring.   3 I wrapped it .... well.
2 We have to work .... hard.   4 It's .... noisy here.

The words you've written are adverbs. How do they change the meaning of the words which follow?

A5 2◀◀ Listen to conversation 3 again. Put the adverbs and adverb phrases on the right into the correct gaps in the sentences. Stop the recording when you need to.

1 Well I can't come ....
2 They .... stop ....
3 The traffic's moving ....
4 She's waiting ....
5 She .... goes ....

outside our house	there
round the corner	patiently	now
always	after school	very slowly
at her friend's house	often
to the station	

Look at the adverbs and adverb phrases you've written. For each one decide if it tells you how often?, how?, where?, or when?

B Grammar

B1 Using adverbs

Adjectives tell us about a **noun**:
He's a careful **cyclist**.

Adverbs tell us about a **verb**:
He **cycles** *carefully*.

Adverbs say how often, where, how much, how and when:

	how often?	verb	how?	where?	when?
I	*often*	*come*		*here*	*on Friday lunchtimes.*
She		*is waiting*	*patiently*	*at her friend's house.*	

Adverbs can be one word or a phrase:
I'm getting on my bike **now**.
I'm **outside my office**.

⚠ Some verbs are followed by adjectives not adverbs. (See Unit 1 Grammar B1.):
You **sound miserable**.   *That's* **unfair**.   *I* **feel happy**.

B2 Forming adverbs

Adjective + *-ly* → adverb
perfect   + *-ly* → *perfectly*
usual   + *-ly* → *usually*

Spelling rules:

adjective ending	adverb
-y — *noisy*	*y* + *-ily* *noisily*
-le *comfortable*	*~~e~~* + *-y* *comfortably*
-e *safe*	keep *-e* + *-ly* *safely*

⚠ Some words look like adverbs because they end *-ly* but they are adjectives (e.g. *friendly, likely, lonely, lovely, silly, ugly*):
He was a **friendly** *man. He told me a* **silly** *story.*
We don't make adverbs from these adjectives. We use a phrase:
He spoke **in a friendly way**.

➡C1

B3 Irregular adverbs

Well is the adverb for *good*:
He's a **good** *boss. He treats us* **well**.

⚠ *Well* is also an adjective (= not ill):
I had stomach-ache last week but I'm **well** *this week.*

Some adjectives and adverbs look the same (e.g. *fast, early, hard, late, daily/weekly/monthly*):

adjective	adverb
*It was a **fast** train.*	*He drove **fast**.*
*He had an **early** breakfast.*	*He always eats breakfast **early**.*
*It's **hard** work.*	*They work **hard**. (**not** They work hardly.) **
*There's a **late** bus on Fridays.*	*We arrived **late**. (**not** We arrived lately.) ***

* The adverb *hardly* = 'almost not'. ** The adverb *lately* = 'recently'.

➡C2

B4 Adverb position

Most adverbs usually go after the verb. If there are several adverbs, they go in this order:

 How?   **Where?**   **When?**

*Josh cycled   **quickly**   **to the station**   **at one o'clock**.*

When? adverbs can sometimes go at the beginning of the sentence.

***At one o'clock** Josh cycled quickly to the station.*

How often? adverbs usually go:
- before a one-word verb: *I **never** see you.*
- before the second part of a two-part verb: *I've **never** forgotten you.*
- BUT after *am/is/are/was/were*: *I'm **often** late.*

The adverbs *already, also, just, still, even* and *only* usually go in the same place as **how often?** adverbs:

*I'm **still** at the station. I've **just** arrived.*

Adverbs do not go between the verb and its object:

*I posted your present on Wednesday. (**not** I posted on Wednesday your present.)*
*I wrapped the present carefully. (**not** I wrapped carefully the present.)*
⚠ We say *He speaks Spanish very well. (**not** He speaks very well Spanish.)*

Too and *as well* = *also* but they usually go at the end of the sentence:
*I sent you a card **as well** / **too**.*

➡C3

B5 Modifying adverbs and adjectives

Some adverbs change the meaning of adjectives or other adverbs:

 extremely   really   very   rather   fairly   quite
 ⟵―――――――――――――――――――――――――――――――――⟶
 strongest   less strong

*She'll be **really** pleased to see you.*
*I cycle **very** quickly.*

➡C4 and C5

2

C Grammar exercises

C1 Look at the adjectives in brackets. For each gap decide whether to make the adjective into an adverb. Write the adverb or the adjective.

Teenagers like to dress (1) ...fashionably.. (fashionable) but their parents don't always think their clothes are (2) .... (suitable). They look (3) .... (unhappy) at their children as they leave the house. Some parents are (4) .... (honest) and say (5) .... (polite) what they think, others get (6) .... (angry) and shout that they don't like the clothes. But the best idea is for parents to sit (7) .... (calm) in their chairs and say nothing. They forget that when they were teenagers they didn't like to dress (8) .... (different) from their friends and they didn't always choose their clothes (9) .... (sensible). But their opinions changed (10) .... (slow) and by the time they were 30, they had started to dress like their own parents!

C2 Look at each word in *italics* and decide whether it is correct. If not, write the correct word.

1 They listened *careful* when the instructor told them what to do. .....*carefully*....

2 The weather today is *well*. ....

3 We trained *hardly* because we had an important match. ....

4 We have a *weekly* spelling test in English. ....

5 I slept *bad* because there was a thunderstorm. ....

6 He answered the question *correctly*. ....

7 I arrived at school *lately* and missed the beginning of the lesson. ....

8 Cara's cousin gave her a *friendly* wave as he left. ....

9 I could understand quite *good* because the teacher spoke *clear*. ....

10 We worked *fast* and finished *early*. ....

C3 Are the adverbs in the correct place in these sentences? Correct any mistakes.

1 You will learn quickly English. ....*You will learn English quickly.*............

2 I missed yesterday the train. ....

3 I enjoyed very much that television programme. ....

4 I usually go to college by bus. ....

5 I never have been to Spain. ....

6 We have just finished painting the room. ....

7 They still were waiting when we arrived. ....

8 This shop always is open on Sundays. ....

9 Taeko and I have already become friends. ....

10 My friends and I went last night to a nightclub. ....

C4 Complete these sentences using an adverb from the box and an adjective you choose.

> very   really   extremely   fairly   rather   quite

1 My town is <u>very crowded in summer.</u>

2 My best friend is ....

3 Some sports are ....

4 In my country the people are ....

5 When I come home from holiday I usually feel ....

6 In winter in Britain the weather is ....

C5 Put the adverbs on the right into the correct place in each line.

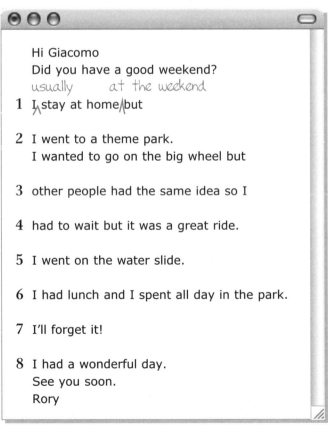

Hi Giacomo
Did you have a good weekend?
1 I *usually* stay at home *at the weekend* but

2 I went to a theme park.
I wanted to go on the big wheel but

3 other people had the same idea so I

4 had to wait but it was a great ride.

5 I went on the water slide.

6 I had lunch and I spent all day in the park.

7 I'll forget it!

8 I had a wonderful day.
See you soon.
Rory

usually   at the weekend

near London   on Saturday

as well

in the queue   patiently   very

also

in a café   at midday

never

there   really

D Exam practice

Reading Part 5

Read the text below and choose the correct word for each space.
For each question, mark the correct letter **A**, **B**, **C** or **D**.

Example:
0 **(A)** every   **B** some   **C** all   **D** most

Family meals

Does your family sit down together **(0)** .... day to share a meal? Does someone plan the food carefully, buy it **(1)** .... and cook it **(2)** .... , so that you really enjoy eating it?

Nowadays, the answer to these questions **(3)** .... often 'no'. Adults are usually working and arrive home late. Granny probably lives too **(4)** .... away to visit regularly. Children eat fast so they never learn that preparing good food and eating healthily **(5)** .... time and thought. In some families, each person eats separately, **(6)** .... television or working at a desk and the children often eat **(7)** ....

By sitting **(8)** .... the table with other people, however, children have the chance to learn that a shared meal is a **(9)** .... for family members to tell each other their news.

But if we can't **(10)** .... eat together, we should try to have family meals at weekends. It's good for our health, it's good for society, and it's fun.

---

1 A local	**B** locally	**C** near	**D** nearly
2 A well	**B** nice	**C** tasty	**D** good
3 A gives	**B** is	**C** has	**D** makes
4 A distant	**B** long	**C** much	**D** far
5 A wants	**B** gets	**C** takes	**D** asks
6 A seeing	**B** looking	**C** watching	**D** attending
7 A single	**B** alone	**C** lonely	**D** privately
8 A at	**B** on	**C** by	**D** in
9 A possibility	**B** chance	**C** situation	**D** event
10 A quite	**B** ever	**C** never	**D** always

Grammar focus task

1 Write the adverbs from the exam task which mean:

1 with care .... 2 in the neighbourhood .... 3 normally ....

4 at the same time each day, week, month etc. .... 5 in a way which is good for your health .... 6 not together .... 7 not in public ....

2 Write the adjectives which the adverbs come from.

1 .... 2 .... 3 .... 4 .... 5 ....

6 .... 7 ....

A   Context listening

A1 You are going to hear someone talking about these three magazines.

Which of the following words do you think she uses?

hairdresser   music   teenagers   homework   posters   holidays   sales
reviews   stadium   journalists   sport   adverts

A2 🎧 3 Listen and tick the words you hear.

A3 3◀◀ Listen to the first part of the recording again and complete the sentences below.

1 *Hits!* seems more ......*colourful*...... than *Buzz*.   4 *Hits!* is .... than *Buzz* too.

2 *Buzz* is as .... as *Hits!*   5 *Buzz* isn't as .... as *Hits!*

3 *Hits!* is less .... than *Buzz*.

A4 3◀◀ Listen to the second part again and tick the correct magazines.

Which magazine:	*Hits!*	*Buzz*	*Smash*
is the newest?			
has got the most reviews?			
is the most expensive?			
has the most adverts?			

A5 Look at A3 and A4. Which exercise is about comparing two things? Which exercise is about comparing more than two things?

B Grammar

B1 Comparative and superlative adjectives

Comparing two people or things:

Hits! *is **smaller than** Buzz.*

Comparing more than two people or things:

Buzz *is the **most expensive** (magazine).*
Hits! *is the **least expensive** (magazine).*

We make comparative and superlative adjectives like this:

adjective	comparative	superlative
one syllable:		
long	+ -er → longer	+ -est → the longest
ending in -e nice	+ -r → nicer	+ -st → the nicest
ending in one vowel + -b, -d, -g, -n, -p or -t big	double the last letter + -er → bigger	double the last letter + -est → the biggest
two syllables:		
famous	+ more → more famous	+ the most → the most famous
ending in -y dirty	-y and + -ier → dirtier	-y and + -iest → the dirtiest
three syllables:		
popular	+ more → more popular	+ the most → the most popular

⚠ Some adjectives are irregular:
good → better → the best, bad → worse → the worst, far → further → the furthest
*His latest song is **better** than his last one. He's **the best** singer in the band.*
*This magazine is **worse** than that one. It's **the worst** magazine I've ever read.*

We also use (*not*) *as... as* and *less ... than* to compare things:
Buzz ***isn't as*** *popular* ***as*** Hits! **or** Buzz *is **less** popular **than*** Hits! (= Hits! *is more popular than* Buzz.)
When two things are the same, we say:
Buzz *is **as** popular **as*** Hits!

▶ more	Hits! *is more colourful than* Buzz.
◀ less	Buzz *isn't as/so colourful as* Hits! / Buzz *is less colourful than* Hits!
= the same	Buzz *is as colourful as* Hits!
▲ the most	Smash *is the most interesting magazine.*
▼ the least	Buzz *is the least interesting magazine.*

➡C1 and C2

B2 Comparative and superlative adverbs

Sometimes we compare **how** we do something:

You can read Hits! ***more easily*** *than* Buzz.
The Smash *journalists write* ***better*** *than some national journalists.*

Adverbs ending in *-ly* form comparatives and superlatives like this:

adverb	comparative	superlative
slowly	*more slowly*	*the most slowly*
beautifully	*more beautifully*	*the most beautifully*
easily	*more easily*	*the most easily*

Other adverbs form comparatives and superlatives like short adjectives:

hard → harder → hardest
My sister works ***harder*** *than I do but Alex works* ***the hardest.***

Some adverbs are irregular:

well → better → the best, badly → worse → the worst
I play the guitar ***well***. *Rob plays the guitar* ***better*** *than me. Rob plays lots of instruments but he plays the guitar* ***the best***.

⚠ We don't use superlative adverbs very often.

➡C3

B3 Comparing nouns

We use *more/the most* to compare both countable and uncountable nouns:

Smash *has* ***more*** *reviews than* Hits!
Hits! *has* ***the most*** *adverts.*
Smash *contains* ***the most*** *information.*

We use *fewer / the fewest* to compare countable nouns:

There are ***fewer*** *adverts in* Smash *than in* Hits!
Hits! *has* ***the fewest*** *posters.*

We use *less / the least* to compare uncountable nouns:

There's ***less*** *rubbish in* Smash *than in* Buzz.
Smash *contains* ***the least*** *rubbish.*

➡C4

C Grammar exercises

C1 Complete these sentences with a comparative adjective.

1 My teacher is friendly but my sister's teacher is ....*friendlier*.... .

2 My bike is big but my brother's bike is ....

3 This biscuit tastes nice but those cakes taste ....

4 Geography is interesting but history is ....

5 I felt nervous but my friend felt ....

6 Tim is rich but John is ....

7 This exercise is easy but the next one is ....

8 Madrid is hot but Bangkok is ....

C2 Write sentences comparing these things.

1 Football / exciting / volleyball. *Football is more exciting than volleyball*

2 Golf / safe / horse-riding. ....

3 Water-skiing / difficult / swimming. ....

4 Motorcycling / noisy / cycling. ....

5 Rugby balls / heavy / tennis balls. ....

Rewrite your answers above in two different ways.

6 *Volleyball isn't as exciting as football. Volleyball is less exciting than football.*

7 ....

8 ....

9 ....

10 ....

C3 Change the adjective in brackets into an adverb.

1 She designed the clothes (*careful*) *She designed the clothes carefully.*

2 She coloured the drawings (*neat*) ....

3 She explained her designs (*good*) ....

4 She sewed her clothes (*beautiful*) ....

Here are the results of a competition for fashion students. Complete sentences 5–8 about Daisy, Jill and Paola using *more* and *the most* with the adverbs in sentences 1–4.

	Daisy	Jill	Paola
designed her clothes	★★★	★★	★
coloured her drawings	★	★★	★★★
explained her designs	★	★★★	★★
sewed her clothes	★★	★★★	★

5 Jill designed her clothes _more carefully_ than Paola but Daisy designed hers _the most carefully_.

6 Jill coloured her drawings .... than Daisy but Paola coloured hers ....

7 Paola explained her designs .... than Daisy but Jill explained hers ....

8 Daisy sewed her clothes .... than Paola but Jill sewed hers ....

C4 Match the words on the left with their opposites on the right.

| expensive   near   old   small   tidy | | big   cheap   far   new   untidy |

Look at the pictures of three houses for sale and correct the sentences below.

A

B

C

Built 1887 £200,000
Two bedrooms,
one bathroom, sitting
room, kitchen, 5kms
from city centre

Built 2004 £155,000
Three bedrooms, two
bathrooms, sitting
room, kitchen, in city
centre

Built 1934 £325,000
Five bedrooms, three
bathrooms, sitting room,
dining room, kitchen,
2 kms from city centre

1 C is the smallest house. _C is the biggest house_ .

2 A is the newest house. _A is_ .

3 B has the most untidy garden. _B has_ .

4 B is the most expensive house. _B is_ .

5 A is the nearest to the city centre. _A is_ .

Now complete these sentences about the three houses using *more, most, fewer* or *fewest*.

6 B has .... rooms than A.

7 C has the .... rooms.

8 B has .... bedrooms than C.

9 A has the .... bedrooms.

10 C has .... bathrooms than B.

D Exam practice

Writing Part 1

Here are some sentences about a radio station.
For each question, complete the second sentence so that it means the same as the first.
Use no more than three words.

Example:

0 Radio 255 is my favourite radio station.

  I think Radio 255 is .... *better* .... **than the other radio stations**.

---

1 Other radio stations have fewer listeners than Radio 255.

  Radio 255 has .... **listeners than other radio stations**.

2 Steve Wood is funnier than all the other disc jockeys.

  Steve Wood is the .... **disc jockey**.

3 I find the sports programmes interesting.

  I .... **in the sports programmes**.

4 The music programmes are less popular than the news programmes.

  The music programmes aren't .... **the news programmes**.

5 I entered a competition but I'm unlikely to win.

  I entered a competition but I .... **likely to win**.

Grammar focus task

Sentences 0, 1, 2 and 4 test comparisons.

Can you complete each of these sentences in a different way so it still means the same?

0 Other radio stations aren't .... Radio 255.

1 Radio 255 has the .... listeners.

2 The other disc jockeys aren't .... Steve Wood.

4 The news programmes are .... than the music programmes.

Present tenses
present simple; present continuous;
state verbs; *have got* and *have*

4

A Context listening

A1 Look at the pictures. What are these places?

A2 🎧4 You are going to hear a tour guide talking to some tourists in a coach. She is telling them about places they can see in a city.

Listen and tick the places in A1 which they see.

A3 4◄◄ Listen again and complete the sentences below.

1 Our tours ~~usually last~~ about one hour.

2 The bus .... into Queens Road.

3 We .... the City Theatre.

4 This Cititour bus .... along the High Street into the market place.

5 At the moment some musicians .... for an outdoor concert there.

A4 Look at your answers to A3 and answer these questions.

1 Which sentences contain the present simple? ....

2 Which sentences contain the present continuous? ....

3 Which sentences tell you about what usually happens? ....

4 Which sentences tell you only about now? ....

A5 Sometimes the tour guide uses *have* and sometimes *have got* before a noun. Look at these words and put them into the correct column.

~~a good time~~   a map   a sore throat   a new entertainment centre   a cinema
air-conditioning   good shops   a walk   lunch

have	have got
a good time	

4◄◄ Look at the recording script on page 182 or listen again and check.

B Grammar

B1 Present simple

+	I/you/we/they + verb he/she/it + verb + **-s**	I **live** in Durrington. She **lives** in Durrington.
–	I/you/we/they **don't** + verb he/she/it **doesn't** + verb	He **doesn't live** in Durrington.
?	Do I/you/we/they + verb Does he/she/it + verb	**Do** you **live** in Durrington?

⚠ We use *do* to make questions and negatives for all verbs except *to be*.

+	I **am** (**'m**) you/we/they **are** (**'re**) he/she/it **is** (**'s**)	I'm here.
–	I **am not** (**'m not**) you/we/they **are not** (**aren't**) he/she/it **is not** (**isn't**)	They **aren't** here.
?	**Am** I ...? **Are** you/we/they ...? **Is** he/she/it ...?	Is she here?

We use the present simple:
- ◆ for habits and things which happen regularly:
  I **go** there most weekends.
  especially with *always*, *never*, *usually*, *often*, and *sometimes*:
  The tour **usually lasts** about one hour.
- ◆ for permanent situations:
  I **live** in Durrington.
  We **don't see** animals in the city centre.
- ◆ for general truths:
  Many tourists **enjoy** coach tours.   ➡C1, C2

(We also use the present simple for the future, see Unit 12.)

B2 Present continuous

+	I **am** (**'m**) + **-ing** you/we/they **are** (**'re**) + **-ing** he/she/it **is** (**'s**) + **-ing**	We're **visiting** Durrington this week.
–	I **am not** (**'m not**) + **-ing** you/we/they **are not** (**aren't**) + **-ing** he/she/it **is not** (**isn't**) + **-ing**	I'm **not visiting** Durrington this week.
?	**Am** I + - **ing** ...? **Are** you/we/they + **-ing** ...? **Is** he/she/it + **-ing** ...?	Are you **visiting** Durrington this week?

We use the present continuous
- ◆ for the present moment:
The bus is now turning into Queens Road.
What are you doing? I'm listening to you.
- ◆ for temporary situations:
This week our tours are taking a little longer.
An international company is using that building for a conference. (= They don't use it all the time.)

(We also use the present continuous for the future, see Unit 12.)   ➡C3

B3 State verbs

Some verbs almost always use simple tenses not continuous tenses:

*Most people **prefer** the new theatre.* (**not** ~~Most people **are preferring** the new theatre.~~)

*I **like** chocolate ice cream.* (**not** ~~I'm **liking** chocolate ice cream.~~)

Here are some important state verbs:

belong, hate, have/have got (= possess, see below), hear, know, like, love, mean, prefer, realise, recognise, remember, see, understand, want, wish   →C4

B4 *Have got* and *have*

+	I/you/we/they **have got** (**'ve got**) he/she/it **has got** (**'s got**)	*I've got a new car.*
−	I/you/we/they **have not got** (**haven't got**) he/she/it **has not got** (**hasn't got**)	*She **hasn't got** a new car.*
?	**Have** I/you/we/they **got** ...? **Has** he/she/it **got** ...?	*Have they got a new car?*

+	I/you/we/they **have** he/she/it **has**	*I **have** a new car.*
−	I/you/we/they **don't have** he/she/it **doesn't have**	*She **doesn't have** a new car.*
?	**Do** I/you/we/they **have** ...? **Does** he/she/it **have** ...?	*Do they **have** a new car?*

We use *have got* or *have* in the present simple (not the present continuous)

◆ for things which we possess:

*We**'ve got** a new entertainment centre. = We **have** a new entertainment centre.*

Has everyone got a map? = Does everyone have a map?

*We **haven't got** any money. = We **don't have** any money.*

◆ for describing things and people:

*It's **got** a cinema and a concert hall.*

*It **doesn't have** enough seats.*

Has he got long dark hair?

◆ for illnesses:

*I've **got** a sore throat.*

⚠ We don't normally use *have got* in the past and the future (see Units 5 and 12).

We use *have* (not *have got*) in many common expressions (*have a bath*, *have a holiday* etc.) to talk about actions. When it means *do, eat, take, enjoy*, etc. we can use simple or continuous tenses:

*I hope you're **having a good time**.*

*Why don't you **have a walk** round there?*

*You can **have lunch** in one of the cafés.*   →C5, C6

4

C Grammar exercises

C1 Read this advertisement for a job as a TV make-up artist. Complete the magazine article below with the correct form of the present simple.

> *Do you want to meet lots of famous people? Can you do this?*
>
> **4 am** Get up.
>
> **5 am** Arrive at the TV studio. Have a coffee.
>
> **5.10** Prepare the make-up room.
>
> **6 am** Do make-up for the newsreaders.
>
> **6.30–11.30** Work with guests on morning TV shows. No time for a break.
>
> **12** Have lunch with colleagues.
>
> **1 pm** Order new make-up.
>
> **2 pm** or later Leave the studio.
>
> Apply to Megalith TV Ltd Box 2343

A hard day at the studio.

Sharon usually 1 _gets up at four o'clock_. She hates that! She 2 .... at the film studio at five and 3 .... a coffee. She 4 .... her room carefully. At six, she 5 .... the make up for the newsreaders and for the next five hours she 6 ....with guests on morning TV shows. She 7 .... time for a break but at noon she 8 .... lunch with colleagues. After lunch she 9 .... new make-up. She 10 .... the studio before two o'clock. It's a tiring job!

C2 Now make some notes about your typical day and then write a short description of it.

I usually get up at ....

C3 Read this mobile phone conversation. Fill in the gaps with a verb from the box in the correct form of the present continuous.

come	come	~~do~~	get	get	leave
read	shout	sit	talk	wait	

Mandy: Dwayn? This is Mandy.

Dwayn: Hi Mandy. Why aren't you here? What 1 _are you doing_ (you)? 2 .... (you) to this party?

Mandy: 3 I .... on the bus.

Dwayn: What?

Mandy: The bus has broken down. We 4 .... for another bus to come and take us to town.

Dwayn: Oh, no.

Mandy: Yes. Some of the passengers **5** .... angrily, but what can the driver do?

Dwayn: **6** .... (he) to them?

Mandy: No, he **7** .... a newspaper. Ah, here's the other bus. I **8** .... on to it now. The bus **9** .... I **10** .... to the party!

C4 Here is part of a student's letter to a penfriend. Fill in the gaps with the correct form of the present simple or continuous.

Dear Pari

1 ...*I'm*... (I/be) a university student. As it's holiday time now, **2** .... (I/work) in a hotel. At the end of every term **3** .... (I/come) back to my home town and
4 .... (I/get) a job in this hotel to earn money.
5 This summer .... (I/share) a room in the hotel with another girl.
6 ....(It/not be) as comfortable as my parents' house, but **7** ....
(I/prefer) it, because **8** .... (I/not want) to travel home late at night. So this year
9 .... (I/save) more money and **10** .... (I/get) more sleep.

C5 For each of these sentences, write another sentence with the same meaning. Use *have got.*

1 There are five bedrooms in our house. _Our house has got five bedrooms._

2 My head hurts. ....

3 Her hair is long and straight. ....

4 Is there a swimming-pool at your hotel? ....

5 I'm not rich. ....

6 Are there locks on these suitcases? ....

7 The doctor is too busy to see you today. ....

C6 Underline the correct form of the verb.

1 I *know/am knowing* this part of town quite well.

2 Amy *has/is having* very small feet.

3 We *go/are going* on holiday with my grandparents every summer.

4 My grandmother *stays/is staying* in my room this week so I *sleep/am sleeping* in the sitting-room.

5 *Do you understand/Are you understanding* my situation?

6 Can I phone you back in ten minutes? We *have/are having* breakfast at the moment.

7 These CDs *belong/are belonging* to my sister.

8 Have you seen John's email? He *has/is having* a great time in Tokyo.

D Exam practice

Look at the Writing Part 2 task below.

Write down some ideas for your answer. Use some of these words if you want.

bed and breakfast   cafés   campsite   hotel   nightclubs   restaurants
shops   sports hall   tennis courts   youth hostel

Grammar focus task

Think about which tenses you will use to:
- describe where you are staying.
- write about the facilities.
- say what you do in the evenings.

1 When will you use the present continuous?
2 When will you use *have got*?
3 When will you use the present simple?

Now do the exam task below.

Writing Part 2

You are on holiday in a seaside town.

Write a postcard to an English friend of yours. In your postcard, you should

- describe where you are staying
- say what facilities the town has got
- tell your friend what you do in the evenings.

Write **35–45 words**.

A Context listening

A1 Look at each picture of Donny. Where is he?

A2 🎧 5 Listen and check if you were right.
What news does Donny tell his mother?

A3 5◄◄ Listen again and answer the questions below.

1 What did Donny's mother do at eight o'clock? ....

2 Why didn't he answer his phone? ....

3 What did she do at nine o'clock? ....

4 Why wasn't his phone switched on? ....

5 What did she do at ten o'clock? ....

6 Why didn't he answer his phone at ten o'clock? ....

5◄◄ Now listen again and read the recording script on p.183 to check your answers.

A4 Look at your answers to A3 and answer these questions.

1 Which sentences contain the past simple? ....

2 Which sentences contain the past continuous? ....

3 Which sentences tell you about a past activity which continued for some time?
....

4 Which sentences tell you about a single event? ....

B Grammar

B1 Past simple – forms

In the past simple
- we add *-ed/-d* to regular verbs: *want → wanted, hope → hoped, shop → shopped*

+	I/you/he/she/it/we/they + verb + **-ed/-d**	*I phoned you.*
–	I/you/he/she/it/we/they **did not** (**didn't**) + verb	*She didn't phone me.*
?	**Did** I/you/he/she/it/we/they + verb	*Did you phone me?*

- some verbs are irregular and do not end in *-ed/-d*: *buy → bought, go → went, make → made* (See p.viii.)

+	I/you/he/she/it/we/they + irregular past verb	*I went to the cinema.*
–	I/you/he/she/it/we/they **did not** (**didn't**) + verb	*They didn't go to the cinema*
?	**Did** I/you/he/she/it/we/they + verb	*Did you go to the cinema?*

- *to be* has two forms (*was* and *were*)

+	I/he/she/it **was** you/we/they **were**	*I was there.*
–	I/he/she/it **was not** (**wasn't**) you/we/they **were not** (**weren't**)	*They weren't there.*
?	**Was** I/he/she/it ...? **Were** you/we/they ...?	*Were you there?*

B2 Past simple – use

We use the past simple
- for completed actions, events and situations in the past:
  *I **wanted** to see the new film.*
  *Your phone was on but you **didn't answer**.*
  *Why **didn't** you **answer**?*
  *She **left** the desk and **ran** out of the building.*

➡ C1

B3 Past continuous – forms

We form the past continuous of all verbs with *was/were* + *-ing*:

+	I/he/she/it **was** + verb + **-ing** you/we/they **were** + verb + **-ing**	*I was having a coffee.*
–	I/he/she/it **was not** (**wasn't**) + verb + **-ing** you/we/they **were not** (**weren't**) + verb + **-ing**	*We weren't having a coffee.*
?	**Was** I/he/she/it + verb + **-ing** ...? **Were** you/we/they + verb + **-ing** ...?	*Were they having a coffee?*

⚠ We do not use state verbs in the past continuous. (See Unit 4.)

➡ C2

B4 Past continuous – use

We use the past continuous

◆ for an unfinished activity around a time in the past:
*At nine o'clock I **was sitting** in the cinema.*

> 8.30 ← ... *I was sitting in the cinema* ... → 9.45
>
> 9 o'clock

⚠ Compare: *At 8.30 I **sat** down.* (= one event at 8.30)

◆ for a past activity beginning before a past event and continuing until or after it. For the event we use *when* + the past simple:
*I **was talking** to the manager **when** you rang **me**.*

> (I started talking to the manager) ... *I was talking* ... (I continued talking)
>
> You rang me

***When** I **went** out, you **were having** a shower.*

> I went out
>
> ← ... *You were having a shower* ... →

*I **was leaving** the cinema **when** I **saw** a notice.*

> ← ... *I was leaving* (I stopped to read it)
>
> I saw a notice

(Compare: *I **left** the cinema then I **saw** a notice.* = 1 I left, 2 I saw. See Unit 30.)

◆ for two activities at the same time in the past (often with *while* or *and*):
*I **was sitting** near the ticket desk **and** the manager **was talking**.*

> I was sitting
>
> the manager was talking

*I **was having** a coffee **while** I **was waiting**.*

> I was having a coffee
>
> I was waiting

→C3, C4, C5

5

C Grammar exercises

C1 Read this postcard and put the verbs in brackets into the past simple.

Hi Niki. We **1** ..made.. (make) a trip to Brighton last week. We
2 .... (visit) the Pavilion, and **3** .... (see) the
nineteenth century kitchen. I'm glad I **4** .... (not work)
there in those days. The dining-room **5** .... (be) my
favourite room. We **6** .... (have) coffee in the restaurant,
then we **7** .... (go) for a walk by the sea and
8 .... (eat) some fish and chips for lunch. We **9** ....
(spend) the afternoon shopping. We **10** .... (find) some
funny little shops where we **11** .... (buy) some unusual
clothes. **12** .... (you/go) anywhere interesting in the
holidays?
Love, Jenny.

C2 Tanya and her brother Tony gave a party together. Use the information below and write sentences with the past continuous to show how they prepared for the party.

	Tanya	Tony
10 am	make a shopping list	email their friends
1 pm	buy the drinks	choose the music
3 pm	tidy the house	prepare the food
6 pm	blow up the balloons	decorate the rooms
7 pm	iron her dress	have a shower

1 At ten o'clock _Tanya was making a shopping list and Tony was emailing their friends._

2 At one o'clock ....

3 At three o'clock ....

4 At six o'clock ....

5 At seven o'clock ....

C3 Complete each sentence with a verb from Box A in the past continuous and a verb from Box B in the past simple.

A	climb	cook	~~dance~~	stay
	study	tidy	work	

B	burn	discover	meet	fall
	paint	~~play~~	see	

1 I ..was dancing.. with my boyfriend when the disc jockey ..played.. our favourite song.

2 My parents .... in a restaurant when they ....

3 I .... grammar when I .... asleep.

4 The chef .... spaghetti when he .... his hand.

5 The artist .... in the South of France when she .... her most famous picture.

6 The scientist .... his laboratory when he .... the new drug.

7 We .... the wall when the gardener .... us.

C4 Read this email and <u>underline</u> the best tense for each verb.

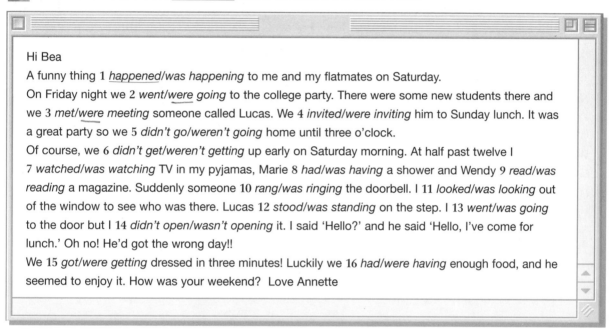

Hi Bea

A funny thing 1 *happened*/*was happening* to me and my flatmates on Saturday.

On Friday night we 2 *went*/*were going* to the college party. There were some new students there and we 3 *met*/*were meeting* someone called Lucas. We 4 *invited*/*were inviting* him to Sunday lunch. It was a great party so we 5 *didn't go*/*weren't going* home until three o'clock.

Of course, we 6 *didn't get*/*weren't getting* up early on Saturday morning. At half past twelve I 7 *watched*/*was watching* TV in my pyjamas, Marie 8 *had*/*was having* a shower and Wendy 9 *read*/*was reading* a magazine. Suddenly someone 10 *rang*/*was ringing* the doorbell. I 11 *looked*/*was looking* out of the window to see who was there. Lucas 12 *stood*/*was standing* on the step. I 13 *went*/*was going* to the door but I 14 *didn't open*/*wasn't opening* it. I said 'Hello?' and he said 'Hello, I've come for lunch.' Oh no! He'd got the wrong day!!

We 15 *got*/*were getting* dressed in three minutes! Luckily we 16 *had*/*were having* enough food, and he seemed to enjoy it. How was your weekend? Love Annette

C5 Read this newspaper article and put the verbs in brackets into the correct tense, past simple or past continuous.

An honest customer

Yesterday Jon Atkins 1 ....*went*........ (*go*) into Harpers' Art Gallery at the end of the afternoon. He 2 .... (*want*) to buy a present for his mother. It 3 .... (*be*) nearly closing time and owner Michael Harper 4 .... (*count*) the money. Quickly Jon 5 ....(*choose*) a small picture and Mr Harper 6 .... (*wrap*) it for him. While 7 he .... (*wait*) for his bus, Jon 8 .... (*decide*) to look at the picture again. In the parcel he 9 .... (*find*) £500 in cash as well as the picture. He 10 .... (*run*) back to the shop. It was closed so Jon 11 .... (*look*) through the window.

Michael Harper 12 .... (*search*) under the counter, and his assistants 13 .... (*look*) in all the cupboards and drawers. 'I 14 .... (*knock*) on the window and 15 .... (*wave*) the money at them' said Jon.

'I was so happy,' said Mr Harper. 'It's wonderful to know that there are honest people like Jon.'

D Exam practice

Look at the Writing Part 3 task below. What tense is used in the first sentence of the story? Here are some sentences which can follow. Put the verbs into the correct tense.

A man 1 <u>was walking</u> (walk) slowly towards the café. He 2 .... (carry) a huge box. Suddenly he 3 .... (stop) and 4 .... (look) around him. A woman 5 .... (follow) him. He 6 .... (drop) the box and 7 .... (run) towards the café.

Now think about your story. You can finish the story above or write your own story. Write down some ideas. Use these questions to help you:

Who are the people in your story?
What were they doing in the market square?
What happened?
How does your story end?
Which tenses will you use?

Now do the exam task below.

Writing Part 3

- Your English teacher has asked you to write a story.

- Your story must begin with this sentence:

  One day last week I was sitting in a café in the market square.

- Write your **story** in about 100 words.

Present perfect and past simple
present perfect and past simple; *have gone* and *have been*

A   Context listening

A1   James shares a flat with his sister Annie. James is having a birthday party. Look at the pictures and guess what happened.

A2   🎧 6   You are going to hear some conversations at the birthday party.
How does Garry know Annie? What happens at the end?

A3   6◀◀   Listen again and complete the sentences below.

1 I .... all the balloons up yet.

2 I still .... my hair.

3 I .... it this morning.

4 .... you two already .... ?

5 I .... there for two months.

6 I .... Annie last week at the cinema.

7 She .... there since April.

8 I .... in the cinema for you on Saturday.

9 But I .... just .... her!

10 She .... an hour ago ...

A4   Look at your answers to A3 and answer these questions.

1 Which sentences are about an action or event in the past which is finished? Which tense is used?

2 Which sentences contain the words *yet*, *still*, *already* and *just*? Which tense is used?

3 Which sentences contain the words *for* and *since*? Which tense is used?

6

B Grammar

B1 Present perfect

We form the present perfect with *has/have* + past participle.

The past participle
- for regular verbs (*want* → *wanted*) and a few irregular verbs (*make* → *made*) is the same as the past simple.
- for most irregular verbs is different from the past simple (*break* → *broke, broken*; *go* → *went, gone*). (See p.viii.)

+	I/you/we/they **have** + past participle he/she/it **has** + past participle	*They've arrived.*
–	I/you/we/they **have not** (**haven't**) + past participle he/she/it **has not** (*hasn't*) + past participle	*He **hasn't arrived**.*
?	**Have** I/you/we/they + past participle ...? **Has** he/she/it + past participle ...?	*Has **it arrived**?*

➡ C1

B2 Present perfect and past simple (for past simple forms see Unit 5)

We use the present perfect **not** the past simple	We use the past simple **not** the present perfect
◆ for past events when the exact time is not important, but the result is interesting now: *They **have moved** to another town.* (= They don't live here now.) *She's **passed** her driving test.* (= She can drive to work.) *The bus **has arrived**.* (= We can get onto it.)	◆ for past events at a particular time: *They **moved** in July.* *She **passed** her driving test yesterday.* *The bus **arrived** at six.*
◆ for a period of time beginning in the past and continuing to now (often with *since* and *for*): *You **have worked** very hard.* some time in the past → now *You've worked very hard.* *I've **worked** there for two months.* *I've **worked** there since April.* (= I still work there now.)	◆ for a period of time beginning and ending in the past (sometimes with *for*): *You **worked** very hard last year.* last year now *You worked very hard.* *She **worked** at the cinema for ten months.* (= But she doesn't work there now.)

◆ *not* with *still* and *yet* and in questions with *yet*:
*I **still haven't dried** my hair.* (= it's wet)
*I **haven't put** the balloons up **yet**.* (= I want to – they're on the floor)
*Have the guests **arrived yet**?*

⚠ *Still* goes before the verb and *yet* goes after it.

◆ for questions asking *how long* until now:
*How long **have** you **known** Annie?*

◆ for actions and events started in the past which are finished, often with *ago*:
*I **dried** my hair half an hour **ago**.* (= it was wet but it's dry now)
*I **didn't put** the balloons up.* (= because I decided not to have a party)

◆ for questions asking *when*:
*When **did** you **meet**?*

B3 Other uses of the present perfect

We use the present perfect

◆ with *just* for an event a short time before now:
*I've **just met** her.* (= a few minutes ago)

◆ with adverbs *already*, *before*, *ever* and *never*, meaning 'before now' (see also Unit 2):
*We've **already met**.*
*Has he **ever met** her?*
*We've **met before**.*

◆ with superlatives (see Unit 3):
*You make **the best** pizza I've ever **eaten**.*

◆ after the expressions *the first/last* etc. *time*:
*That's the **second time** you've **asked** me.*

➡C3

B4 *Have gone* and *have been*

⚠ *To go* has two forms in the present perfect: *have gone* and *have been*. The meanings are different.

He's been to the shops.
(= He went there and then returned home.)

She's gone to the city centre.
(= She went there and she's there now.) ➡C4

C Grammar exercises

C1 Rhiannon is preparing for a trip abroad with her friend Ellen. Look at the list she made yesterday evening and then complete the email she has sent to Ellen, using the present perfect.

To do
photocopy passport ✓
collect travellers' cheques ✓
buy money belt ✓
check camera ✗
choose clothes ✓
pack rucksack ✗
phone Granny ✓
see my cousins and say goodbye ✓
find my address book!! ✗ Ellen look?
get coach ticket ✗

Hi Ellen
Are you ready? I am, almost!
Today 1 I *'ve photocopied my passport*, 2 I*'ve collected* my travellers' cheques and 3 I*'ve bought* a money belt. 4 I*'ve checked* my camera, but 5 I *'ve chosen* my clothes. 6 I *'ve packed* my rucksack. I can do that tomorrow. 7 I .... Granny and 8 I .... my cousins and 9 I .... goodbye to them. One problem: 10 I still .... my address book. 11 .... (you) .... for it in your flat?
Phone me if you find it. I'm going to the coach station now because I 12 .... my ticket to the airport.
See you tomorrow evening at the check-in desk!
XX R

C2 A film has just won a prize. Journalist Ali has interviewed the director, Mike, and the star, Nika, for his magazine. Fill in the gaps using the verbs in brackets in the present perfect or the past simple.

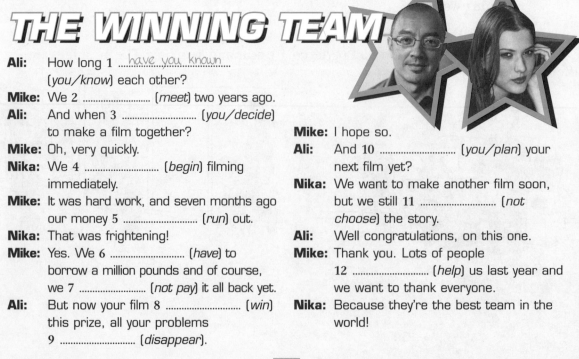

THE WINNING TEAM

Ali: How long 1 *have you known* (*you/know*) each other?

Mike: We 2 .... (*meet*) two years ago.

Ali: And when 3 .... (*you/decide*) to make a film together?

Mike: Oh, very quickly.

Nika: We 4 .... (*begin*) filming immediately.

Mike: It was hard work, and seven months ago our money 5 .... (*run*) out.

Nika: That was frightening!

Mike: Yes. We 6 .... (*have*) to borrow a million pounds and of course, we 7 .... (*not pay*) it all back yet.

Ali: But now your film 8 .... (*win*) this prize, all your problems 9 .... (*disappear*).

Mike: I hope so.

Ali: And 10 .... (*you/plan*) your next film yet?

Nika: We want to make another film soon, but we still 11 .... (*not choose*) the story.

Ali: Well congratulations, on this one.

Mike: Thank you. Lots of people 12 .... (*help*) us last year and we want to thank everyone.

Nika: Because they're the best team in the world!

C3 Complete each sentence with a word or phrase from the box.

> ago   already   ever   for   how long   just   never
> since   still   when   yet

1 I don't want to swim now because I've ....*just*......... had lunch.
2 My family has lived in this house .....*since*..... thirty years.
3 Elena has ....*Never*.... played volleyball. She doesn't enjoy sport.
4 Jordan left school a year .....*ago*..... .
5 ..*how long*.. have you been a member of the swimming team?
6 I haven't seen my boyfriend ....*for*........ last weekend.
7 ....*when*.... did Zoe join the theatre company?
8 We've ...*already*... booked our holiday. We're going to Corfu.
9 Have you ....*ever*....... worked in a shop before or is this your first job?
10 Neil ......*still*...... hasn't paid me the money he owes me.
11 The boss hasn't arrived ......*yet*...... so we needn't start work.

C4 Look at each pair of sentences. Mark S if their meaning is the same or D if it is different.

1 Have you ever ridden a motorbike?
   Have you ridden a motorbike recently? .....*D*.....

2 She's worked here since the summer.
   She didn't work here after the summer. ....

3 I've been to London twice this year.
   I've just come back from London. ....

4 This is the most expensive holiday I've ever had.
   I've never had such an expensive holiday before. ....

5 My father hasn't been to the theatre for ten years.
   My father didn't go to the theatre ten years ago. ....

6 We've already seen this film.
   We've seen this film before. ....

7 He still hasn't read that book.
   He hasn't read that book yet. ....

8 This is the second time I've visited Crete.
   I've been to Crete once before. ....

6

> ⚠ This task tests grammar from the rest of the book as well as the grammar in this unit.

Writing Part 1

Here are some sentences about a visit to a new sports centre.
For each question, complete the second sentence so that it means the same as the first.
Use no more than three words.

Example:

0 This is the first time I've been to this sports centre.

   I've ....*never*............ **been to this sports centre before.**

---

1 The old sports centre isn't as big as the new one.

   The new sports centre is .... **the old one.**

2 The sports centre doesn't have a swimming pool.

   The sports centre hasn't .... **a swimming pool.**

3 They're still building the squash courts.

   They .... **finished building the squash courts yet.**

4 My friend started work here three weeks ago.

   My friend .... **here for three weeks.**

5 He finds the work enjoyable here.

   He .... **working here.**

> ### Grammar focus task
>
> **Check your answers. Now look at these pairs of sentences. Are they the same or different?**
>
> **1** I've never been to this sports centre before.
>
>   I've already been to this sports centre. ....
>
> **2** They haven't finished building the squash courts yet.
>
>   They've just finished building the squash courts. ....
>
> **3** I haven't been to the sports centre yet.
>
>   This is the first time I've been to the sports centre. ....

A Context listening

A1 You are going to hear Peter talking on the radio about a city he visited last week. Here are two pictures of the city. Which is from last week? Which is from seven years ago?

A2 🎧 7 **Listen and check if you were right.**

Why did Peter go there?
What changes did he see?

A3 7◀◀ **Listen again and complete the sentences below. Stop the recording if you need to.**

1 Well, last week I ....visited.......... my home city.

2 When I .... , Stefan .... his work for the day ...

3 When we .... lunch, we .... by the river.

4 The riverside .... the factory area ...

5 There didn't .... a sports centre in the city.

6 The engineers .... it the year I ....

7 I .... to become an engineer ...

8 I .... into the restaurant and I .... all my old friends.

A4 Look at your answers to A3 and answer these questions.

1 Look at sentences 4 and 5 and complete this statement.

We use .... to talk about things that were different in the past.

2 Look at the other sentences. Which contain two different verb forms? ....

In these sentences did one event happen before the other? ....

B Grammar

B1 Past perfect

We form the past perfect with *had* + past participle. (See notes on past participles in Unit 6 and the table of irregular verbs on p. viii.)

+	I/you/he/she/it/we/they **had** + past participle	*We'd eaten lunch.*
–	I/you/he/she/it/we/they **had not** (**hadn't**) + past participle	*I hadn't eaten lunch.*
?	**Had** I/you/he/she/it/we/they + past participle ...?	*Had they eaten lunch?*

→C1

B2 Past perfect and past simple

We use the past perfect

♦ to talk about something that happened before a past event:
*Last week I **visited** my home city. It **had changed** a lot.*

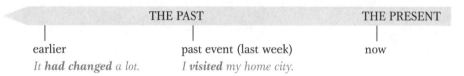

	THE PAST		THE PRESENT
earlier	past event (last week)		now
*It **had changed** a lot.*	*I **visited** my home city.*		

*I **walked** into the restaurant and I **saw** all my old friends. Stefan **had invited** them to join us.*

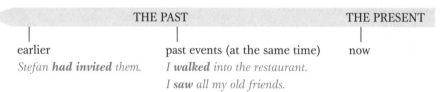

	THE PAST		THE PRESENT
earlier	past events (at the same time)		now
*Stefan **had invited** them.*	*I **walked** into the restaurant.*		
	*I **saw** all my old friends.*		

♦ in sentences that have *when* + past simple, to show that one event happened before the other:

When I arrived, Stefan **had finished** his work. =	1 He finished work
	2 (later) I arrived.

The two actions are separate.

Compare:

When I arrived, Stefan **stopped** work. =	I arrived and he stopped work at that time.

The two actions are probably connected.

B3 Past perfect not past simple

We always use the past perfect not the past simple with *already*, *ever*, *never* and *just* when we mean before a time in the past:

They **'d just started** the year I left. (**not** ~~They just started the year I left.~~)

I **had already decided** to become an engineer. (**not** ~~I already decided~~)

I **'d never seen** anything like it. (**not** ~~I never saw~~)

⚠ *Already*, *ever*, *never* and *just* go between the auxiliary and the main verb.   ➡C2

B4 *used to*

+	I/you/he/she/it/we/they **used to** + verb	I **used to live** in the city.
−	I/you/he/she/it/we/they **did not** (**didn't**) **use to** + verb	They **didn't use to live** in the city.
?	**Did** I/you/he/she/it/we/they **use to** + verb...?	**Did** she **use to live** in the city?
	We make negatives and questions with *did* like a regular verb in the past simple (see Unit 5).	

⚠ There is no present tense of *used to* (**not** ~~I use to~~ etc.). We use the present simple (see Unit 4).

I meet my friends on Saturday evenings. **not** ~~I use to meet my friends on Saturday evenings~~

We use the verb *used to* to talk about the past when we want to emphasise that things are different now:

*It **used to be** the factory area.* (= It isn't the factory area now.)

THE PAST		NOW
It **used to be** the factory area.	The factories were knocked down.	It's a park.

*I **used to watch** the engineers.* (= I don't watch them now.)

*We **used to see** a lot of big lorries in the city.* (= We don't see them now.)

*There **didn't use to be** a sports centre in the city.* (= There is now.)

***Did** there **use to be** less traffic?* (= There's a lot of traffic now, but I want to know if it has increased.)   ➡C3, C4, C5

C Grammar exercises

C1 Complete this email by putting the verbs in brackets into the past perfect.

Hi Billy
Well, I'm home from Africa. The late flight from Paris caused some problems at first but the holiday was great
Because 1 ...we'd never visited... (never/visit) that part of the world before, 2 ....
(we/ask) the holiday company to book us seats on the bus to the city centre to meet the tour manager. Our plane was an hour late and we ran through the airport to the car park but when we arrived the bus 3 .... (just/leave). We got a taxi to the main square and found the company's local office, but the staff 4 .... (already/go) home for the day.
We 5 .... (not/bring) our mobiles, because they don't work in that country. At last we found a post office and luckily it 6 .... (not/shut) yet, so we called the company's head office in Canada.
In ten minutes the tour manager was with us. He 7 .... (go) to the airport to meet us, because he 8 .... (realise) our plane was late, but we 9 .... (not/see) him. Anyway, he took us to the hotel he 10 .... (book) for us and bought us dinner.
So everything was fine in the end. And our trip to the jungle was amazing!! I'll show you the photos when I see you.
XXXX Julie

C2 In each of these sentences, one of the verbs should be in the past perfect. Underline the verb and write the correction at the end.

1 I wanted to have a shower when I got home, but my sister <u>just had</u> a bath and there wasn't any hot water. ...had just had.

2 The concert started when we got to the theatre, so we missed the first two songs. ...
....

3 I couldn't tell my teacher about the film because I never saw it. ....

4 Freya didn't finish breakfast when I arrived, so I had a coffee while she ate her toast. ....

5 The children were very excited about flying because they were never in a plane. ....

6 Colin didn't know the poem but the other students already studied it. ....

7 We just visited Japan so we told our friends some good places to visit when they went there.
....

C3 Fill in the gaps in this conversation with the correct form of *used to* and a verb from the box.

be	not go	have	not have	live	know	travel	walk

Mina: There's Dahlia in her dad's sports car. Where do they get their money from?

Sara: Don't you know? Her family won the lottery.

Mina: Wow!

Sara: I knew her before that, though. Her family **1** *used to live in our road.* She **2** .... to school like all the other children in those days.

Mina: **3** .... (you) them very well?

Sara: Oh, yes. They **4** .... friendly people. And her father grew all their vegetables because they **5** .... much money.

Mina: They go on holiday a lot now. **6** .... (they) abroad then?

Sara: No, they **7** .... away at all.

Mina: They're very lucky now.

Sara: Mmm, but they **8** .... more friends.

C4 Complete each sentence to show what was different in the past. Use the word in brackets and any others you need with *used to/didn't use to* + verb.

1 Patrick *didn't use to take many photos* (photos) but he loves using his new camera.

2 You .... (lazy) but you're working very hard this term.

3 I .... (slim) but I've lost weight.

4 Bobby .... (a bike) but he drives a car now.

5 Bertie .... (my brother) but they've become friends recently.

6 Nora .... (the cinema) very often but she sees lots of films now.

7 My sister .... (shy) but she enjoys parties now.

8 We .... (sport) but we often play tennis these days.

9 Joanna .... (a vegetarian) but she had a sausage for breakfast.

10 They............................... (the city centre) but their new house is in the country.

C5 Write true sentences about when you were very young using *used to/didn't use to* + verb.

1 *I didn't use to do my homework on a computer.*

2 ....

3 ....

4 ....

5 ....

7

D Exam practice

Reading Part 5

Read the text below and choose the correct word for each space.
For each question, mark the correct letter **A**, **B**, **C** or **D**.

Example:

0 Ⓐ takes   **B** introduces   **C** offers   **D** brings

The Roman Baths

The city of Bath **(0)** .... its name from the public baths **(1)** .... were built there by the Romans. By the middle of the first century, they'd already **(2)** .... planning the baths. The biggest bath, **(3)** .... as the Great Bath, was **(4)** .... a swimming pool. In the next 300 years, the Romans **(5)** .... the baths with changing rooms, a sauna and other smaller baths. They used to come there not only to wash **(6)** .... also to meet friends. The baths were, in **(7)** .... , at the heart of Roman life. This way **(8)** .... life ended in the year 400 when the Romans left Britain. By that time, they'd built towns, roads and bridges across Britain. The Great Bath was discovered again in the eighteenth century after being buried for years and the baths then **(9)** .... as famous as they had been in Roman times. Many tourists **(10)** .... visit the baths today.

1 A who	**B** what	**C** which	**D** where
2 A began	**B** begun	**C** begin	**D** beginning
3 A named	**B** called	**C** titled	**D** known
4 A like	**B** as	**C** same	**D** similar
5 A joined	**B** expanded	**C** added	**D** grew
6 A and	**B** because	**C** so	**D** but
7 A turn	**B** case	**C** fact	**D** place
8 A from	**B** of	**C** to	**D** for
9 A became	**B** developed	**C** changed	**D** turned
10 A already	**B** just	**C** first	**D** still

Grammar focus task

Answer the questions with full sentences.

1 What had the Romans done by the middle of the first century? ....

2 What did they use to do at the baths? ....

3 What had the Romans done in Britain by the year 400? ....

A Context listening

A1 **⌂8a** You are going to hear some advertisements and announcements on a local radio station. Look at the pictures and match them to what you hear.

A    B    C

A2 **8a◀◀** Listen to the first advertisement again and complete these sentences using the places in the box. You sometimes need to add *the*.

> Alps   Andes   Atlantic Ocean   Greece   Lake Garda
> New York   Rome   Sahara Desert

1 You can go climbing in the Alps or ....
2 We're not suggesting sailing across .... but you can sail around the coast of .... or on ....
3 You can watch the sun set over ....
4 Go on one of our city breaks to .... or ....

Do we use *the* before the names of:
countries? .... cities? .... mountain ranges? .... deserts? .... lakes? .... oceans? ....

A3 **8a◀◀** Listen to the second advertisement again. What does he talk about?

jeans   pyjamas   shirts   shorts   shoes   socks   trousers

Which words above can you use only in the plural?

A4 **8a◀◀** Listen to the announcement again. Complete these sentences.

1 The .... on 555FM is perfect for a Friday afternoon.
2 Are you sitting in your car in the .... ?
3 We bring you the latest .... every hour.
4 Then it's your chance to phone us and ask us a question about ....
5 Mark Sherlock, is here to give you ....

Look at the nouns you wrote. Can you make them plural?

8

B Grammar

B1 Plurals

Some things we wear or use are always plural. They are made of two parts which cannot be separate: *trousers, pyjamas, shorts, jeans, tights, pants, sunglasses, glasses, scissors*. They have a plural verb:

*My **trousers** are new.* (**not** *My trouser is new.*)
*These **shorts** are dirty.* (**not** *This short is dirty.*)

Other things we wear can be singular. They are made of two parts which can be separate: *shoe/shoes, sock/socks, earring/earrings*.

⚠ The word *clothes* is never singular: *I bought some new clothes.* (**not** *I bought a new clothe.*)   ➡C1

B2 A(n), the and no article

	means:	use for:	use with:
A(n)	one of many: *My sister works in **a** cinema.*	new information: *My friend was talking to **a** girl.*	countable* nouns (*cinema, girl*)
The	the only one(s) or the particular one(s): ***The** cinema opened last week.*	things already introduced: ***The** girl was very angry.* when we already know what we are talking about: *Where's **the** money I lent you?*	countable* nouns (*cinema, girl*) and uncountable* nouns (*money*)
No article	all: *Cinemas show films.*	things in a general sense: *Money makes people happy.* *I like music.*	plural countable* nouns (*cinemas*) and uncountable* nouns (*money, music*)

*See B3 below.   ➡C2, C3

B3 Countable and uncountable nouns

Countable nouns (e.g. *shoe, passport*)

♦ can be singular with *a, the*:
   *a passport, **the** phone*
   *I've got **a** problem.* (**not** *I've got problem.*)

♦ can be plural with no article, *some* or *the*:
   *shoes, **some** cars, **the** cars*

♦ have a singular or plural verb:
   *The car **is** new. The cars **are** new.*

Uncountable nouns (e.g. *air, bread, food, help, ice, music, money, pollution, rain, sand, travel*):

♦ use *the, some* or no article but not *a*:
   ***the** money, **some** money, money* (**not** *a money*)

♦ cannot be plural:
   money (**not** *moneys*)*, music* (**not** *musics*)

♦ always have a singular verb:
   *The music **is** perfect.* (**not** *The musics are perfect.*)

⚠ These nouns are usually uncountable in English (but are countable in some other languages): *advice, furniture, hair, homework, information, luck, luggage, money, news, traffic, travel* (but *trip* and *journey* are countable), *weather, work*.

⚠ *news* ends in *s* but is uncountable.

When we want to count things which are uncountable nouns, we use words like *a bag, a bottle, a box, a cup, a glass, a packet, a piece*:
*I need **a bottle** of water.* (**not** *I need a water.*)

Many drinks can be countable or uncountable:
*Would you like **a coffee**?* (= a cup of coffee)
*I'd like **two coffees** and **a tea**, please.* (= 2 cups of coffee + 1 cup of tea)
*I bought **some coffee** in the market.* (= a packet of coffee) ➡C2

B4 *The* or no article

Places
There is no article before
◆ continents, most countries, states, cities, towns, villages:
Europe, Italy, London, Florida **but we say** *the Netherlands*.
◆ buildings and places that use the name of their town:
Manchester Airport, Cardiff Station, Edinburgh Castle, Durham University
⚠ We say *at school, at work, at home* and *in bed*.

We put *the* before
◆ names of countries that include a word like *Republic* or *States*:
the United States, the Czech Republic
◆ oceans, seas and rivers: *the Pacific Ocean, the Danube* but not before lakes: *Lake Ontario*.
◆ regions: *the Far East, the north*
◆ groups of islands: *the Philippines*
◆ deserts and mountain ranges: *the Kalahari, the Himalayas* but not before one mountain: *Mount Everest*
◆ the environment: *the sea, the coast, the seaside, the beach, the country, the mountains, the hills, the sky, the sun, the moon*

Jobs
We say *I'm **a** doctor.* (**not** *I'm doctor.*)

Entertainment
We *listen to **the** radio* but we *watch television*.
We *play **the** guitar* (a musical instrument) but we *play tennis* (a sport).
We *go to **the** cinema, **the** theatre* etc.

Travel
We *travel by train, bus etc.* (**not** *by the train.*)

Meals
We *have lunch, dinner etc.* (**not** *the lunch* etc.) ➡C3, C4

8

C Grammar exercises

C1 Which of the plural words in the box can we also use in the singular form?

> boots   bracelets   clothes   earrings   gloves
> jeans   shorts   socks   shoes   tights

C2 Look at this notice from a holiday cottage. For each of the <u>underlined</u> words, add *s* if it is plural countable.

Rose Cottage, Hobbs Farm, Newton, Near Norwich

Welcome!

To help you enjoy your stay, we offer some 1 *advice* .... for 2 *visitor* ˢ............ .

You can use 3 *euro* .... in Norwich city centre but you need English 4 *money* .... at the shop in Newton village. This shop sells good 5 *bread* .... and you can buy fresh 6 *vegetable* .... from the farmhouse. For other 7 *food* .... use the 8 *shop* .... in Ridby or Walcot.

If you want some 9 *information* .... about 10 *travel* .... and 11 *traffic* .... in the Ridby area, try the local radio station.

Notes
If you want to listen to 12 *music* .... please remember to keep the volume down.
Please use only garden 13 *chair* .... in the garden. Do not take any sitting-room 14 *furniture* .... outside.
Please be careful not to bring any 15 *sand* .... or 16 *stone* .... into the cottage from the beach.

Thank you – enjoy your stay!

C3 Read these short newspaper articles. Add *the, a* or *an* or nothing to the gaps.

1

THAT WAS LUCKY!

Last weekend 1 ......ᵃ...... group of tourists had 2 .... lucky escape near 3 .... Mount Rushmore in 4 .... United States. Their car was hit by 5 .... small plane making an emergency landing. 6 .... pilot broke two toes. 7 .... tourists were not hurt, but their car and 8 .... plane were damaged.

2

NO MORE FOREIGN HOLIDAYS?

'We must do more to prevent pollution,' 1 .... professor at Exeter University in 2 .... South of England said yesterday. Professor Kirkwell said that pollution is increasing all over 3 .... world. 'Places like 4 .... Andes mountains and 5 .... Sahara desert will get warmer, and some small islands will disappear. Everyone wants to travel by 6 ....plane but this cannot continue. People must think more carefully about 7 .... environment when they choose 8 .... holiday.'

3

THE WRONG JOB

Janice Miller left her job at 1 .... cinema near 2 .... Bristol in 3 .... west of England yesterday after only one day because she didn't want to watch 4 .... horror film. 'I didn't know I'd see any films,' she explained. 'I saw 5 .... horror film once, and I was very frightened. I thought my job was just selling tickets.'
Stanley Greenham, 6 .... manager of 7 .... cinema, said that he was sorry.

'I didn't really explain 8 .... job to Janice at her interview,' he added. '9 .... horror films we show aren't very frightening. 10 .... young people usually like them.'

C4 There is one mistake in each of these sentences. Find them and correct them.

1 I want to buy some trouser/s so I'll meet you by the new clothes shop.

2 Tom Cruise was wearing a black jacket, black jean and black shoes.

3 I'm happy with a furniture in my room, but I want to change the curtains.

4 I'm sending this card to wish you a good luck for your driving test.

5 My cousin's just been on a travel round France.

6 I listen to musics when I'm working so I feel more relaxed.

7 The weather was marvellous so we went to beach and swam in the sea.

8 I'll go to the swimming-pool for some informations about diving lessons.

9 If I send you a money, will you buy me some earrings like yours?

10 We saw some lovely old towns in Czech Republic on our last holiday.

8

D Exam practice

Listening Part 3

Before you listen, look at questions **1–6** in the notebook below. Which of the spaces need a noun?

🎧 **8b** You will hear a tour guide talking to some tourists about the town of Medbury.
For each question, fill in the missing information in the numbered space.

<u>Tour of Medbury</u>

The craft market has been in Medbury since **(1)** ....

The guide recommends buying **(2)** .... for presents.

The shoe factory is now a **(3)** ....

The nearest bank is next to the **(4)** ....

The fastest way to travel from London to Medbury is by **(5)** ....

(6) .... is available in the kiosk.

Grammar focus task

Look at the words you put in the spaces.

1 Which words are nouns? ....

2 Which of these are countable? ....

3 Which are uncountable? ....

4 How many words did you write in (5)? ....

A Context listening

A1 Look at the four people in the pictures below. They've all left a message on Mia's answerphone. Where is each person? Why do you think they're phoning?

A2 🎧 9 Listen to the four messages. Were you right?

A3 9◀◀ Listen again and answer these questions.

Tom	1	Why doesn't he need a taxi? _because he hasn't got much luggage_
	2	What does he offer to buy? ....
Giorgio	3	Why is he surprised? ....
	4	Who has he already rung? ....
Chloe	5	What has she found in the newspaper? ....
	6	Why is she worried? ....
Roseanne	7	Who is coming to the picnic? ....
	8	What should Mia bring? ....
	9	What has Roseanne bought? ....

A4 9◀◀ In each message, you hear people say the same thing in two different ways. Complete the two sentences so they mean the same. Listen again if you want.

1 I haven't got ...._much_........ luggage. = I've only got a .... small bags.

2 There isn't .... here. = There's .... here.

3 I've found .... = I haven't found ....

4 I've got .... experience. = I haven't got .... experience

5 .... of people are coming. = There'll be a .... people.

6 I bought a .... of cakes. = I got .... cakes.

B Grammar

B1 *Some* and *any*

We use *some* and *any* before both countable and uncountable nouns.

		Countable (e.g. *bag*)	Uncountable (e.g. *luggage*)
+	a/some	*He's got* **a** *bag /* **some** *bags.*	*He's got* **some** *luggage.*
–	any	*He hasn't got* **any** *bags.*	*He hasn't got* **any** *luggage.*
?	any	*Has he got* **any** *bags?*	*Has he got* **any** *luggage?*

We often use *some* in questions which are requests or offers:

Can you buy **some** *crisps?*   *Shall I buy* **some** *food?*

No means 'not any'.

He's got **no** *bags. = He has***n't** *got* **any** *bags.*   *He's got* **no** *luggage. = He has***n't** *got* **any** *luggage.*

⚠ **not** *He has any bags*   ➡C1

B2 *Somebody/anybody/nobody/everybody* etc.

	People	Things	Places
+	*somebody (someone)*	*something*	*somewhere*
–	*not anybody (not anyone) / nobody (no-one)*	*not anything / nothing*	*not anywhere / nowhere*
?	*anybody (anyone)*	*anything*	*anywhere*

We'll find **somewhere** *quiet.*   *Have I forgotten* **anything***?*   *I haven't found* **anything***.*

⚠ *not anything = nothing; not anybody = nobody; not anywhere = nowhere*:
There isn't **anybody** *here. / There's* **nobody** *here.* (**not** *There isn't nobody here.*)

⚠ *Everybody, everyone, everything* and *everywhere* have a plural meaning but they are followed by a singular verb:
Where **is everybody***?*
Everything is *organised.*

(See Unit 10 for *every* and *all*, *every* + noun.)   ➡C2, C3

B3 *Much / many / a lot / a few / a little*

We use *a lot of / lots of* with both countable and uncountable nouns.
We use *a few* (= more than two but less than a lot) and *many* with countable nouns but we use *a little* and *much* with uncountable nouns.

	Countable (e.g. bag)	Uncountable (e.g. luggage)
+	*He's got* **a lot of** */* **lots** *of bags.*	*He's got* **a lot of** */* **lots** *of luggage.*
	He's only got **a few** *bags.*	*He's only got* **a little** *luggage.*
–	*He hasn't got* **many** *bags.*	*He hasn't got* **much** *luggage.*
?	*Has he got* **many** *bags?*	*Has he got* **much** *luggage?*
	How **many** *bags has he got?*	*How* **much** *luggage has he got?*

We can also use *a couple of* (= two) and *several* (= more than a few) with countable nouns:
He's got **a couple of** */* **several** *bags.*

(See Unit 28 for *too much/too many*.)   ➡C4

C Grammar exercises

C1 Read this conversation between some art students and their teacher. Fill in the gaps with *a, an, some, any* or *no*.

Rex: Hi, I'm Rex. Are you **1** ....*a*........ new student?

Jenny: Yes, I'm Jenny. I haven't been to **2** .... art class before.

Rex: The classes in this college are good. Have you brought **3** .... equipment?

Jenny: I've got **4** .... brushes and **5** .... pens, but I haven't got **6** ....
            paint. I didn't know what kind to buy.

Rex: That's OK. I can lend you **7** .... paint.

Jenny: Thanks very much.

Rex: Now we need **8** .... paper. Let's ask the teacher. Excuse me, is there
            9 .... thick paper? There's **10** .... paper in the drawer because we
            used it all last week.

Teacher: Oh. Well, I'll fetch some from the store cupboard now.

C2 Read this short story and underline the correct words.

Last month my husband and I went to a wedding in the north of the country. We needed to stop for a night on the journey. We didn't have **1** *anywhere/nowhere* to stay, so I rang the tourist information office to find a bed and breakfast. I asked for **2** *somewhere/everywhere* near the main road and was given the address of a small inn.

When we arrived it was almost dark. The inn was an old-fashioned place with a garden that **3** *anyone/no-one* had tidied for a long time. The front door was locked. We soon began to feel that **4** *nobody/somebody* didn't want visitors. When we rang the bell **5** *anybody/nobody* answered, but we heard a noise inside the building. We called out but **6** *nothing/everything* happened. After several minutes we decided to look for **7** *anywhere/somewhere* else to stay. We found a modern hotel in the nearest village. When we asked about the old inn, **8** *everybody/somebody* in the hotel was really surprised. **9** *Anybody/Nobody* knew it.

'It's on the main road, just before this village,' we explained.

At last the hotel owner asked her father, a very old man. 'There was an inn many years ago, but it burned down,' he said. '**10** *No-one/Anyone* goes there now.'

After the wedding, we drove past the place again. There wasn't **11** *nothing/anything* there. It seemed like a dream. But we know we saw **12** *something/anything*. We just don't know what it was.

9

C3 Look at each pair of sentences. Write S if their meaning is the same and D if it is different.

1 I didn't bring my boots because I didn't have any space in my suitcase.

   I didn't bring my boots because I had no space in my suitcase. ....S......

2 Is there anything in that box?

   Does that box have anything in it? ....

3 Has everyone in the class read this book?

   Has anyone in the class read this book? ....

4 There's nowhere to buy a coffee in the bus station.

   There isn't anywhere to buy a coffee in the bus station. ....

5 I've got several jobs to do before I go out.

   I don't have much work to do before I go out. ....

6 We're looking everywhere for our passports.

   We don't know where our passports are. ....

7 Everything in that shop is expensive.

   Nothing in that shop is cheap. ....

8 Did you eat anything at the barbecue?

   Did you eat everything at the barbecue? ....

9 Do you want some help with your homework?

   Would you like any help with your homework? ....

C4 Look at the nouns in this box. Which are countable and which are uncountable?

CDs	homework	money	fruit	magazines	parties	jewellery	T shirts

Which of the following words can you use with countable nouns? Which can you use with uncountable nouns?

a couple of	a few	a little	lots of	many	much	several

Write some true sentences about yourself or your friends using words from the two boxes.

1 I bought several CDs when I went shopping last week.

2 ....

3 ....

4 ....

5 ....

6 ....

D Exam practice

Reading Part 3

Look at the sentences below about a music festival.
Read the text to decide if each sentence is correct or incorrect.
If it is correct, mark **A**.
If it is incorrect, mark **B**.

---

1 If you arrive at the same time as last year, the gates will be closed.
2 Nobody will be able to buy a ticket on arrival.
3 Everyone who has bought a ticket will receive it in the post by 14 August.
4 You need to prove who you are when you get to the festival.
5 One adult with a ticket can take several children into the festival.
6 Arrange to meet friends near the gates if you have their tickets.
7 You will receive a souvenir programme when you show your ticket.
8 You should bring enough food to eat over the weekend.
9 You can find signs in Shipton to tell you the way to the festival.
10 There is a small charge for the buses which go direct to the festival site.

The Festival will take place on 24, 25 and 26 August. Gates open at 10am on Wednesday 22 August. This is two days before the start of the Festival. Please note that this is an hour later than in other years. You will not be allowed to enter the site if you arrive before that time. This website has lots of information and is updated every day.

Tickets

Tickets will be sent out by post between 1 August and 14 August to people living in the UK. For those living abroad, tickets have to be collected from an office in Willesbrook. See below for more details.

There will be no tickets on sale at the site. Please do not come without a ticket, and if you know anyone who is planning to come without a ticket, tell them not to.

When you arrive, your name will be put on your ticket so don't forget to bring a passport or identity card. After that, the ticket is yours and cannot be given to someone else to use.

All children aged twelve and under are admitted free but they must be with an adult who holds a ticket. There is no limit to the number of children who can attend with an adult. Please note that there is lots of entertainment provided for kids but they must stay with an adult at all times.

If you have bought tickets for friends, give them to them before they leave for the Festival. It is impossible to meet anyone at the gates because of the crowds. If you have to meet up, do it at least five miles away from the Festival site.

What's on?

Click on Events below for information. Everyone who has a ticket will be given a free souvenir programme. You can buy extra programmes at Information Points.

What shall I bring?

Don't bring much luggage. You need a tent and don't forget suncream and a torch. You can eat really well and cheaply on the site, so it really isn't necessary to carry food.

Where is the site?

The village of Shipton is three kilometres from the site. There are signs from Willesbrook which is the nearest town. Please follow these signs which take you around Shipton. No traffic should go through Shipton itself which has very narrow streets.

How do I get there?

If possible, leave your car at home because there'll be a lot of traffic. There are coaches and trains to Willesbrook. From there you can take a Festival bus. The price of the bus fare is included in your Festival ticket so only those who can show a Festival ticket will be allowed onto these buses.

Grammar focus task

Answer these questions about the text.

1 What does the website have? ....

2 What is provided for kids? ....

3 What is everyone given? ....

4 What should you not carry? ....

5 Why should you leave your car at home?

Look at your answers.

Which nouns are countable? .... Which are uncountable? ....
Can you put *a few* in front of any of these nouns? ....
Can you put *a little* in front of any of these nouns? ....

A Context listening

A1 Look at the pictures below. They show a 'makeover' TV programme. What do you think 'makeover' means? What happened in this programme?

A2 🎧 10 The room belongs to Kirsty. You are going to hear her talking on the radio about her room. Does she like it now?

A3 10◀◀ Listen again and complete these sentences.

1 ....*each*............ of them had a different job to do.

2 .... colour was OK with me ...

3 .... of the colours looks very nice.

4 .... teenagers watch TV ...

5 .... people have a TV in their room ...

6 .... room in our house has a TV.

7 .... bedrooms have fridges in them ...

8 .... of them are really nice.

9 .... of them are modern.

10 .... of them want to copy it!

A4 Look at the words you wrote in A3.

Which words are about more than two things or people? *each* ....

Which words are about two things or people? ....

B Grammar

B1 *This, that, these* and *those*

We can use *this/these* and *that/those* as adjectives:

This T shirt suits me. (I'm wearing it.)
That T shirt suits you. (You're wearing it, not me.)

or as pronouns:

This is a good concert. (I'm at the concert now)
That was a good concert. (I'm not at the concert now.)

When we don't want to repeat a countable noun, we use *one*:

Which picture do you like? **That/This one**. **The one** *of a sunset.*
Which pictures do you like? **Those/These ones**. **The ones** *by Van Gogh.*

We often use *the one(s)* with an adjective:

Which chair do you want? *The* **red** *one.*

→C1

B2 *All, most, some, no* and *none*

all	most	some	none

Things/people in general	Things/people in a particular group
All + noun: *All* **teenagers** *watch TV.*	*All (of)* + *the/my/this* etc. + noun: *All (of) the* **teenagers** *went home early. (the teenagers = a particular group of teenagers)*
Most/some + noun: *Most* **people** *have a TV in their bedroom.* (not *Most of people have a TV in their bedroom.*)	*Most/some of* + *the/my/this* etc. + noun: *Most of my* **friends** *like it.* (my friends = a particular group of people) (**not** *Most my friends*)
No + noun without *the*: *No* **bedroom** *has a fridge.* **or** *No* **bedrooms** *have fridges.*	*None of* + *the* + noun: *None of the* **paintings** *is modern.* **or** *None of the* **paintings** *are modern.*
	All/most/some/none + *of* + pronoun: *All/Most/Some/None of them* *were very old.* ⚠ *All of them* (**not** *All them*)

→C2

B3 *Both/either/neither*

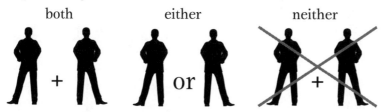

both   either   neither

We use *both/neither/either* when we talk about two things. We can use them

◆ with a noun or pronoun:
   Both lights are *nice.* or ***Both (of) the lights/them are*** *nice.* (plural verb)
   Either colour is *OK.* (singular noun and verb) **or**
   Either of the colours/them is/are *OK.* (singular or plural verb)
   Neither colour looks *good.* (singular noun and verb) **or**
   Neither of the colours/them looks/look *good...* (singular or plural verb)
◆ or alone:
   Which colour would you prefer? ***Neither (of them).*** */* ***Either (of them).***
   Which picture do you like? ***Both (of them).***

⚠ *All* and *both* can go with a verb:
They're all *mad.*
We've both *finished.*

(See Unit 30 for *both ... and, either ... or*.)   ➡ C3

B4 *Each* and *every*

Each and *every* often have the same meaning:
Every/each star has a light in it.

but sometimes they have different meanings.
Each = separate things or people in a group:
We tried ***each*** *colour on the wall.* (= The colours were different.)
Every = all the people or things in a group together:
Every *room in the hotel has a TV.* (= The rooms are the same.)

⚠ We use a singular verb after *each* and *every*.

We use *each/every* + singular noun:
Every/each room has a TV.
We use *each* **not** ~~every~~ with *of* + noun or pronoun:
Each of the people */* ***Each of them*** *had a different job.* (**not** ~~Every of the people / Every of them~~
~~had a different job.~~)

⚠ *Every* and *all* often have a similar meaning:
Every *wall* ***is*** *blue.* (singular verb)
All *the walls* ***are*** *blue.* (plural verb)
But when we talk about time, they have different meanings:
They go to a different place ***every*** *week.* (= regularly)
They spent ***all*** *week in my room.* (= one complete week)   ➡ C4

C Grammar exercises

C1 <u>Underline</u> the correct words in this conversation between Nyree and Ian.

Nyree: Can we stop here a moment? I want to look in the window of **1** *this/that* shoe shop. I need to buy some new shoes.

Ian: OK. But **2** *these/those* ones you're wearing look really good. And they go with **3** *this/that* jacket.

Nyree: Yes, but **4** *these/those* aren't very comfortable now the summer is here. I'd like something lighter for **5** *this/that* warm weather.

Ian: What about **6** *these/those*, at the back of the window?

Nyree: Mm, they look cool, but I don't like the colour. I prefer **7** *the one / the ones* in front of them.

Ian: Let's go in and you can try them on.

C2 Look at this table of information about language courses in Upton and complete the sentences below. Use *all of*, *most of*, *some of* or *none of*.

Language Schools in Upton – a quick guide

	Courses for children	Qualified teachers	Library	Evening classes	Sports facilities	Weekend activities	City centre
Abbey Languages	✓	✓		✓		✓	
Brown's School		✓	✓	✓		✓	✓
Cottle's College	✓	✓		✓			✓
Drake's Academy	✓	✓	✓	✓			✓
Egmont Institute	✓	✓		✓			✓

1 ......Most...... of the schools in Upton offer courses for children.

2 .... the schools employ qualified teachers.

3 .... the schools have libraries.

4 .... them offer evening classes.

5 .... the schools have sports facilities for their students.

6 .... them organise weekend activities for their students.

7 .... the schools are in the city centre.

C3 There is one mistake in each of these sentences. Underline it and write the correction.

1 We had a drink but <u>none</u> food was available. ....no...........

2 Neither these jackets fits me. ....

3 We stopped for a meal because both of us was hungry. ....

4 I was surprised that most the people staying in the hotel were Italian. ....

5 Either of the restaurant you suggested is fine with me. ....

6 He's tidied the garden and put away all chairs. ....

7 I liked both pairs of jeans, but I chose the black one for the party. ....

8 This was an awful meal we had yesterday. We won't go to that restaurant again.

....

9 We're having a party for my father and we're inviting all of old friends. ....

10 Some of airports have several restaurants. ....

C4 Read this hotel brochure and underline the correct word for each question.

The Regent Hotel ★★★★

This attractive hotel offers accommodation for families and business visitors. **1** *Both/Every* groups can find everything they need.

The Main Building has ten luxury rooms and the Garden House has ten family rooms.

2 *Each/Both* buildings have a dining-room. Adult guests and older children may use

3 *either/every* of them at any time. **4** *All/Both* of them offer the same menu but in the evening children under six may only eat in the Garden House dining-room.

5 *All/Every* bedroom has a DVD and CD player and **6** *all/every* of them have private bathrooms. The decoration is different in **7** *either/each* room, and is changed **8** *every/all* year.

There is a swimming-pool available for **9** *all/both* the guests. It is open on weekday evenings and **10** *both/all* day at weekends.

D Exam practice

⚠ This task tests grammar from the rest of the book as well as the grammar in this unit.

Writing Part 1

Here are some sentences about some twins.
For each question, complete the second sentence so that it means the same as the first.
Use no more than three words.

Example:

0 When they were small, the twins spoke a strange language together.

When they were small, the twins used ......*to speak*..... a strange language together.

---

1 Their father understood them better than their mother.

Their mother didn't understand them .... as their father.

2 At first, neither twin enjoyed school.

At first, neither .... twins enjoyed school.

3 They've only got a few friends because they prefer each other.

They haven't got .... friends because they prefer each other.

4 There isn't anybody in the school who can tell which one is which.

There's .... in the school who can tell which one is which.

5 Every teacher in the school has problems because of this.

All of .... in the school have problems because of this.

Grammar focus task

Look at sentences 2 and 5. Which determiners are there? ....

Can you follow them with *of*? ....

Here are the other determiners from this unit:

both	each	either	most	none	no	some

Can you follow them with *of*?

A Context listening

A1 'Market Street' is a soap opera which appears on TV every evening. You are going to hear a girl tell her friend what happened last night. Look at the pictures. The end of the story is missing. Can you guess what happened?

A2 🎧 11a Listen and check if you were right.

A3 11a◀ Here are some sentences about the recording. Fill in the gaps with the words in the box. Then listen again and check your answers.

his	her own	herself	hers	their	~~her~~	his own	himself

1 Sally lent ....*her*........ key to .... cousin Tony.

2 Tony doesn't have .... flat.

3 Tony broke .... leg.

4 Cara was looking forward to being in the flat on ....

5 Tony was sitting there by .... when he had an idea.

6 They were friends of ....

7 Cara really enjoyed ....

A4 Here are some sentences from the recording. Can you put the apostrophe (') in the correct place?

1 I missed last night's programme.

2 Cara is Sallys sister.

3 He wants to leave his parents house.

4 He works in the newsagents.

5 He used Sallys key.

B Grammar

B1 Possessive 's/of

We use 's with people and animals:
The boy's bedroom was very untidy. (**not** ~~the bedroom of the boy~~)
The dog's teeth are very sharp.
and with time expressions:
I missed last night's programme.
but we usually use *of* instead of 's with things:
*What's the price **of** that holiday?* (**not** ~~the holiday's price~~)

Sometimes we don't say the second noun when it is a home or a business:
I stayed at Sally's (= Sally's flat)
He works in the newsagent's. (= the newsagent's shop)

The apostrophe s ('s) goes in a different place for singular and plural nouns:
my cousin's friends (= one cousin), *my cousins' friends* (= more than one cousin)

B2 Personal pronouns, possessive pronouns and possessive determiners

Subject pronouns:	I/you/he/she/it/we/they	Possessive pronouns:	mine/yours/his/hers/ours/theirs
Object pronouns:	me/you/him/her/it/us/them	Possessive determiners:	my/your/his/her/its/our/their

We use *I, you, he* etc. for the <u>subject</u> of the verb and we use *me, you, him* etc. for the object of
the verb:
She gave him her key.   *He invited them to a party.*

We use possessive determiners (*my, your, his* etc.) before a noun:
*I went with **my** friends.*
⚠ *His* means 'of a boy or a man' and *her* means 'of a girl or a woman':
*He sees **his** girlfriend every night.*
*She shares a flat with **her** brother.*

We always use *my, your* etc. with parts of the body and clothes.
*Tony broke **his** leg.* (**not** ~~Tony broke the leg.~~)
*They changed **their** shoes when they came in.*

We use possessive pronouns (*mine, yours* etc.) without a noun:
*Give that key to her. It's not **yours**.* (= it's not your key)

This bicycle is **mine**.
This is **my** bicycle.
This bicycle belongs to **me**.

This bicycle is the boy's.
This is the boy's bicycle.
This bicycle belongs to the boy.

We can say *my friends* or *some friends of mine (yours/his/hers/ours/theirs* etc.) (**not** ~~some friends of me~~)
We use *own* to emphasise that something belongs to someone:
He doesn't have his own flat. (= a flat just for him)   ➡C1, C2

B3 Reflexive pronouns

I → myself, you (singular) → yourself, he → himself, she → herself, it →
itself, we → ourselves, you (plural) → yourselves they → themselves

We use *myself, yourself* etc.

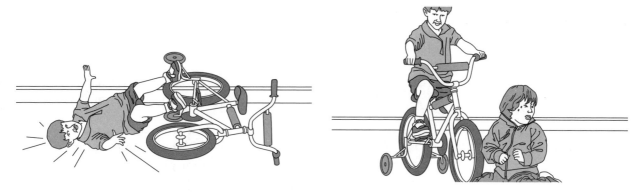

♦ when the <u>subject</u> and the object are the same person/thing:
Tim hurt himself when he fell off his bike. (= Tim (subject and object) was hurt)
but *Sam cried when Tim hurt him.* (= Sam (object) was hurt)

♦ with *enjoy (your)self, behave (your)self, help (your)self*:
Help yourself *to some food.*
*Sally really **enjoyed herself**.*

By (your)self means alone. We can also say *on (your) own*:
*Sally wanted to be **by herself**. or **on her own**.*   ➡C3

B4 *There* and *it + to be*

We use *there + to be* to say somebody/something exists, especially when we talk about them for
the first time:
There's *a party in Cara's flat.*
There were *lots of people in the flat.*
Is there *a newsagent's near here?*

⚠ We say *There is* before a singular noun and *There are* before a plural noun.

⚠ We can't use *it is* in the same way as *there is*. We use *it is* to talk about something we have
already discussed:
There's a *newsagent in this street.* ***It's*** *on the corner.*
(**not** ~~It's a newsagent in this street. It's on the corner.~~)

We can use *it + to be* to talk about time, weather and distance:
It's *sunny here and **it's** nine o'clock in the evening.*
It's *ten kilometres from here to the city centre.*   ➡C4, C5

C Grammar exercises

C1 Complete this table.

That is (1) _my bicycle_ .	That bicycle is mine.	That bicycle belongs to me.
That is my father's jacket.	That jacket is (2) _my father's_ .	That jacket belongs to (3) ....
These are our skis.	These skis (4)	These skis (5) ....
Is this your CD?	Is this CD (6)............................. ?	Does this CD belong to (7) .... ?
This (8)	This (9)	This car belongs to my grandparents.
(10)	(11)	Those videos belong to them.

C2 Fill in the gaps with the correct word (*me/my/mine*, *you/your/yours* etc.).

1 Sorry, I can't pay you because I've left ...._my_........ wallet at home.

2 My brother invited six of .... friends from school to stay the night.

3 My sister's hair is longer and thicker than ....

4 My uncle had grown a beard and I didn't recognise .... at first.

5 My parents have an old car. My car is new and it's more comfortable than ....

6 Our bags are almost the same. Where did you buy .... ?

7 My mother was really pleased when I told .... the news.

8 Maurice can't play tennis because he's hurt .... back.

9 Sarah told .... father a lie.

10 That woman is a neighbour of .... She lives in our road.

C3 Complete each sentence with the correct reflexive pronoun.

1 Help ......_yourself_...... to a sandwich and a drink and then take it to the checkout.

2 Children, behave .... please.

3 The boys hurt .... when they fell out of the tree.

4 I went to the dentist with Jane because she doesn't like going by ....

5 I cut .... when I was making soup.

6 The actor looked at .... in the mirror before he went on stage.

C4 Fill in the gaps in this email with *it's* or *there is/are*.

To: Silva

Cc:

Subject: tomorrow

Hi Silva

I'm glad you can come tomorrow. You can walk to my house from the station as
(1) ......it's...... only about 500 metres. (2) .... some interesting shops on the
way. My favourite is the music shop. (3) .... the best one in town.
Anyway my house is easy to find. (4) .... on the corner and (5) ....
quite modern. Number 54. (6) .... a garage opposite.
I hope (7) .... sunny so we can have lunch in the garden. (8) .... a
tree we can sit under if (9) .... hot.
I can't wait to see you. (10) .... a train which arrives at 11.
Love
Alice

C5 Underline the correct words.

A few years ago my brother, Alan, decided to travel round the world with a friend of
(1) *his/him* called Sam. They flew to Australia because a friend of our (2) *fathers'/father's*
had said they could stay with him. After a few weeks they found a flat because they
preferred to be on (3) *themselves/their own* so they could enjoy (4) *them/themselves*.
My brother met (5) *her/his* wife in Australia and stayed there. Now they live in a
beautiful house. (6) *It/There* is much bigger than (7) *my/mine* in London but they invite
(8) *me/myself* there every year. (9) *There/It* is even a swimming pool and a tennis court.
Alan and Sam are still friends although Sam now lives in Africa and his life is very
different from (10) *Alans'/Alan's*!

D Exam practice

🎧 11b Listening Part 2

You will hear an interview with Helen, who is a basketball player.
For each question, put a tick (✓) in the correct box.

1 Helen went to the United
States because

A she was offered a place at a college there. ☐

B her friend was living there at the time. ☐

C her sister persuaded her that it was a good idea. ☐

2 What do the sisters have to pay
for in the United States?

A their sports training ☐

B their lectures ☐

C their accommodation ☐

3 What does Helen say about
herself and her sister?

A They are less strong than the rest of the team. ☐

B They are shorter than the rest of the team. ☐

C They have had some injuries. ☐

4 What does Helen say about the
sports students?

A They don't have to study as hard as the other students. ☐

B They can study fewer subjects than the other students. ☐

C They can't play in the team if they don't attend their classes. ☐

5 Helen and her sister first
played basketball

A four years ago. ☐

B six years ago. ☐

C ten years ago. ☐

6 What do Helen and her sister
do in their free time?

A watch TV with their friends ☐

B relax together in their room ☐

C spend time shopping ☐

Grammar focus task

**Here are some phrases from the recording with their meanings. Complete them.
Play the recording again if you want.**

1 ...A friend of ours... told us. = One of our friends told us.

2 We have our .... trainer. = We have a personal trainer.

3 They .... = They get injured.

4 His team isn't as good as .... = His team isn't as good as our team.

5 We sit in our room by .... = We sit in our room on our own.

A Context listening

A1 Elliot is talking to his friend Kelly about the weekend. Look at the pictures. What are Elliot's plans? What are Kelly's plans?

A2 🎧 **12** Listen and check if you were right.

Why is Kelly annoyed with Elliot?

A3 **12◀◀** Listen again and complete the sentences below.

1 What does Kelly say about tonight? 'We ʼre going to see the new James Bond film.'

2 What does Elliot say about tonight? 'I .... for exams tonight.'

3 What does Kelly say about Saturday and Sunday? 'We .... the weekend at the seaside.'

4 What are Elliot's plans for Saturday? 'I .... a designer at 10.30 on Saturday.'

5 What does Elliot tell us about his journey from Rome? 'My flight .... Rome at 11 pm on Saturday and it .... in London at 1 am.'

6 What does Elliot say about Sunday? 'I expect I .... asleep all day on Sunday.'

7 What does Kelly agree to do? 'OK. I .... a coffee with you.'

8 What does Elliot say about the future? 'I .... really rich. I .... a fast car and I .... you all to the seaside ...'

A4 Look at your answers to A3 and find the sentences which contain:

1 present simple .... 2 *going to* .... 3 present continuous .... 4 *will* future? ....

5 a timetable .... 6 what someone believes about the future ....

7 plans someone has already made .... 8 what someone decides at that moment? ....

B Grammar

To talk about the future, we use *will*, *going to*, the present simple and the present continuous.

B1 *Will*

+	I/you/he/she/it/we/they **will** (*'ll*) + verb	*I'll pay.*
–	I/you/he/she/we/it/they **will not** (**won't**) + verb	*She **won't pay***
?	***Will*** I/you/he/she/it/we/they + verb?	***Will** you **pay**?*

We use *will*
◆ to say what we know or believe about the future (often with *maybe, I think, I expect* and *I hope*):
I'll be 17 next week. (= he knows this)
*Everybody **will do** shopping by computer in a few years' time.* (= he believes this)
*I **expect I'll be** asleep all day.*
◆ when the speaker decides something at the moment he/she speaks.
*I'll **have** a coffee with you.* (= she decides now)   →C1

B2 *Going to*

+	am/is/are going to + verb	*We're **going to see** the film.*
–	am/is/are not going to + verb	*I'm **not going to see** the film.*
?	am/is/are ... going to + verb?	*Are you **going to see** the film?*

We use *going to*
◆ when we can see that something is certain to happen:
*The plane **is going to land**.*
◆ to talk about plans:
*We're **going to see** the new James Bond film.* (= we decided earlier)
⚠ We can often use *going to* or *will* to talk about the future:
*I'm **going to be** 17 next week.* = *I'll **be** 17 next week.*
We use *will* more often when we write, but *going to* when we speak.   →C2, C3

B3 Present continuous
We use the present continuous (see Unit 4)
◆ for plans already made when we know or guess the time:
*What **are you doing** tonight?* (= what plans have you got?)
*I'm **meeting** a designer at 2.30.* (= he has an appointment)
⚠ We can often use the present continuous or *going to* to talk about plans:
*We're **spending** the weekend at the seaside.* = *We're **going to spend** the weekend at the seaside.* →C4

B4 Present simple
We use the present simple (see Unit 4) for timetables (trains, planes etc.) and for programmes (films, classes etc.):
*My flight **leaves** Rome at 11 pm on Saturday and it **arrives** in London at 1 am.*
*The film **starts** at nine o'clock.*   →C5

C Grammar exercises

C1 Complete each sentence with a verb from the box and the correct form of *will*.

be become come leave need ~~phone~~

1 I think ......*I'll phone*...... Rob because I haven't heard from him for a long time.
2 I (*not*) .... my bag here because it's got my camera in it.
3 My grandmother .... 65 on her next birthday.
4 No thanks, I (*not*) .... to the swimming pool with you because I've got a cold.
5 During the next hundred years the world .... warmer and warmer.
6 How much money (*you*) .... for the weekend?

C2 Write a sentence with *going to* about each picture. Use the verbs in the box.

be join play rain ~~wash~~ win

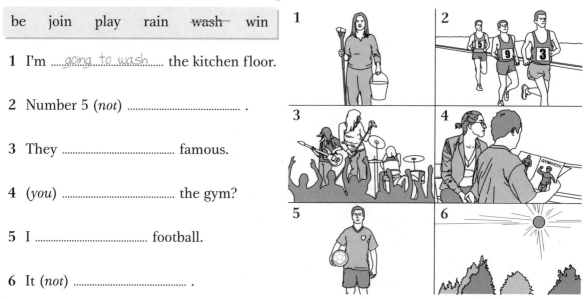

1 I'm .....*going to wash*..... the kitchen floor.

2 Number 5 (*not*) ....

3 They .... famous.

4 (*you*) .... the gym?

5 I .... football.

6 It (*not*) ....

C3 Read this conversation and fill in the gaps with the correct form of *will* or *going to*.

Colin: Hello Darius. **(1)** ....*We're going to go*.... (*we/go*) to a music festival this summer.
Darius: Are you? That sounds good.
Colin: Do you want to come? **(2)** .... (*we/buy*) tickets this afternoon.
Darius: **(3)** .... (*I/think*) about it.
Colin: **(4)** .... (*Paul and Ros/come*) too. It's quite cheap.
Darius: **(5)** .... (*I/check*) my diary. When is it?
Colin: 5–8 August.
Darius: OK, OK, **(6)** .... (*I/buy*) a ticket.

C4 Melissa wants to interview Liam O'Neill, a famous DJ. She is talking to Joe, his assistant. Look at the diaries and fill in the gaps using the present continuous.

Melissa: I can meet Liam any time on Monday. What (1) ....*is he doing*.... during the day?

Joe: We (2) .... to new CDs all day. He can't see you then.

Melissa: And what (3) .... in the evening?

Joe: He (4) .... to the *Daily Post* at 7.30.

Melissa: Oh. And where (5) .... on Tuesday?

Joe: He (6) .... to the TV studio early and he (7) .... there all day.

Melissa: Oh, that's great. I (8) .... the day at the TV studio.

Joe: But in the evening he's (9) .... his TV show. He can't see you before that. But the production team (10) .... a meal together after that. Perhaps you can join them?

Melissa Really? That's great! Thank you so much.

MONDAY ——————— Liam —
Listen to new CDs (with Joe)
evening
- give an interview to the Daily Post at 7.30

TUESDAY
morning
- go to the TV studio early (stay all
evening
- present the TV show
- the production team have a meal toge

MONDAY ——————— Melissa

TUESDAY
Spend the day at the TV studio

C5 Read this conversation between a hotel receptionist and a guest. <u>Underline</u> the best form of the verb.

Guest: Excuse me. I (1) *'m staying* / *stay* here till Friday. I'm (2) *going to look* / *I'm looking* around the city now but I want to do some walking in the mountains while I'm here.

Receptionist: OK. There's a guided tour tomorrow. It (3) *is leaving* / *leaves* from outside the hotel at 10 am and it (4) *is returning* / *returns* at 5 pm.

Guest: Oh good. I think I (5) *'m doing* / *'ll do* that.

Receptionist: Would you like to order a packed lunch? Cheese or chicken sandwiches?

Guest: I (6) *'ll have* / *have* cheese please. And are there any evening activities in the hotel?

Receptionist: There's a concert tonight which (7) *is starting* / *starts* at 7.30.

Guest: Oh I (8) *'m meeting* / *'ll meet* an old friend at 6 and I don't think I (9) *'m* / *'ll be* back in time.

Receptionist: OK. (10) *Are you going to have* / *Do you have* dinner in the hotel tonight?

Guest: No thanks.

D Exam practice

Reading Part 1

Look at the text in each question.
What does it say?
Mark the letter next to the correct explanation – **A**, **B** or **C**.

1

> **Sale starts Monday.**
> Shop opens normal time
> but closes late every day
> except Wednesday.

A The shop is open longer on Monday than on Wednesday.

B The shop is open the same hours as usual during the sale.

C The shop is open the same number of hours each day during the sale.

2

Lewis
Can you give me a lift home from the concert tonight? I'm working late so I expect I'll miss the beginning of it.
Don't wait for me outside.
Jack

A Lewis will probably arrive at the concert after Jack.

B Lewis will probably pick up Jack on his way to the concert.

C Jack will probably meet Lewis inside the concert hall.

3

Dear Mum
We're staying in the mountains tomorrow night after we've spent the day walking. Then, before we travel to the coast, we're going to spend two days in the city.
Paula

A Paula is travelling from the coast to the city.

B Paula is walking in the mountains before she goes to the city.

C Paula is staying on the coast before she travels to the mountains.

4

> Mr Johnson has a meeting this morning. Please do not disturb him until after lunch.

A You can talk to Mr Johnson at lunchtime if you want.

B Mr Johnson is going to arrange a meeting for this afternoon.

C You cannot talk to Mr Johnson until this afternoon.

5

> Kezia
>
> Jenny rang. You left your mobile at her house. She'll probably bring it here on her way to college.
> Alex.

A Kezia has to fetch her mobile from Jenny's house.

B Jenny hopes to give Kezia her mobile before she goes to college.

C Kezia should meet Jenny at college to get her mobile back.

Grammar focus task

Look at the exam questions. Find some verbs which have a future meaning.

1 Find two verbs which tell us about a timetable. Write them here.

....

2 Find two verbs which tell us about plans someone has already made. Write them here.

....

3 Find two verbs which tell us about what someone believes about the future. Write them here.

....

A Context listening

A1 Mr Kent, Maria and Alex work together. Where do you think they work? What are their jobs?

A2 🎧 **13a** You are going to hear three conversations. In which conversation:

1 does Alex make suggestions or offer to do things? ....

2 does Maria ask Alex to do things? ....

3 does Alex ask for permission to do things? ....

A3 **13a◄** Listen again and complete these sentences.

1 ....*Can*........ I sit here for a minute?

2 .... I get a drink of water?

3 .... I use the phone?

4 .... you do those tables over there?

5 .... you help me put out today's menus?

6 And .... you check the salt and pepper?

7 Then .... you sweep the floor?

8 But .... we move some tables outside?

9 And we .... serve more interesting food perhaps.

10 I .... make one of my special recipes if you like.

A4 Look at the recording script on page 187 and check your answers.
Now put the expressions in the box under the correct heading.

~~Can I~~ ...	Would you ...	We could ...	Will you ...	Could I ...
Shall we ...	I can ...	Can you ...	Could you ...	May I ...

Asking for permission   **Asking someone to do something**   **Making offers or suggestions**

........*Can I*........   ....

....

....

....

B Grammar

B1 Modal verbs: general notes

Modal verbs (e.g. *can, could, may, might, must, shall, should, will, would*) are special auxiliaries which add to the meaning of other verbs. (See also Units 14 and 15.) They follow these rules:

+ Modal verbs never change (we don't add *-s* or *-ed* or *-ing* to them): *He **might help**.*
  Another verb follows the modal verb, e.g. *can + help → I **can help**.*
⚠ We don't put *to* before the second verb: *I **can help*** (not *I can to help*).

− *not* follows the modal verb: *That **will not** (or **won't**) be necessary.*

? The modal verb goes first: *Could you **sweep** the floor?*

⚠ *Ought* is like other modal verbs but we put *to* after it:
*I/You/He/We/They **ought to help**.* (not *They **ought help**.*)　　　　　　**→C1**

⚠ *need* can be a modal verb and a normal verb. (See Unit 14B3.)

B2 Asking someone to do something

Less polite	More polite	Answer +	Answer −
*Can/Will you **help** me?*	*Could/Would you **help** me?*	*Yes, of course. / Certainly.* (etc.)	*I'm afraid not. / Sorry.* (etc.)

⚠ We never use *May you?* to ask someone to do something. (**not** *May you help me?*)　　**→C2**

B3 Making suggestions and offers

To make a suggestion, we can say:
***Shall** I/we **move** some tables outside?*　　　　　*I **can make** one of my special recipes if you like.*
If we are less sure of what we are suggesting, we say:
*We **could serve** more interesting food perhaps.*
We can also use these expressions:
***Why don't** I/we **move** some tables outside?*　　　*Let's **move** some tables outside.*
*How about / What about **moving** some tables outside?*
⚠ We say *moving* not *move* after *How about / What about …*

When we offer to do something, we usually use *shall*:
*Shall I **put** the advert back in the window?* (**not** *Will I put…?*)　　　　　**→C3**

B4 Asking for, giving and refusing permission

When we **give** permission or talk about **having** permission, we use *can*:

Less polite	More polite	Answer +	Answer −
*Can I **sit** here?*	*Could/May I **sit** here?*	*Yes, of course. / Certainly.* (etc.)	*I'm afraid not. / Sorry.* (etc.)

*You **can borrow** my camera.*
*We **can finish** work early tomorrow.*
When we refuse permission, we use *can't*:
*You **can't use** the phone.*　　　　　　　　　　　　　　　　　　　　　**→C4, C5**

C Grammar exercises

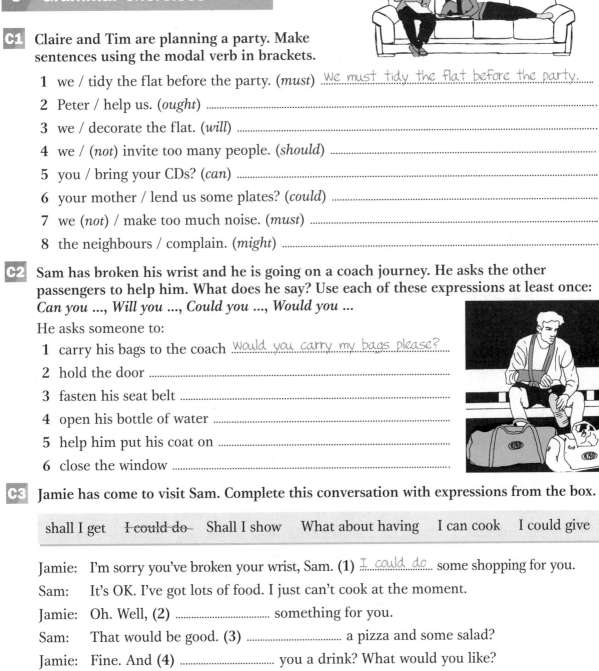

C1 Claire and Tim are planning a party. Make sentences using the modal verb in brackets.

1 we / tidy the flat before the party. (*must*) We must tidy the flat before the party.

2 Peter / help us. (*ought*) ....

3 we / decorate the flat. (*will*) ....

4 we / (*not*) invite too many people. (*should*) ....

5 you / bring your CDs? (*can*) ....

6 your mother / lend us some plates? (*could*) ....

7 we (*not*) / make too much noise. (*must*) ....

8 the neighbours / complain. (*might*) ....

C2 Sam has broken his wrist and he is going on a coach journey. He asks the other passengers to help him. What does he say? Use each of these expressions at least once: *Can you ..., Will you ..., Could you ..., Would you ...*

He asks someone to:

1 carry his bags to the coach Would you carry my bags please?

2 hold the door ....

3 fasten his seat belt ....

4 open his bottle of water ....

5 help him put his coat on ....

6 close the window ....

C3 Jamie has come to visit Sam. Complete this conversation with expressions from the box.

shall I get	~~I could do~~	Shall I show	What about having	I can cook	I could give

Jamie: I'm sorry you've broken your wrist, Sam. **(1)** I could do some shopping for you.

Sam: It's OK. I've got lots of food. I just can't cook at the moment.

Jamie: Oh. Well, **(2)** .... something for you.

Sam: That would be good. **(3)** .... a pizza and some salad?

Jamie: Fine. And **(4)** .... you a drink? What would you like?

Sam: Can you open that orange juice in the fridge? I can't do it with one hand.

Jamie: OK. Look, I've brought some work from college. **(5)** .... you?

Sam: Actually, I'm coming into college this afternoon.

Jamie: I'm going too. **(6)** .... you a lift. I've got my motorbike outside.

C4 Underline the correct words.

1 I know you want to learn to sail. I _could_/may teach you.

2 Why don't we *eat*/eating in the new Chinese restaurant?

3 *Could/Would* I speak to Silvana please?

4 *Can/May* you drive me to school today?

5 *Shall/Will* I carry that for you? It looks very heavy.

6 *Shall/Will* you give me Maria's phone number please?

7 I enjoyed playing tennis with you. *Shall/Would* we play again next week?

8 How about *inviting/invite* my sister too?

9 '*Would/May* you help me to write this letter?' 'I'm sorry. I'm busy.'

10 Let's *meet/meeting* in the café at 7.

C5 What did these people say? Use a different expression in each question.

1 Anan suggested meeting outside the supermarket.
   Anan said: '_Shall we meet outside_ the supermarket?'

2 Mirsad asked for permission to leave work early.
   Mirsad said: '.. work early?'

3 Fernando asked me to buy some stamps.
   Fernando said: '.. some stamps?'

4 Jasmina offered to paint her grandmother's kitchen.
   Jasmina said: '.. your kitchen?'

5 Martina suggested leaving a message for Luca.
   Martina said: '.. a message for Luca?'

6 Michael offered to do the washing up.
   Michael said: '.. washing up.'

7 The teacher gave the boy permission to use the computer.
   The teacher said: '.. the computer.'

8 Katharine asked the shop assistant to find a bigger size.
   Katharine said: '.. a bigger size?'

9 Ellie suggested buying a CD for Tom's birthday.
   Ellie said: '.. a CD for Tom's birthday?'

10 Sanja asked for permission to put a poster on the wall.
   Sanja said: '.. a poster on the wall?'

D Exam Practice

Listening Part 1

🎧 13b

There are seven questions in this part.

For each question there are three pictures and a short recording.

Choose the correct picture and put a tick (✔) in the box below it.

---

1 What does the woman order?

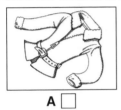
A ☐

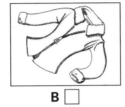
B ☐

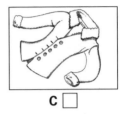
C ☐

2 Where is the boy?

A ☐

B ☐

C ☐

3 When will the man see Dr Browning?

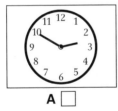
A ☐

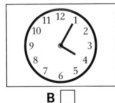
B ☐

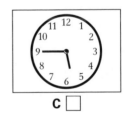
C ☐

4 Where will the man park his car?

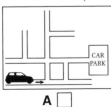
A ☐

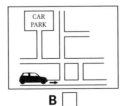
B ☐

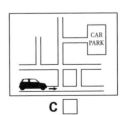
C ☐

5 What do they decide to do?

A ☐

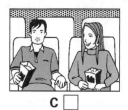

B ☐

C ☐

6 What does Jane want Maria to do?

A ☐

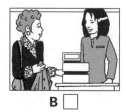

B ☐

C ☐

7 How will the woman travel to the city centre?

A ☐

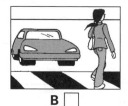

B ☐

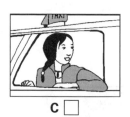

C ☐

Grammar focus task

Here are some sentences from the conversations you heard. There is one mistake in each sentence. <u>Underline</u> it and write the correction.

1 <u>Could</u> I have a look on the computer for you? ....*Shall*........ (an offer)

2 Will I try on that skirt? .... (asking for permission)

3 So may you come and pick me up? .... (a request)

4 Why don't you calling a taxi? .... (a suggestion)

5 Shall I change it please? .... (asking for permission)

6 Excuse me, would I leave my car here? .... (asking for permission)

7 What about go to see a film at the cinema? .... (a suggestion)

8 Will we go to that new restaurant? .... (a suggestion)

9 Shall you help me please? .... (a request)

10 So may you do it? .... (a request)

11 Would I book you a taxi? .... (an offer)

12 Or you may take the underground. .... (a suggestion)

Look at the recording script to check your answers.

A Context listening

A1 This is a scene from a television programme. What kind of programme is it?

A2 🎧14 You are going to hear one of the girls in the picture telling her mother about the TV programme. Were you right?

A3 14◀◀ Listen again. Rosie talks about all the things below. Tick the correct columns in the table.

	We have to	We mustn't	We don't have to	We needn't
look after the animals	✓			
be good at acting				
use mobile phones				
take modern equipment				
wear a microphone				
take our own clothes				
cook the meals				
stay there				

A4 Look at the recording script on page 188 and check your answers. <u>Underline</u> each sentence as you find it.

Example: <u>We have to look after the animals</u> and things like that.

Does *mustn't* mean the same as *don't have to*? ....
Does *needn't* mean the same as *don't have to*? ....

B Grammar

B1 Obligation – *must* and *have to*

Must and *have to* = it is essential or necessary:
*You **must read** the letter carefully.*
*We **have to wear** a microphone.*

must is a modal verb.	**have to** isn't a modal verb.
*I **must go**.* *You **must go**.* *He **must go**. (See Unit 14.)*	*I **have to go**.* *You **have to go**.* *He **has to go**.*

When we ask a question we say:
***Must** she go?* or ***Does** she **have to go**?*

We can often use either *must* **or** *have to*:
*I **must go** now.* or *I **have to go** now.*
We use *must*
◆ when we give orders or advice:
  *You **must read** the letter carefully.*
◆ when we decide something is important for us:
  *I **must phone** my friends.*
We normally use *have to*
◆ when we talk about rules:
  *I **have to wear** a microphone.*
  *We **have to cook** the meals.*
  *She **has to follow** the rules in the castle.*

➡C1

In the present tense, we use *must* or *have to*. For other tenses, we use *have to*:

Past simple	*I **had to go** home.* *I **didn't have to go** home.* ***Did** he **have to go** home?*
Future	*I **will have to go** home.* *I **won't have to go** home.* ***Will** I **have to go** home?*
Present perfect	*She's **had to go** home.* *She **hasn't had to go** home yet.* ***Has** she **had to go** home yet?*

➡C2

B2 Obligation – *mustn't* and *don't have to*

Although *must* and *have to* have similar meanings (see B1), *mustn't* ≠ *don't have to*.

mustn't = don't do it (a rule):
*We **mustn't use** mobile phones.*
*I **mustn't use** a diary.*
We can also say *It's not allowed*:
*We're **not allowed to use** mobile phones.*

don't have to = it's not necessary:
*We **don't have to take** our own clothes.*

B3 Necessity – *need*

need = it is necessary
Need is a normal verb:
*I **need to buy** some bread. (**not** I need buy some bread.)*
***Do** you **need to take** any food with you?*

In the negative, *need* can be
◆ either a modal verb:
   *You **needn't worry**.*

◆ or a normal verb:
   *You **don't need to worry**.*

Needn't and *don't need to* = it isn't necessary = *don't have to*:
*You **needn't worry** = You **don't need to** worry. = You **don't have to worry**.*

In the past we say:
+   *They **needed to look** after the animals. (= It was necessary to look after the animals.)*
−   *They **didn't need to work** hard. (= It wasn't necessary to work hard.)*
?   ***Did** they **need to grow** their own food? (= Was it necessary to grow their own food?)*   **➡C3, C4**

B4 Orders and advice

We use *must*, *should*, *ought to* and *could* to give advice.

strong advice		less strong advice
You **must** check the details .	You **should** / **ought to** take a diary.	You **could** take some books.

In the negative, we use *shouldn't* or *ought not to*:
*You **shouldn't sign** the letter.*
*You **ought not to go** there.*
⚠ We don't use *couldn't* to give advice. (**not** You couldn't sign the letter.)

We use *should* and *ought to* when we are talking about the right thing to do:
*I **should learn** to cook.*
*We **ought to send** her a postcard.*
*I **shouldn't worry** so much.*
*I **ought not to eat** that cake.*   **➡C5, C6**

14

C Grammar exercises

C1 Complete these sentences using the correct form of *must* or *have to*. Think about the tense of *have to*.

1 I _didn't have to_ (not) get up early yesterday because it was Saturday. (*have to*)
2 You .... always tell the truth. (*must*)
3 I .... buy a new computer next year. (*have to*)
4 .... (*we*) wash up now? (*have to*)
5 When he was in the school team, Simon .... train every Saturday. (*have to*)
6 Children .... (*not*) go in the pool without an adult. (*must*)
7 I .... (*not*) pay to use the health club because I'm a member. (*have to*)
8 How long .... (*you*) wait for the bus last night? (*have to*)

C2 For each sentence, <u>underline</u> *mustn't* or *don't have to*.

1 Tell John he *mustn't* / <u>*doesn't have to*</u> drive me to the station because Martha can.
2 The students *mustn't* / *don't have to* eat in the library.
3 He can stay at home. He *doesn't have to* / *mustn't* come with us.
4 You *mustn't* / *don't have to* tell Chloe because it's a surprise.
5 I *mustn't* / *don't have to* forget to phone Jan tonight – I promised her.
6 You *mustn't* / *don't have to* bring any football boots because you can borrow mine.
7 We *mustn't* / *don't have to* clean this room because it's not dirty.
8 We *mustn't* / *don't have to* be late because we don't want to miss the beginning of the film.

C3 Complete these conversations with *need to* or *needn't*.

1 'I'm going walking in the mountains.'
   'You **(1)** _need to_ take some suncream because the sun's very strong.'
   'Yes you're right but at least I **(2)** .... carry my raincoat.'
2 'Can I get ready for the party at your flat? I **(1)** .... have a shower after work.'
   'Of course and you **(2)** .... bring a hair-dryer because you can use mine.'
3 'I'm going to town now.'
   'Why?' 'I **(1)** .... buy a birthday present.'
   'Have you got some cash?'
   'No, I **(2)** .... take cash because I've got my credit card.' 'What about the bus fare?'
   'I've got a bus pass so I **(3)** .... pay.'

C4 Read this conversation between two friends about going camping. Fill in the gaps with the correct form of *need*.

Rena: I'm going to that campsite by the beach next week. When you went,
(1) ...*did you need*... (*you*) to take a sleeping bag?

Dominic: Of course. It was very cold. And we (2) .... to take plenty of food too as there were no restaurants.

Rena: So (3) .... (*you*) to make a fire to cook your food on?

Dominic: No, because we took a small cooker with us. We had one small frying pan so we cooked everything in that . We (4) .... (*not*) to use any saucepans.

Rena: Maybe I could borrow that frying pan and cooker.

Dominic: Sure.

C5 You have a part-time job in a shop. Your friend is starting work at the shop next week. Give your friend some advice. Use each expression in the box once.

> You must ...   You ought to ...   You could ...   ~~You should~~ ...
> You shouldn't ...   You mustn't ...

1 be polite to the customers ...*You should be polite to the customers.*...
2 offer to work extra hours ....
3 arrive at work on time ....
4 look tidy ....
5 look bored ....
6 lose the key to the safe ....

C6 Fill in the gaps in this email with one of the words or phrases in the box.

> had   'll have   ~~must~~   should   needn't   didn't have   shouldn't

Dear Sarah

I (1) ....*must*........ tell you about my weekend with my friend Erica who lives in Leeds. The journey wasn't easy because I (2) .... to change trains three times. But Erica lives near the station so I (3) .... to take a taxi or the bus to her flat. We spent all weekend chatting and shopping. You (4) .... come with me next time. You (5) .... spend every weekend studying. I need to study hard this week. If I don't pass my maths exam, I (6) .... to take it again. I want to visit Erica again next weekend. Why don't you come with me? You (7) .... decide yet. You can tell me on Friday.

83

D Exam practice

Grammar focus task

Look at the Writing Part 3 task below. Make a list of things you have to do and things you mustn't do in your school.

We have to	We mustn't
arrive by 8.30	leave the school during the day

Now do the exam task below.

Writing Part 3

- This is part of a letter you receive from your English friend Claire.

> We have lots of rules in my school. We have to arrive by 8.30 and we mustn't leave the school during the day. What are the rules at your school? Do you agree with them?

- Now write a letter to Claire, telling her about the rules at your school.
- Write about **100 words**.

A Context listening

A1 Look at these photos of two ordinary objects. What are they?

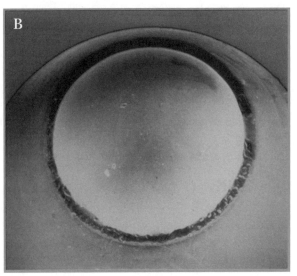

A2 🎧 15 You are going to hear part of a quiz programme. Were you correct?

A3 15◀◀ Listen again and complete these sentences.

Photo A	Photo B
1 It ......*might*...... be an insect.	5 It .... be a headlight.
2 It .... be a hairbrush.	6 It's the wrong shape. It .... be a needle.
3 It .... be a flower.	7 It .... be a pencil.
4 It .... be a book.	8 It .... be a pen because that looks like ink.

A4 Look at the sentences in A3.

1 In which sentences does the speaker feel sure? ....

2 In which sentences does the speaker feel unsure? ....

A5 Look at the recording script on page 189. Complete what the questioner says to the teams.

1 Team A, ... say what's in your photo?

2 Team B, ... say what the object is?

Look at the words you've written. Do they mean the same? ....

B Grammar

B1 Certainty and possibility

When we're sure something is true, we use *must*:

*It **must be** a pen because that looks like ink.*
*They **must be** at home because the light is on.*

When we think something is possible, we use *might/could/may*:

*It **could be** a butterfly because those are its wings.*
*He **might be** her brother but I'm not sure.*

When we're sure something isn't true, we use *can't*:

*It **can't be** a butterfly because it hasn't got a body.* (**not** *It mustn't be a butterfly.*)
*That **can't be** Sue's car because hers is at the garage.*

⚠ We also use *might/could/may* when we are uncertain about the future:

*I **may go** to Greece next month.* (= it's possible but I'm not certain)
*My football team **might win** the cup.*

➡C1, C2

B2 Ability (*I can ..., I'm able to ..., I could ...*)

I can = I know how to do something or it is possible for me to do something.
In the present we use *can* (a modal verb) or *be able to* (not a modal verb).

+   *The children **can swim** but they can't dive yet.*
    *I **can help** you on Monday but not on Tuesday.*
–   *I **can't decide** what it is.*
?   ***Can** you **say** what's in your photo?*

be able to is less common:

*My grandfather **is able to cook** his own meals but he **isn't able to walk** to the shops.*
*I'm **not able to answer** that question.*

In the past we use *could* or *was able to*:

*He **could** / **was able to walk** when he was one.*
*The athletes **couldn't**/**weren't able to** train because the weather was bad.*

For all other forms, we use *be able to*:

Future: *Team A **will be able to come** back next week.*
Present perfect: *Team A **hasn't been able to answer** the question yet.*
Infinitive: *Team A hopes **to be able to come** back next week.*

We also use *can* and *could* for permission, offers and requests. (See Unit 13 Modals 1.) ➡C3, C4

C Grammar exercises

C1 Underline the correct verbs.

Carlotta: I can't find my keys and I'm late. There **(1)** *might/must* be a lot of traffic in town so I need to hurry. They're not in my bag so they **(2)** *must/can't* be in the flat somewhere.

George: Have you looked in the kitchen?

Carlotta: They **(3)** *can't/could* be there because I haven't been in the kitchen. They **(4)** *must/might* be in the bedroom because I changed my clothes there or they **(5)** *could/must* be on the table in the hall. I'll go and look. No, they're not there.

George: Did you leave them in the car?

Carlotta: They **(6)** *could/can't* be in the car because I opened the door with them. They **(7)** *can't/must* be here somewhere.

George: I can't see them. Let's think. They **(8)** *might/can't* be in your coat pocket because you weren't wearing one but they **(9)** *can't/might* be in your jeans pocket. Have you looked there?

Carlotta: Oh, thanks. I've found them. I **(10)** *can/may* be home a bit late tonight. Bye.

C2 Look at these photographs. Where are they? Write three sentences for each photograph beginning *It might be ...*, *It could be ...*, *It can't be ...*, *It must be ...* Use the places in the box.

| Sweden | Nepal | Australia | India | Brazil | South Africa |

It can't be Australia.

It might be Nepal.

It must be

C3 Write *can*, *can't*, *could* or *couldn't* in the spaces.

1 I'm sorry I ....*can't*........ come to your party. I'm busy on Saturday.

2 You .... sing much better than that when you were younger.

3 Rachel's son .... count to 20 and he's only two!

4 We didn't speak the language so we .... understand what the woman said.

5 .... you read that notice from here? I haven't got my glasses with me.

6 I know that man but I .... remember his name.

7 Anne-Marie likes to sit close to the stage so she .... see the actors' faces clearly.

8 I'm afraid of going on a boat because I .... swim.

9 When I was a teenager I walked everywhere because I .... drive.

10 .... you write your name when you started school?

11 He looked everywhere for the ring but he .... find it.

12 .... you open this window? I've tried, but it's too heavy.

C4 Fill in the gaps with words from the box.

are	be	is	to be	hasn't been	haven't been	isn't	will
weren't	wasn't	won't be	~~were~~				

1 None of the students ....*were*........ able to read the teacher's writing.

2 Your sister speaks very good Spanish. .... you able to speak any foreign languages?

3 .... you be able to finish that homework by tomorrow?

4 They .... able to see anything from the plane because it was cloudy.

5 I'm sorry, I .... able to come to your wedding next month because I've got exams.

6 He .... able to take a holiday since last summer.

7 If you want to do the diving course, you have .... able to swim.

8 I looked everywhere but I .... able to find the photograph because Laura had it.

9 .... Rebecca able to lend you some money or do you want me to give you some?

10 Let's phone the theatre. We may .... able to get seats for tonight.

11 I wanted to invite James but I .... able to contact him.

12 The manager .... able to see you now. Can you come back tomorrow?

D Exam practice

Reading Part 1

- Look at the text in each question.
- What does it say?
- Mark the letter next to the correct explanation – **A**, **B** or **C**.

1

We can't accept credit cards if
you spend £5 or less.
Please have enough cash.

A It is possible to pay bills of more than £5 by credit card.

B We can give you cash if you pay your bill by credit card.

C We will charge you extra if you pay bills of under £5 by credit card.

2

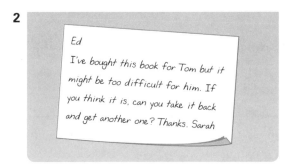

Ed

I've bought this book for Tom but it might be too difficult for him. If you think it is, can you take it back and get another one? Thanks. Sarah

A Sarah is happy to go and get a different book if Ed wants her to.

B Sarah is worried that the book isn't suitable for Tom.

C Sarah wants Ed to give the book to Tom.

3

One free concert ticket
for students who can
serve refreshments
during interval.

A Refreshments are included in the price of concert tickets.

B Students who help with the concert get free refreshments.

C Students don't pay for concert tickets if they help with the refreshments.

4

> **To: Katie**
> **From: Gemma**
>
> Can you look for my gloves? They might be in your bedroom because I put my coat there. I've looked everywhere here so they must be in your flat.

A Gemma is sure her gloves are in Katie's bedroom.

B Gemma has searched everywhere for Katie's gloves.

C Gemma thinks her gloves are in Katie's bedroom.

5

> Simon, Trudi phoned. She hasn't been able to contact Nick. She knows he can't be on holiday because he's got an exam tomorrow! Can you tell her if you know where he is?

A Trudi thinks Nick is still on holiday.

B Trudi wants Simon to phone Nick for her.

C Trudi hopes Simon can help her find Nick.

Grammar focus task

Rewrite these sentences using a modal verb – *can, can't, must* or *might*. It is not possible to change one of the sentences.

1 We are not able to accept credit cards if you spend £5 or less.

....

2 It is possible that the book is too difficult for Tom.

....

3 Are you able to take it back?

....

4 One free concert ticket for students who are able to serve refreshments.

....

5 Gemma thinks her gloves are in Katie's bedroom.

....

6 Gemma is sure her gloves are in Katie's flat.

....

7 She hasn't been able to contact Nick.

....

8 He definitely isn't on holiday.

....

A Context listening

A1 Della Dombey is an American singer. She's at a radio station in Manchester in England to take part in a phone-in. Her fans are going to ask her some questions. What questions would you like to ask your favourite singer?

Write three ideas here.

1 ....   2 ....   3 ....

A2 🎧 16a Listen to the interview. Did any of Della's fans ask one of your questions?

A3 16a◀◀ Listen again and complete the questions below. Stop the recording when you need to.

1 ...._Do you like_................ Manchester?
2 .... stay here?
3 .... in public for the first time?
4 .... any clubs in Manchester?
5 .... your boyfriend now, Della?
6 .... best?

A4 Look at the questions you completed in A3 and match them to these answers.

a ....._6_..... My boyfriend Dean's.
b .... Yes, I do.
c .... No, I haven't.
d .... Dean Bradley.
e .... Only four days.
f .... At my high school concert.

A5 Look again at A3 and A4.

1 Which of the questions in A3 begin with question words? ....
2 Which of the questions in A3 do not begin with question words? ....
3 What is different about the answers to these two groups of questions? ....

B Grammar

B1 Yes/No questions

When we make questions which can be answered with *Yes* or *No*

◆ we put an auxiliary or modal verb before its subject:
(For modals, see Units 13, 14 and 15.)

We're (*We are*) *going clubbing tonight.* → *Are we going clubbing tonight?*
You've (*You have*) *been to that clubs.* → *Have you been to that club?*
We must go to London. → *Must we go to London?*

◆ we use *do(es)* or *did* to make questions in the present simple or past simple. (See Units 4 and 5.)

You like Manchester. → *Do you like Manchester?*
Manchester has fantastic clubs. → *Does Manchester have fantastic clubs?*
(**not** ~~*Does Manchester has fantastic clubs?*~~)

They went clubbing. → *Did they go clubbing?*

◆ we put the verb *to be* before its subject:

She's (*She is*) *in Manchester today.* → *Is she in Manchester today?* ➡C1

B2 Short answers

We answer a *Yes/No* question using the same auxiliary or modal verb as in the question.

If the answer is *Yes*:

Are you going to London? Yes, I *am*.
Do you like Manchester? Yes, I *do*.
Has he been clubbing? Yes, he *has*.
Could they ask questions? Yes, they *could*.

If the answer is *No*:

Are you going to London? No, *I'm* not.
Did you sing well? No, I *didn't*. ➡C2

B3 Question words

Who	*What*	*Where*	*Why*	*How*	*Which*	*How often*		*How long*
How far		*How many* (+ countable noun)			*How much* (+ uncountable noun)			
What (+ noun)		*Which* (+ noun)		*Whose* (+ noun)				

Wh... questions begin with the words in the box above.

We make most *Wh...* questions in the same way as *Yes/No* questions.

Della might marry Dean. → *Who might Della marry?*
(Answer: *Dean.*)

I wrote a love song. → *What did you write?*
(Answer: *A love song.*)

She can't sing because she's tired. → *Why can't she sing?*
(Answer: *Because she's tired.*)

*They'll leave **at two o'clock**.*	→ ***What time** will they leave?* (Answer: *At two o'clock.*)
*I've known Dean **for three years**.*	→ ***How long** have you known Dean?* (Answer: *(For) three years.*)
*I like **this song**.*	→ ***Which song** do you like?* (Answer: *This song* or *This one.*)
*I like **Dean's music** best.* ✓	→ ***Whose music** do you like best?* (Answer: *Dean's.*)
*She earned **a million pounds**.*	→ ***How much money** did she earn?* (Answer: *A million pounds.*) ⚠ Remember *money* is uncountable. (See Unit 8.)

⚠ Remember the difference between these questions with *like*:
*What **does** Della **like**?* (= What does Della enjoy?) *She **likes** dancing.*
*What **does** Della **look** like?* (= describe her) *She's very tall.*
*What's (**is**) Della **like**?* (= tell me about her) *She's clever and very tall.*   ➡C3, C4, C6

B4 Questions about the subject of the verb

When we make a question about the subject of the verb we do not change the word order. We don't use *do* in the present simple or *did* in the past simple.
Compare these questions about the subject and object of a sentence:

Matt enjoyed the concert.
Who enjoyed the concert? (Answer: *Matt.*) **not** ~~Who did enjoy the concert?~~
What did Matt enjoy? (Answer: *The concert.*) **not** ~~What enjoyed Matt?~~
Which CDs cost £5? (Answer: *These CDs.*) **not** ~~Which CDs do cost £5?~~

⚠ In a subject question, *who* has a singular verb
Who is going to the concert? (**not** ~~Who are going?~~ although we know there must be more than one!)
unless there are two or more people in the question:
Who are your favourite singers?   ➡C4, C6

B5 Agreeing with statements

We use *So* to agree with positive statements and *Neither* or *Nor* to agree with negative statements. We put the verb before the subject:

◆ with the verb *to be*:
I'm looking forward to that concert.	*So am I.*
We're going to Leeds.	*So am I.*

◆ with an auxiliary or modal verb:
She's been to Manchester.	*So have I.*
I don't know this song.	*Neither do I.*
He can't dance.	*Nor can I.*

◆ with the present or past simple, using *do* or *did*:
They enjoyed the concert.	*So did we.*
He likes this song.	*So do I.*
We didn't hear it.	*Neither did I.*
    ➡C5

93

16

C Grammar exercises

C1 Change these sentences into *Yes/No* questions.

1 I live in Barcelona.   <u>Do you live in Barcelona</u> ?
2 Alex is a student.   <u>Is Alex a student</u> ?
3 Sam and Emma are getting married.   ....?
4 Bob drove to Malaga.   ....?
5 Joanne's got lots of CDs.   ....?
6 I can dive very well.   ....?
7 Eddy watches football every Saturday.   ....?
8 Adam's seen that film.   ....?
9 Marc had dropped his watch.   ....?
10 I was late for school yesterday.   ....?

C2 Which of these answers can you match with the questions you wrote in C1?

1 ...f... 2 .... 3 .... 4 .... 5 .... 6 .... 7 .... 8 .... 9 .... 10 ....

> **a** Yes he did.   **b** No, I wasn't.   **c** Yes, they are.   **d** No, he doesn't.   **e** Yes, he had.
> **f** Yes I do.   **g** Yes, I can.   **h** No, he isn't.   **i** No, he hasn't.   **j** Yes, she has.

C3 Read the questions and answers
then complete the questions with
the correct question words.

> I called at your house yesterday,
> but you weren't in.

1 ....<u>Where</u>.......... were you?   In Bristol.
2 .... did you go there?   Because I wanted to go shopping.
3 .... did you travel?   By car.
4 .... car did you go in?   My father's.
5 .... did you go with?   My sister and her friend.
6 .... were you there?   Five hours.
7 .... shops did you go to?   About twenty.
8 .... did you buy?   A new jacket and some boots.
9 .... did they cost?   £120.
10 .... did you have for lunch?   I didn't have any. I'd spent all my money!
11 .... did you get home?   Ten o'clock.

94

C4 Read this magazine article and then write questions to match the answers below.

Top fashion model Charles Decker shocked his fans yesterday when he flew into London. He'd been on holiday in the Caribbean and he was wearing old shorts and a T-shirt. 'I was on the island of Grenada, but I had to come home suddenly because of a family emergency,' he explained. 'I was on the beach. My secretary phoned from London. I jumped onto my motorbike and went straight to the local airport. It took twenty minutes to get there. I'm going to visit my brother now. He's in hospital. I'll change my clothes after I've seen him.'

1 Who shocked his fans yesterday ....?   Charles Decker.
2 ....?   In the Caribbean.
3 ....?   Old jeans and a T-shirt.
4 ....?   Grenada.
5 ....?   Because of a family emergency.
6 ....?   His secretary.
7 ....?   By motorbike.
8 ....?   Twenty minutes.
9 ....?   In hospital.
10 ....?   After he's seen him.

C5 Which of these sentences do you agree with? Write what you say.

1 I like playing volleyball. _So do I._ ....

2 I don't go out very often. _Nor do I or Neither do I._ ....

3 I've got a CD player. ....

4 I'm going to meet my friends this weekend. ....

5 I was at school last week. ....

6 I didn't go out last night. ....

7 I'd like to learn to fly a plane. ....

8 I couldn't speak English when I was five. ....

C6 Write six questions to ask someone you admire (for example an actor or sportsperson). Begin five questions with the words given and add one *Yes/No* question. If you like, you can add answers too!

1 Why .... ?   4 Who .... ?

2 How often .... ?   5 How long .... ?

3 Where .... ?   6 .... ?

95

D Exam practice

Listening Part 4

🎧 16b

Look at the six sentences for this part.

You will hear a conversation between a teenager, Amy, and her mother about a trip.

Decide if each sentence is correct or incorrect.

If it is correct, put a tick (✔) in the box under **A** for **YES**. If it is not correct, put a tick (✔) in the box under **B** for **NO**.

		A YES	B NO
1	Amy's mother thinks that Amy should ask for her job back.	☐	☐
2	Amy is glad she no longer has to work in the café.	☐	☐
3	At first, Amy's mother is confused about who Amy will travel with.	☐	☐
4	Amy last heard from Ricky on her birthday.	☐	☐
5	Ricky has travelled to Asia before.	☐	☐
6	Amy and her mother agree she should meet Ricky before she goes.	☐	☐

Grammar focus task

Here are some questions and answers from the conversation. Can you remember the questions? Listen again if you need to.

1 'What plans .... ?' 'We're going to travel.'

2 'How long ....?' 'At least six months.'

3 'Which countries .... ?' 'First of all Thailand and India and then maybe China.'

4 'Who .... with you?' 'Ricky.'

5 '................................... his mum .... in the library?' 'No, Mum, not him.'

6 'But .... doing the same kinds of things?' 'Yes, we do.'

Now complete these sentences from the conversation.

7 'I haven't seen him since he was about 15.' 'No, neither .... I.'

8 'I always liked him when he was little.' 'So .... I.'

9 'I like sports and adventure and so .... Ricky.'

10 'I think we ought to get together before we set off.' 'So .... I.'

A Context listening

A1 Isobel is the receptionist at Forest Adventure, a holiday park. She is telling some new guests about the park. Which of the facilities in the pictures do you think she mentions?

A2 🎧17 Listen and check if you were right.

A3 17◄◄ Listen again and mark the places A–G on the map below.

A cottages
B bicycle store
C swimming pools
D shops
E gym
F equipment kiosk
G barbecue

YOU ARE HERE

A4 Read these sentences. Are they are true or false? Write T for True or F for False and correct the false sentences. Check your answers by looking at the map and listening again.

1 The cottages are across the lake.

2 You can drive round the lake.

3 The swimming pools are beside the restaurants.

4 The gym is opposite the disco.

5 The barbecue is on the island.

B Grammar

B1 *In, at* and *on*

We say *in*

◆ a continent, a country, a town, a park, a garden, a building, a room:
*You can cycle anywhere **in** the park.*
*Uruguay is **in** South America.*

◆ a cupboard, a box, a bag, a wallet, a book, a file:
*There's a lot of money **in** this bag.*
*We found a picture of the castle **in** our guide book.*

◆ a car or a taxi:
*They arrived **in** a taxi.*

We say *on*

◆ an island, the coast:
*There is a barbecue **on** the island twice a week.*

◆ a wall, the floor or the ceiling:
*I put the picture **on** the wall.*

◆ a public transport vehicle (bus, train, plane etc.)
*I do my homework **on** the bus.*

We use *into, onto, off* and *out of* for movement:
*We got **onto/off** the bus.*
*He walked **into/out of** the shop.*

We say *at*

◆ a place where we arrange to meet:
*I'll see you **at** the station.*

◆ after *arrive*:
*When you arrive **at** your cottage you'll find details ...*
but for countries and cities, we use in:
*When do we arrive **in** Athens?*

◆ when we give directions:
*Go left **at** the traffic lights.*

◆ a place where something happens (a cinema, a station, someone's home, school).
*Did you have a good time **at** Alex's house?*
*I saw that film **at** the local cinema.*

◆ an event (a party, a conference, a concert):
*My favourite band played **at** the concert.*
*There were lots of students **at** the conference.*

◆ the top/bottom/side:
*Please sign this form **at** the bottom of the first page.*

➡ C1

B2 *Under* and *on top of*; *above/over* and *below/under*

We use *under* and *on top of* for things which are touching:
*The DVD player is **under** the television.*
*The magazine is **on top of** the television.*
We use *below* or *under* and *above* or *over* for things which are not touching:
*The books are **below/under** the DVD player.*
*The picture is **above/over** the television.*
Above and *below* are used in books:
*Please do the exercise **below**.*

➡C2

B3 *Along, through* and *round*; *across* and *over*

*I followed the man **along** the river, **round** the car park and **through** the wood.*

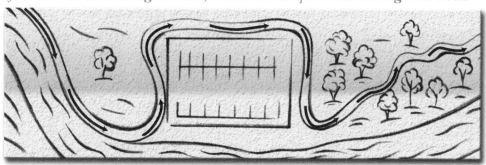

Across and *over* have similar meanings:
*The cottages are **across/over** the lake.* (= They're the other side of the lake from here.)

➡C3

B4 *In front of, behind, opposite, between*; *by, beside* and *next to*

*The woman is **in front of** the television.*
*The television is **behind** the woman.*
We say *between* two places, things or people:
*The mother is **between** her sons.*
By, beside and *next to* mean the same:
*The girl is **by/beside/next** to her father.*
Opposite means two things are on two facing sides.
*The girl is **opposite** her mother.* (= The girl is on the other side of the table from her mother.)
⚠ opposite ≠ in front of

➡C4, C5, C6

C Grammar exercises

C1 **Match the halves of the sentences.**

1 The Prado is in ......h......
2 Part of New York is on ....
3 Tunisia is in ....
4 Chile is on ....
5 Michelangelo painted on ....
6 This exercise is at ....
7 John Lennon was at ....
8 Trains from Cardiff arrive at ....
9 Cairo is on ....
10 The British Crown jewels are in ....

a the coast of the Pacific Ocean.
b North Africa.
c the top of the page.
d art college before he was famous.
e the river Nile.
f the Tower of London.
g the island of Manhattan.
h ~~Madrid.~~
i Paddington Station in London.
j the ceiling of the Sistine Chapel.

C2 **Complete each sentence with a preposition from the box.**

above	~~at~~	at	below	in	in	into	off	on top of	onto

1 What time will Ali arrive ....at.......... the restaurant?
2 There are lots of examples .... a good dictionary.
3 I climbed .... a wall to see what was happening.
4 From the top of the hill, we had a good view of the village .... us.
5 There are lots of shoe shops .... the city centre.
6 I saw Terry get .... a taxi, but I don't know where it took him.
7 You can leave your bike .... the side of the house.
8 I couldn't find my book because someone had put the newspaper .... it.
9 We keep medicines in the cupboard .... the basin so the children can't reach them.
10 Harry got .... the bus at the wrong stop because he was dreaming about his girlfriend.

C3 **Underline the correct preposition in each sentence.**

1 We can walk to the shops more quickly if we go *along/across* the sports field.
2 I was really annoyed when I found our cat asleep *on top of/above* my clean jumper.
3 We drove *round/along* the market square several times but we didn't see Simon.
4 There's a small shelf for your books *on top of/over* the bed.

5 Joseph ran quickly *along/through* the corridor to the office.

6 Nicky found her mobile *under/below* a cushion on the sofa.

7 To get to the lifts, walk *over/through* the perfume department.

8 Please write your name clearly *on top of/above* your signature.

9 You can see *through/across* the harbour from our balcony.

10 The ball flew *over/along* the goal and landed in the crowd.

C4 Look at the picture and fill in the gaps in these sentences with prepositions.

The bed is **1** ...between... the door and the window.
There are four pictures **2** .... the wall
3 .... the bed. There are some clothes
hanging **4** .... the head of the bed. In the
corner is a table with a mirror **5** .... it
and a jug and other things **6** .... it.
There's a chair **7** .... the head of the bed
and another chair **8** .... the foot of the
bed **9** .... a door. There's a towel hanging
10 .... this door.

C5 Write a description of the room you are in or another room you know well. Use the language in C4 to help you.

C6 In each of these sentences there is one wrong preposition. <u>Underline</u> each mistake and write the correction.

1 There are lots of art galleries at Amsterdam. ......in......

2 She watched the children run onto the park to play. ....

3 Timmy saw Mel in the party but he didn't speak to her. ....

4 Andy ran through the beach to the next village and came back by bus. ....

5 I took the ticket out from my bag and gave it to the man by the door. ....

6 Please don't park behind my window – I can't see anything. ....

7 We were very tired when we arrived at Paris after a long flight. ....

8 Jacky hid between a car when she saw Lewis because she didn't want to speak to him. ....

9 I called in Rebecca's house, but she wasn't at home. ....

10 The guide held a small flag on top of her head so that the tourists could follow her easily. ....

D Exam practice

Read the letter in the Writing Part 3 task below. Write down the names of the important buildings in your town. Use these ideas if you want.

town hall   sports centre   railway station   museum   art gallery   hospital

Grammar focus task

Write some sentences describing where the buildings are. Use these prepositions.

opposite   in front of   behind   between   by   beside   next to

Now do the exam task below.

Writing Part 3

- This is part of a letter you receive from your English friend George.

> I'm looking forward to visiting your town. Can you describe the town centre to me? Where are the most important buildings?

- Now write a letter to George, telling him about the buildings in the town centre.

- Write your **letter** in about 100 words.

A Context listening

A1 Dea and Simon are talking about sport on the radio. Before you listen, look at the photographs and write the names of the sports. Which sports do you think they will talk about?

A2 🎧 18 Listen and check if you were right. As you listen, put the sports in the order in which you hear about them.

A3 18◀ Listen again and fill in the gaps below. If there is no word in the gap, mark – .

1 ... .*in*.......... ten days there's one of my favourite events.

2 I run every day .... one or two hours.

3 .... next month there's the Cup Final.

4 That's .... the 18th, right?

5 ... the European Champions' final, which is .... the end of the month.

6 ... don't forget the British Grand Prix .... July.

7 ... fans will arrive .... sunrise and queue .... hours.

8 ... it's worth waiting .... five o'clock.

9 I did that .... my birthday.

10 ... if it rains .... a match ...

11 ... that's sport .... the summer.

12 We haven't got any more time .... the moment.

A4 Look at your answers to A3 and write the words which follow:

1 *in* _ten days_____   5 *for* _____

2 *at* _____   6 *until* _____

3 *on* _____   7 *–* _____

4 *during* _____

18

B Grammar

B1 *At,* *on* and *in*

We use *at* with
◆ a point of time, seasonal holidays:
   at *the beginning/end of the month,* *at* *six o'clock,* *at* *sunrise,* *at* *lunchtime,* *at* *Christmas*
We also use *at* in some expressions:
at *the weekend,* *at* *first* (= at the beginning), *at* *last* (= finally), *at* *present / at* *the moment* (= now)

We use *on* with
◆ dates, days of the week, special days:
   on *8th July* (note that we say *on* *the eighth of July*), *on* *Sunday,* *on* *my birthday,* *on* *the day of the race*

We use *in* with
◆ parts of the day, months, seasons, years, decades, centuries:
   in *the afternoon/morning/evening* (but *at* *night*), *in* *July,* *in* *(the) summer,* *in* *1953,* *in* *the 90s,* *in* *the twenty-first century*

⚠ We do not use a preposition before *today, tomorrow, yesterday, this/next/last:*
Next month there's the Cup Final. (**not** ~~In next month there's the Cup Final.~~)   ➡C1

⚠ Be careful with these expressions.
in the end ≠ *at the end*
in *the end* = the final result **but** *at* *the end* = the last event:
I looked everywhere for my shoe. *In* *the end* *I found it under my bed.*
The film was very exciting with a long car chase *at* *the end.*

on time ≠ *in time*
on *time* = at the correct time **but** *in* *time* = early enough:
If the train's *on* *time, I'll be home at six.*
If we leave now, we'll be home *in* *time to see the news.*

B2 *By* and *until/till*

We use *by* to show something happens before or at a time:
Can you clean the car *by* *four o'clock?* (= Will the car be clean before or at four o'clock?)

We use *until/till* to show something happens up to, but not after, a time:
Don't wait *until/till* *July to get your tickets.* (= Buy your tickets before July.)
They played *until/till* *it got dark.* (= They stopped when it got dark.)   ➡C2

B3 *In, during* and *for*

In and *during* often mean the same when we talk about a period of time:
There will be some good sport *in/during* *the next few months.*
But when we talk about an activity or an event we use *during* not *in:*
It rained *during* *the match.* (= the players were playing tennis when the rain started)

For tells us how long: *I run every day* *for* *one or two hours.*

In tells us how soon: *In* *ten days there's one of my favourite events.*   ➡C3, C4

C Grammar exercises

C1 Complete each sentence with one of the words or phrases in the box.

> last   the moment   ~~Monday~~   14th June   the 1950s   New Year   the evening
> the end of this lesson   the nineteenth century   their wedding anniversary

1 I'll meet you on ....Monday............ .

2 Did you visit your cousins at .... ?

3 The exam took place on ....

4 Ian looked everywhere for his camera and at .... he found it in his bag.

5 Women first came to this university in ....

6 We took my parents to a restaurant on ....

7 Where is Michael living at .... ?

8 My grandparents went to Australia in ....

9 We don't often go shopping in .... because we're too tired.

10 Let's go to the café at ....

C2 Fill in the gaps in this note with *at, on, in, by, until* or mark – if no word is necessary.

Hi Tabitha

I hope you're all ready for our trip to Glasgow. Remember to bring a jacket
because Scotland can be very rainy, even **1** ....in........ summer and it may be cold
2 .... night. But I'm sure we'll have a good time. My brother was there
3 .... 2004. I spoke to him **4** .... last week and he says it's a great
place. Our plane arrives there **5** .... lunchtime so we'll have plenty of time to
find somewhere to stay. Then we can go out **6** .... the evening and go to
some art galleries **7** .... Friday. I've booked tickets for a guided tour
8 .... the weekend. But we'll have time for shopping, don't worry. You can
phone me **9** .... tomorrow if you want to ask me anything, I'll be at home
10 .... about two, but I have to go out after that.
That's it, really. I'll meet you at the airport **11** .... quarter past eleven
12 .... Thursday. I know the flight's not **13** .... 12.30 but we have
to check in **14** .... 11.30 at the latest so please make sure you're there
15 .... time!

Love

Francine

C3 Underline the correct prepositions in this magazine article.

New Year Romance

The singer Petunia is getting married again! She told our reporter the news:

I've known Carlo 1 *in/for* six months. He's a wonderful person and I'm so happy. I met him 2 *during/at* my European tour last autumn. He asked me to marry him and of course I said 'Yes' immediately. But we didn't want to make an announcement 3 *for/until* we'd told our families. We're having a house built near Milan. The architect promises it'll be ready 4 *by/till* the summer so we can move in straight away. I'm so excited. 5 *On/In* three weeks I'll be Mrs Bianchi! And I'm going to be Mrs Bianchi 6 *in/for* the rest of my life. Isn't that wonderful?

C4 Chuck is planning to visit his English cousin, Rick. Fill in the gaps in this online chat with a preposition.

Hi Rick. A few questions, if you have time?

Hi Chuck. Ask anything.

I'll be in classes 1 *on* weekdays. Will I have time for shopping?

Of course! You can go shopping 2 .... weekends. Most shops are open all day 3 .... Saturdays, but they don't open 4 .... ten or eleven o'clock 5 .... Sundays.

What about getting home if I stay out late 6 .... the evening? Do buses run 7 .... the night in your town?

There are some buses 8 .... the middle of the evening, but not after that, so if you're not home 9 .... ten, you'll have to get a taxi. Or cycle.

I don't really want to cycle in England 10 .... winter. Perhaps I could hire a car.

I don't think you can hire a car 11 .... your twenty-first birthday actually! But don't worry. You'll be here 12 .... six weeks and you'll soon get used to everything. Anyway, I'll make sure you have a good time.

That's great. Thanks for the help. See you. Bye.

D / Exam practice

Reading Part 4

Read the text and questions below.
For each question, mark the correct letter **A**, **B**, **C** or **D**.

Portmeirion

Last week I visited the village of Portmeirion in north Wales. During my childhood, I'd enjoyed holidays in the area, which is one of the most beautiful parts of Britain. However, I'd never been to the village and I had always wanted to. I visited the village in the autumn, which was a good choice as it was less crowded than in the summer. I'd read about its history and knew that the buildings were from many different styles and periods but hadn't realised how colourful they would be.

Portmeirion didn't exist in the nineteenth century. The first building didn't go up until 1926 and the last in 1976. It was built by Sir Clough Williams. From the age of 5, he dreamed of building his own village. He wanted to show that it was possible to build a village in a lovely area and not spoil it. In 1919 he sailed around the British coast for several months looking for a suitable spot. He visited 22 possible sites before he found the place of his dreams at last, just 8 km away from his family home.

Sir Clough had to build cheaply and quickly and I discovered that some of the buildings even have painted windows which were cheaper than putting in real windows! Some were built so that they look grander than they are. The windows in the bell tower, for example, are smaller as you go up the tower, so it seems taller from the ground than it really is.

On my second day there I stood on the balcony of my hotel at dawn. As I looked over the Austrian-style houses and Italian piazzas with the wonderful view of the Welsh coastline in the background, I realised what Clough Williams was trying to do.

1 What is the writer trying to do?

   A give information about where to stay in Portmeirion

   B compare Portmeirion to other similar villages

   C describe a visit to Portmeirion

   D suggest what improvements could be made to Portmeirion

2 What surprised the writer about the village?

   A the mixture of buildings

   B the beauty of the area

   C the number of visitors

   D the different colours used

3 What was the aim of Clough Williams in 1919?

    A to build a village without damaging the natural surroundings

    B to make an existing village more beautiful

    C to build a village as close to his home as possible

    D to visit as many villages as possible before building his own

4 What did the writer find out about some of the buildings?

    A They cost more to build than expected.

    B They aren't as big as they look.

    C There was a mistake in their design.

    D Some of the windows need replacing.

5 Which of these postcards did the writer send from Portmeirion?

A
> It's my first visit to the area, and I hadn't realised how lovely this coast is. We should have a holiday together in Portmeirion.

B
> I discovered Portmeirion by chance. I've really enjoyed finding out about its history and looking at the unusual buildings.

C
> I hadn't been to Portmeirion before but I'm pleased I came. I now realise what a special place it is.

D
> Portmeirion village is getting bigger all the time. I don't think they should add any more new buildings.

Grammar focus task

Put the correct prepositions in the spaces. Use the exam task to help you. There are similar expressions in it.

Last week I visited the city of York. I'd enjoyed holidays there
(1) ....during........ my childhood and I'd always wanted to go back. This year
I went there again (2) .... last. When I was a child we went (3)
.... the summer but this time I visited (4) .... the
autumn. I was there (5) .... five days. The first place
I went to was the Cathedral or Minster. There was a church there
(6) ....the fourth century but the present building was started
(7) .... 1220 and wasn't completed until 1472.

A Context listening

A1 Look at the picture of Katie, Emma and Olivia. What can you guess about them?

Emma   Olivia   Katie

A2 🎧 19 You are going to hear Katie talking to her teacher, Mr Orwell. Why is she worried?

A3 19◀◀ Listen again and complete the sentences below.

1 Emma and Olivia insist ....on........ applying for the same university as me.

2 Well I approve .... that plan.

3 You're interested .... studying different subjects.

4 They're both so good .... their subjects.

5 You think your sisters may succeed .... getting places at university.

6 You may find that they're also worried .... getting places at university.

7 They're really excited .... going away to study.

8 I'm looking forward to congratulating you all .... your exam results.

9 Thank you .... listening to me.

A4 Look at your answers to A3 and answer these questions.

1 What kind of word have you written in the gaps?

2 What kind of word follows the gaps in 1, 3, 5, 6, 7 and 9?

3 What kind of word follows the gaps in 2, 4 and 8?

A5 Match the words in the box with the sentences 1–3. <u>Underline</u> the words in the sentence which mean the same as the words in the box.

| fill in   get on well   look through |

1 I'll check it with you.

2 They've already started to complete the forms.

3 You usually have a good relationship with your sisters.

B Grammar

B1 Expressions with prepositions

We go somewhere:

by air/land/sea/road, by plane/car/bus/rail/train/bike, on foot, on holiday, on business.

We can be:

at work, at home, at school, at university, at lunch, in love, in danger, in bed, in a hurry, on the phone.

We do things:

by chance, by accident, by mistake, in secret, in private, in public, on purpose.

Things can be:

in stock, for/on sale, for hire, on fire.

➡C1

B2 Verb + preposition

We use prepositions after some verbs:

	verb	preposition	
They **apologised**	*for*	*starting without me.*
She doesn't **approve**	*of*	*that.*
They **insist**	*on*	*applying for the same university.*
Your sisters may **succeed**	*in*	*getting places at university.*

⚠ Don't forget that a noun, pronoun or the *-ing* form follows a preposition.

B3 Verb + object + preposition

We use prepositions after the object of some verbs:

verb	object	preposition	
He **congratulated**	*me*	*on*	*my success.*
Thank	*you*	*for*	*listening to me.*
You can **forgive**	*them*	*for*	*doing that.*
We will **prevent**	*the students*	*from*	*leaving.*

Some verbs are followed by different prepositions with different meanings:

I **asked** *my teacher* **about** *the new books.* (I wanted information) ≠ *I* **asked** *my teacher* **for** *the new books.* (I wanted her to give me the books)

⚠ When we ask someone to **do** something, we say:

I **asked** *my teacher* **to give** *me the books.* (**not** ~~I asked my teacher for giving me the books.~~)

⚠ Don't forget that a noun, pronoun or the *-ing* form follows a preposition.

 ➡C2

B4 *to be* + adjective + preposition

We use prepositions after some adjectives when they follow the verb *to be*:

to be	adjective	preposition	
He **was**	good	*at*	*football.*
We **were**	angry	*with*	*our friends.*
She **will be**	angry	*about*	*losing the match.*
Were they	happy/excited/worried etc.	*about*	*their exam results?*
I **was**	pleased	*with*	*the present.*
We **mustn't be**	unkind	*to*	*our cousins.*
Don't be	rude	*to*	*anyone at the party.*
Please **be**	polite	*to*	*my parents.*
Are you	interested	*in*	*football?*

⚠ Don't forget that a noun, pronoun or the *-ing* form follows a preposition. **➡C3, C4**

B5 Phrasal verbs

Phrasal verbs are two-word or three-word verbs. They have a main verb + one or two short words (preposition or adverb) which are really part of the verb.

The meaning of some phrasal verbs is clear:
*Please **put down** your pencils.* (= put + down)

The meaning of some phrasal verbs is not so clear. You have to learn what they mean:
*He **looks after** his little brother.* (= He takes care of his little brother.)
***Look out**! There's a car coming.* (= Be careful!)
*They **looked up** the word in the dictionary.* (= They found the word in the dictionary.)
*I am **looking forward to** meeting them.* (= I believe I will enjoy meeting them.)

Some phrasal verbs have several meanings. We understand which meaning by looking at the other words in the sentence:
*She **put on** her clothes.* (= She got dressed.)
*She **put on** weight.* (= Her weight increased.)
*She **put on** the television.* (= She switched the television on.)

Here are some more phrasal verbs which are useful for PET:
fill in = complete a form
find out = discover
get into = enter
get out of = leave
get on with = have a good relationship with someone
get up = get out of bed
give back = return something to someone
give up = stop doing something e.g. smoking
go on = continue
go with = match e.g. a coat and boots
hang up = end a telephone call
hold up = delay

join in = take part in
leave out = not do something
look for = try to find something
put off = do something later
put through = connect a telephone call
run out of = finish something e.g. petrol
set off/set out = begin a journey
take away = remove
take off = remove clothes
turn into = become
turn down = refuse an invitation/offer
turn up = arrive **➡C5**

C Grammar exercises

C1 Fill in each gap with one preposition.

1 I didn't buy any new boots because the shop didn't have my size ....*in*.......... stock.

2 Most of our guests arrived .... car but my brother came .... foot.

3 You shouldn't be .... work with that awful cough, you should be .... home, ... bed.

4 I deleted your email .... mistake, I didn't do it .... purpose.

5 I usually travel .... train when I go to Scotland .... business.

6 The movie star met her lover .... secret because they didn't want to be seen together .... public.

7 Every time I try to see the manager he's either .... lunch or .... the phone.

8 They met .... chance on a train and they've been .... love ever since.

9 If you're not .... a hurry, we could go to the city centre .... bike.

C2 Complete the sentence describing what happened in each picture. Use the verb in brackets.

1 She congratulated Eric ..*on winning the cup*.. . (*win*)

2 He prevented .... (*come in*)

3 She insisted .... (*help*)

4 He thanked .... (*help*)

5 Sue apologised .... (*break*)

6 He forgave .... (*break*)

7 They succeeded .... (*pass*)

8 She asked .... (*help*)

C3 Match the sentence halves.

1 The taxi driver was angry. ......*e*......   a in football.

2 My brother is very good ....   b with the present.

3 Peter was worried ....   c to my neighbour.

4 David was pleased ....   d about losing his job.

5 The postman was rude ....   e ~~with the cyclist.~~

6 We're not interested ....   f at doing word puzzles.

C4 In each of these sentences there is one wrong preposition. <u>Underline</u> each mistake and write the correction.

1 We saw that the house was <u>in</u> fire, but luckily no one was in danger. ....*on*..........

2 The nurses have been very kind to you, you mustn't be rude with them. ....

3 There are boats at hire here, or we can go for a swim. ....

4 Are you in this country for holiday or are you working? ....

5 My parents don't approve on some of my friends. ....

6 Did the manager insist in changing your day off? ....

7 My mother's in work at the moment, but she can phone you this evening. ....

C5 There are eight phrasal verbs in this story. <u>Underline</u> each one, then match it with a verb in the box that has the same meaning.

arrived	became	connected ....
delayed	entered	refused ....
removed	started ......*set off*......	

Last night I had dinner with some friends and <u>set off</u> around eleven o'clock to walk home. Passing an office block, I saw a moving light through a window so I phoned the police station. I was put through to a detective and told him what I'd seen. He promised to come immediately, but he was held up for three-quarters of an hour by a traffic jam. All the city centre roads were blocked by an accident. While I was waiting for him, a man turned up in a car. He asked me why I was there. I explained I'd seen a light, and he told me he was a policeman on his way home. We went to the back of the building and found a broken window. The man got into the building through the window. I said I could help him but he turned down my offer, so I waited for the detective. At last he arrived with a colleague and I told him about the man in the car. He made a note of the number and phoned the police station. Some more police came. One took away the car and the others watched the building. When the man and his friend tried to leave, the detectives arrested them. I'd planned a quiet walk, but it turned into an adventure!

D Exam practice

Grammar focus task

Look at the Writing Part 2 task below.

1 Which prepositions follow
   congratulate someone?   ....
   thank someone?   ....
   apologise?   ....

2 What word do we use when we apologise to a friend? ....

Now do the exam task below. Make sure you use the correct prepositions.

Writing Part 2

An English friend of yours has passed an important exam and has invited you to a party but you can't go.

Write a note to your friend. In your note, you should

• congratulate him or her

• thank him or her

• apologise.

Write **35–45 words**.

A Context listening

A1 Look at this list of things people use computers for. Do you use a computer for any of these things? Do you know other people who do?

> booking accommodation   buying tickets   doing homework
> downloading music   finding out information   having online conversations
> paying bills   planning holidays   playing games   writing emails

A2 🎧 20 You are going to hear Mickey and Cristina having a conversation.

1 What doesn't Cristina enjoy?

2 What has Mickey used the computer for this afternoon?

A3 20◀◀ Listen again and match the questions to the answers below. Stop the recording if you need to.

1 What does the manager's new notice say? ......D......

2 How long has Mickey been on the internet? ....

3 When do Mickey and Cristina need to get plenty of information? ....

4 When did Mickey find the website about Doubtful Sound? ....

5 What did Mickey promise Cristina? ....

6 What is one of the main attractions of the trip? ....

7 What is a possibility on the trip? ....

8 When should people tell the company if they are vegetarians? ....

9 When does Cristina need a good coffee? ....

A While looking for ideas about South Island.

B To go walking with her on holiday.

C After working in that office all day.

D No talking except on business.

E Before planning their holiday.

F Since finishing his essay.   H Seeing penguins.

G Taking photographs.   I When booking.

A4 Look at your answers to A3.

What kind of word follows *since, before, while, when* and *after*?

B Grammar

B1 The *-ing* form as subject

We often use the *-ing* form as the subject of a verb:
Running is good exercise.
We can use a noun with the *-ing* form:
Running a marathon is good exercise.
You often see *-ing* and *No* + *-ing* in signs and notices:
Parking is not allowed.
No talking except on business.

→C1

B2 *Before, after, when, while* and *since* + *-ing*

Before or *after* + *-ing* shows what happens first and what happens second:
We'll look at the website before booking our trip. (– 1 We'll look at the website. 2 We'll book our trip.)
We booked our trip after looking at the website. (= 1 We looked at the website. 2 We booked our trip.)
When + *-ing* shows that two actions happen at the same time:
I dropped my passport when getting off the train. (= I got off the train and I dropped my passport at the same time.)
While + *-ing* shows that one action happens in the middle of another:
I found this website while looking for ideas about South Island. (= I looked for ideas about South Island for some time. I found the website during that time.)
Since + *-ing* shows when an action began:
I haven't had a pleasant day since joining that company.

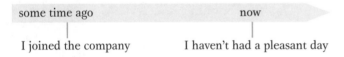

some time ago	now
I joined the company	I haven't had a pleasant day

We can also use *before, after, when, while* and *since* at the beginning of a sentence:
Since finishing my essay, I've been on the internet.
⚠ The subject of the -ing form must be the same as the verb in the other part of the sentence:
Before leaving the room, I turned the computer off. (= **I** turned the computer off,
I left the room.)

→C2, C3

B3 *By, without* and *for* + *-ing*

We use *by/without/for* + -ing to show how we do something, or how something happens.
We can book by filling in this form online.
We can do it without leaving the house.
I use my computer for downloading music.

B4 *go* and *come* + *-ing*

We use *go* + *-ing* to talk about some sports and other activities:
Can we go walking there?
When we invite someone to join us, we use *come* + the *-ing* form:
Would you like to come swimming with me?

→C4

C Grammar exercises

C1 Complete the notices so that they mean the same as these sentences. Use the *-ing* form and any other words you need.

1 Only employees can park here.

......No parking......
EXCEPT FOR EMPLOYEES.

2 You aren't allowed to smoke.

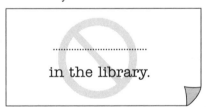

NO ....

3 You are forbidden to eat or drink in the library.

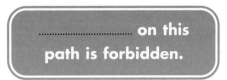

4 You must not cycle on this path.

.... **on this path is forbidden.**

5 Do not talk to the driver when the bus is moving.

.... **to the driver when the bus is moving.**

6 Do not play games on school computers.

....

ON SCHOOL COMPUTERS
IS FORBIDDEN.

C2 Make each pair of sentences into one sentence, using the word given + *-ing*.

1 Use the kitchen. Clear the table. (*after*) ...Clear the table after using the kitchen....

2 Check the address. Post the parcel. (*before*)

....

3 Read the instructions. Connect the mouse to the keyboard. (*before*)

....

4 Ask the price. Book seats for the concert. (*when*)

....

5 Pass your exam. Take a holiday. (*after*)

....

C3 Fill in the gaps in this mobile phone conversation.
Use *before*, *after*, *when*, *while* or *since*.

Tom: Hello?

Kai: Tom, I know it's late, but I need to tell you something.

Tom: It's OK. I'm not home yet. I'm back at the taxi office.

Kai: But I thought you got a taxi immediately **1** ....after........... leaving the club.

Tom: I did. But **2** .... getting into the taxi, I haven't been able to find my wallet. I can't pay the taxi driver.

Kai: I know where your wallet is. But it's empty.

Tom: What?

Kai: Well, I left the club soon after you, and **3** .... waiting for my bus, I noticed a wallet on the pavement. I looked round **4** .... picking it up, but there wasn't anyone near. **5** .... looking in it for a name or address, I thought about taking it to the police station. But then I noticed the initials on it and guessed it might be yours. Someone probably dropped the wallet **6** .... taking the money.

Tom: Oh no. I guess I was robbed **7** .... leaving the club. Can you come to the taxi office and explain?

Kai: Yeah, I suppose someone's got to rescue you. But next time, check your wallet **8** .... taking a taxi, OK?

C4 Complete this email with words or phrases from the box.

after eating   before going   ~~being~~   by emailing   for texting   shopping
since starting   studying   swimming   without dieting

Dear Parissa

How are you? I'm fine now the school holiday has started.

1 ....Being..... at home is great because **2** .... is horrible when the weather is hot.
Could we meet some time soon? We can go **3** .... and have lunch together.
And then, **4** .... we can see a film or something. Perhaps you'd like to come
5 .... with me at the new pool. I go there almost every day.
6 .... to that pool, I didn't really like swimming, but it's really great, with slides
and waves and so on. And the really good news is that I've lost two kilos **7** ....
to swim regularly. And I've done it **8** .... !
Let me know which day is best for you **9** .... me. Or you can text me. I've got a
new mobile and I can use it **10** ....
I look forward to getting your email. Love Abby

D Exam practice

Reading Part 1

Look at the text in each question.
What does it say?
Mark the letter next to the correct explanation – **A**, **B** or **C**.

1

Dear Grant

I'm resting in Glasgow this weekend after spending the week climbing in the Scottish mountains! Then, before flying back to Canada, I'm going to spend two weeks in England.

Elaine

A Elaine is flying from Canada to England.

B Elaine is resting before going to England.

C Elaine is staying in Glasgow after leaving England.

2

Students can only see the nurse if they have an appointment.

Ring 3600 before 10am.

A It is not possible for students to see the nurse without making an appointment.

B Students can get an appointment with the nurse by arriving before 10 am.

C Students can see the nurse up to 10 am without having to make an appointment.

3

Taking photographs is forbidden except in the new gallery where you must request permission.

A You are not allowed to take photographs of the new gallery.

B You are allowed to use a camera in the new gallery if you ask.

C You are allowed to use a camera anywhere except the new gallery.

4

Make sure the door shuts behind you when leaving the building in the evening.

A The door to this building should be kept closed until the evening.

B The door to this building should be left open during the day.

C Don't leave the building in the evening without checking that the door is closed.

5

Sonia
Since joining the health club I swim every day. Would you like to come swimming with me next Friday when I can take a guest free of charge?
Andrew

Andrew wants Sonia to

A join the health club so they can swim together.

B swim with him on a particular day.

C bring a friend to swim at the health club.

Grammar focus task

Look at the exam task. Find an example of:

1 *-ing* as subject ....
2 *go* or *come* + *-ing* ....
3 *when* + *-ing* ....
4 *without* + *-ing* ....
5 *since* + *-ing* ....

A   Context listening

A1 Look at these pictures of necklaces.

1   Which necklace is made of
    wire and beads?

2   Which is made of leather
    and stones?

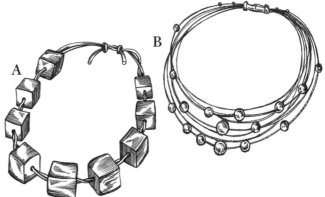

A2 🎧 **21** You are going to hear a man, Jeff, talking to two students, Garth and Mary, about making jewellery.

1   What is Mary's reason for making jewellery? ....

2   What is Garth's reason for making jewellery? ....

3   Which necklace in A1 does Mary make? ....

4   Which necklace in A1 does Garth make? ....

A3 **21◀◀** Listen again and fill in the gaps below.

1   ... think about what you intend ......*to do*...... with it.

2   I don't mind .... something which isn't completely perfect.

3   I suggest .... with simple things.

4   I hate .... heavy jewellery.

5   ... remember .... the weight.

6   I remember .... some earrings for a customer.

7   She made .... lots of heavy stones.

8   I'll let ....

9   Well, I plan .... this one myself.

10 I'd like .... these square black ones.

A4 Look at your answers to A3 and answer these questions.

1   Which verbs are followed by the *to* infinitive? ....

2   Which verbs are followed by an *-ing* form? ....

3   Which verb is in both lists? ....

4   Which verbs are not in either list? ....

B Grammar

B1 We often use one verb followed by another. The first verb decides the form of the second verb:

first verb	second verb		second verb form
I *want*	*to make*	*a necklace.*	*to* infinitive
I *hate*	*wearing*	*heavy jewellery.*	*-ing* form

The second verb is usually either the *to* infinitive or the *-ing* form.

B2 Verbs + *to* infinitive

Some verbs are followed by the *to* infinitive:

> (can't) afford   agree   aim   appear   arrange   choose   decide   demand
> deserve   expect   fail   hope   learn   manage   offer   plan   prepare   pretend
> promise   refuse   seem   (can't) wait   wish

*I **can't afford to buy** a lot of materials.*
*Do you **hope to sell** it?*

For the negative we put *not* before *to*:
*They **agreed not to leave**.*

Some verbs are followed by the *to* infinitive and always have an object:

> advise   encourage   force   invite   order   persuade   remind   teach   tell   warn

*I'm going **to teach** you **to make** necklaces.*
*I **advise** students **to make** several things.*

Some verbs are followed by the *to* infinitive and sometimes have an object:

> ask   expect   help   intend   want
> would like   would love   would hate   would prefer

*We **expect to be** late.* (= we will probably be late) or *We **expect** Tom **to be late**.* (= he will probably be late)
*We **would like to stay** longer.* or *We **would like** them **to stay** longer.*

⚠ Remember the difference between *would like* and *like*:
***Would** you **like to play** tennis?* (= an invitation to play)
*Do you **like playing** tennis?* (= asking about your opinion) (see B5)

➡C1

B3 *make* and *let*

Make and *let* are followed by the infinitive without *to*. They always have an object:

*I'll **let** you **decide**.*
*She **made** me **use** lots of heavy stones.*

➡C2

B4 Verbs + *-ing*

Some verbs are followed by *-ing*:

avoid	carry on*	consider	delay	dislike	enjoy	feel like*	finish	give up*	
imagine	involve	keep	keep on*	(not) mind	miss	practise	put off*		
recommend	suggest								

***Avoid making** heavy jewellery.*
*I **suggest practising** with simple things.*

For the negative we put *not* before the *-ing* form:
*Can you **imagine not having** a car nowadays?*
(*See Unit 19 B5 for more information about phrasal verbs.)

➡C3

B5 Verbs followed by the *to* infinitive or *-ing*

These verbs are usually followed by *-ing* but sometimes by the *to* infinitive:

begin	continue	like	love	prefer	hate	start

*He **continued** talking loudly.* **or** *He **continued** to talk loudly.*
*I **prefer using** a dictionary.* **or** *I **prefer to use** a dictionary.*

Some verbs are followed by the *to* infinitive or *-ing* with a different meaning:

forget	remember	try	stop

Verb + *to* infinitive	Verb + *-ing*
remember to	remember -ing
Remember to check the weight.	I **remember making** some earrings.
(= an action which will be necessary)	(= a memory of an action in the past)
forget to	forget -ing
Don't **forget to phone** me.	I'll never **forget meeting** her.
(= an action which will be necessary)	(= a memory of an action in the past)
try to	try -ing
Try to walk quickly. (= if you can)	**Try taking** more exercise. (= an experiment)
stop to	stop -ing
She **stopped to rest**.	He **stopped shouting** at us.
(= because she wanted to rest)	(= he finished doing it)

➡C4, C5

C Grammar exercises

C1 Complete the second sentence so that it means the same as the first. Use a verb from the box and any other words you need.

> advised   agreed   asked   expected   intended
> invited   ordered   promised   refused   warned

1 'Don't touch the wire, Claire.' said the teacher. The teacher _warned Claire not to touch_ the wire.

2 'You should eat more fruit, Jane.' said the nurse. The nurse _advised Jane to eat_ more fruit.

3 'OK, I'll help you, Amina.' said Nat. Nat .... Amina.

4 'I won't tell you anything, Sally.' said Lorna. Lorna .... anything.

5 'Don't use this computer, Euan.' said Grant. Grant .... the computer.

6 'Can you open the box for me, Zena?' asked Paul. Paul .... the box for him.

7 'I won't forget the tickets.' said Mel. Mel .... the tickets.

8 'I'm going to read ten books in one week.' said Brian. Brian .... in one week.

9 'Would you like to stay at my house, Aziza?' said Helen. Helen .... at her house.

10 'I'll probably see my sister at the weekend.' said Michael. Michael .... his sister at the weekend.

C2 Match the beginnings and endings of these sentences.

1 The official demanded ......_e_......   a people to forget my birthday.

2 My maths teacher pretended ....   b me to check my email.

3 My music teacher made ....   c the children watch a video.

4 My boss reminded ....   d not to see me at the disco.

5 I'd hate ....   e ~~to see my passport.~~

6 I let ....   f me take the exam.

C3 Fill in the gaps in this conversation with the correct form of the verb in brackets.

Mum: Hi Ben, you're home early. I didn't expect 1 ......_to see_...... (see) you before midnight. Are you hungry?

Ben: No, you carry on 2 ......_eating_...... (eat). I don't feel hungry.

Mum: What's the matter?

Ben: Oh, I planned **3** .... (*go*) to the city centre with Maria, but she didn't manage **4** .... (*get*) to the station in time. I didn't feel like **5** .... (*go*) alone, so I decided **6** .... (*come*) home. I'm going to give up **7** .... (*see*) her.

Mum: I suggest **8** .... (*talk*) to her. She seems **9** .... (*be*) a nice girl.

Ben: I don't mind **10** .... (*wait*) for a good reason, but she never even phones.

Mum: You'll miss **11** .... (*spend*) time with her if you break up.

Ben: Perhaps. But I don't like **12** .... (*waste*) my evenings.

C4 **Complete each sentence with the correct form of a verb from the box.**

> change   check   contact   look   phone   ~~send~~   spend   travel

1 Remember ....*to send*.... your grandmother a card on her birthday next week.

2 She stopped .... at a poster and missed the train.

3 Do you remember .... alone for the first time?

4 I'll never forget .... three weeks in the rainforest.

5 Don't forget .... your email before you leave home.

6 He tried .... his hair colour, but he still looked awful.

7 Please stop .... me at work, my boss doesn't allow personal calls.

8 I tried .... my boss, but he was on a climbing holiday.

C5 <u>Underline</u> the correct form of each verb.

Hi Pete

How are you? I'm on holiday by the sea. I'd hoped **1** <u>*to go*</u>/*going* abroad but I couldn't afford **2** *fly/to fly* anywhere because I started **3** *to save/saving* too late. But I don't mind **4** *not to travel / not travelling* abroad because this is a great place. My brother encouraged me **5** *to come/coming*. I'd love you **6** *seeing/to see* it. You should try **7** *to get/getting* a few days holiday so you can come here. My landlady will let you **8** *share/to share* my room. I hope **9** *hear/to hear* from you soon.

Love Eric

PS Don't forget **10** *to book/booking* a seat on the coach if you travel at the weekend!

D Exam practice

Reading Part 5

Read the text below and choose the correct word for each space.
For each question, mark the correct letter **A**, **B**, **C** or **D**.

Example:

0 Ⓐ last   **B** earlier   **C** following   **D** late

SLEEP

People's sleeping habits have changed over the **(0)** .... 500 years. Before electric
lights **(1)** .... invented, most people went to bed soon after it got dark. Today, we
can sleep whenever we want to. Most people **(2)** .... to sleep between six and eight
hours per night during the week and **(3)** .... to ten hours per night at weekends. The
problem is that if we **(4)** .... getting up at the weekend, then we don't want to get
up on Monday morning either! Many of us **(5)** .... like sleeping after lunch and in
some hot countries people do sleep in the afternoon. In **(6)** .... countries however,
people **(7)** .... to keep working all day with only a short break. We all have dreams
(8) .... most of us fail to remember them. Some people find it difficult to
(9) .... asleep. The advice for them is to **(10)** .... taking more exercise and
remember not to drink coffee in the evening.

1	**A** have	**B** had	**C** were	**D** are
2	**A** encourage	**B** choose	**C** consider	**D** advise
3	**A** beyond	**B** above	**C** over	**D** up
4	**A** delay	**B** refuse	**C** fail	**D** force
5	**A** wish	**B** enjoy	**C** prefer	**D** feel
6	**A** any	**B** every	**C** another	**D** other
7	**A** might	**B** have	**C** should	**D** must
8	**A** because	**B** so	**C** but	**D** therefore
9	**A** make	**B** fall	**C** get	**D** go
10	**A** prepare	**B** try	**C** decide	**D** manage

Grammar focus task

Look at Question 2. Which is the correct answer? ....
Why are the other answers wrong? ....
Do the same with Questions 4, 5, 7 and 10. ....

....

A Context listening

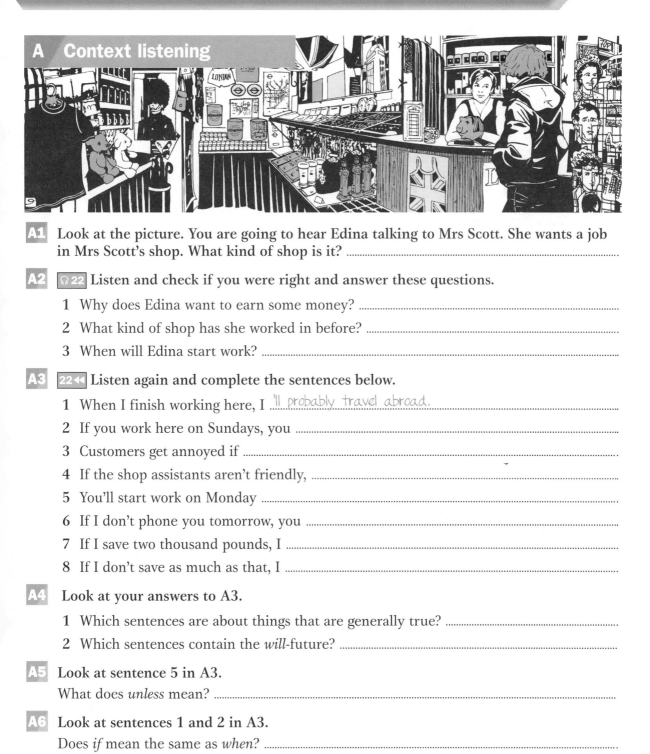

A1 Look at the picture. You are going to hear Edina talking to Mrs Scott. She wants a job in Mrs Scott's shop. What kind of shop is it? ....

A2 🎧 22 Listen and check if you were right and answer these questions.

1 Why does Edina want to earn some money? ....

2 What kind of shop has she worked in before? ....

3 When will Edina start work? ....

A3 22◀◀ Listen again and complete the sentences below.

1 When I finish working here, I *'ll probably travel abroad.*

2 If you work here on Sundays, you ....

3 Customers get annoyed if ....

4 If the shop assistants aren't friendly, ...

5 You'll start work on Monday ....

6 If I don't phone you tomorrow, you ....

7 If I save two thousand pounds, I ....

8 If I don't save as much as that, I ....

A4 Look at your answers to A3.

1 Which sentences are about things that are generally true? ....

2 Which sentences contain the *will*-future? ....

A5 Look at sentence 5 in A3.
What does *unless* mean? ....

A6 Look at sentences 1 and 2 in A3.
Does *if* mean the same as *when*? ....

B Grammar

B1 Conditional sentences

Conditional sentences have two parts, a condition and a result:

      condition   **result**

If you work here, your evenings will be free.

      result   **condition**

Your evenings will be free if you work here.

⚠ When the *if* part comes second, there is no comma.

The condition part usually starts with *if*. Different kinds of conditional sentences use different tenses. (See B2, B3, and Unit 23 B2.)

⚠ *When* does not mean the same as *if*:

When I have £2000, I'll go to South America.   *If I have £2000, I'll go to South America.*
(= I'll certainly have £2000 one day and   *(= Perhaps I'll have £2000 one day and perhaps*
then I'll go to South America.)   *I'll go to South America.)*   →C1

B2 Zero conditional

We use this for things which are generally true:

if +	**present**	**present**		**present**	*if* + **present**

*If customers **have** to wait they **get** annoyed. = Customers **get** annoyed **if** they **have** to wait.*   →C2

B3 First conditional

We use this to talk about possible situations:

if + **present**	**future**		**future**	*if* + **present**

*If I **save** £2000, I'**ll go** to South America. = I'**ll go** to South America **if** I **save** £2000.*
(**not** *If I'll save...*)
*If I **don't save** £2000, I'**ll go** round Europe. = I'**ll go** round Europe **if** I **don't save** £2000.*
(**not** *If I won't save...*)
*If I **save** £1000, I **won't go** to South America. = I **won't go** to South America **if** I **save** £1000.*
(**not** *If I won't save...*)   →C3

B4 *Unless*

Unless means 'if not'. We use it with zero and first conditionals:

*Unless I **phone** you tomorrow, you'**ll start** at nine o'clock.*
*= **If** I **don't phone** you tomorrow you'**ll start** at nine o'clock.*
*The shop **loses** customers **if** the assistants **aren't** friendly.*
*= The shop **loses** customers **unless** the assistants **are** friendly.*   →C4, C5

C Grammar exercises

C1 Read this conversation and <u>underline</u> *if* or *when*.

Liz: I'm going to walk to the station to catch the London train.

Dan: But it may rain. Why not get a taxi?

Liz: Don't worry, I'll use my umbrella **1** *if/<u>when</u>* it rains.

Dan: Well, hurry up! **2** *<u>If</u>/When* you don't leave now, the train will go without you.

Liz: OK, I'm going. Goodbye.

Dan: Will you phone me **3** *if/<u>when</u>* you arrive in London?

Liz: I'll try to phone from the hotel **4** *<u>if</u>/when* I have time before my first meeting.

Dan: Leave a message **5** *<u>if</u>/when* I'm not in. I might be at the shops. Bye.

Liz: Bye.

C2 Complete each sentence with your own idea.

1 Coffee tastes good *if you put sugar in it.* ....

2 Parties are fun if ....

3 Children are naughty if ....

4 People steal things if ....

5 I always phone my friends if ....

6 Politicians lose elections if ....

C3 Complete each sentence with the correct form of a verb from the box.

become	buy	die	eat	not enjoy	give	learn	~~make~~	take	tell

1 If you're tired, I*'ll make* .... some coffee for you.

2 These flowers .... *die* .... if you forget to water them.

3 Many students ...... *learn* ...... faster if they work with a friend.

4 We .... *buy* .... some fruit if we go to the market this afternoon.

5 If you don't want that sausage, the cat .... *eat* ...... it.

6 The bus driver .... *tell* .... us when we reach our stop if we ask him.

7 Children *not enjoy* school if the lessons are boring.

8 My boyfriend's parents .... *give* .... him a car if he passes all his exams.

9 If people don't get enough sleep, they ..... *become* ... ill.

10 I ...... *Take* ...... you to the cinema if you help me finish this exercise.

C4 Fill in the gaps so that the second sentence means the same as the first.

1 I'll give you a lift unless you want to walk.

I'll give you a lift if ...*you don't*... want to walk.

2 I get up early if I'm not ill.

I get up early .... I'm ill.

3 No-one will see us if we don't put the light on.

No-one will see us .... we put the light on.

4 I'll go to the disco unless I have a headache.

I .... to the disco if I have a headache.

5 I don't sleep well if I'm worried about something.

I sleep well .... I'm worried about something.

6 I'll go clubbing unless I'm tired.

I'll go clubbing if .... tired.

C5 Complete this phone conversation with the correct tenses of the verbs in brackets.

David: Do you want to go to the cinema this afternoon?

Tara: Oh, yes. I'm so bored, if **1** ....*I don't do*......... (*I /not do*)
something, **2** ....*I'll go*............ (*I /go*) mad.

David: If **3** .... (*I /come*) to your house at
three o'clock, **4** .... (*you/be*) ready?

Tara: Yeah. But don't ring the doorbell.

David: Why not?

Tara: **5** .... (*The dog /bark*) if **6** .... (*you/ring*) the
doorbell.

David: So?

Tara: My father likes a sleep after lunch. If **7** .... (*the dog/bark*),
8 .... (*it/disturb*) my father. If **9** .... (*he /wake*) up
10 .... (*he/be*) angry. **11** .... (*He /not let*) me go out
if **12** .... (*he/be*) angry. OK?

David: OK. But **13** .... (*you/see*) me if **14** .... (*I/wait*)
outside?

Tara: Sure. I'll watch out for you from the window.

David: I'll probably come on my bike unless **15** .... (*it/rain*).

Tara: Right. See you soon.

David: Sure. Bye.

D Exam practice

Reading Part 3

Look at the sentences about a race in Canada called The Adventure Race.
Read the text to decide if each sentence is correct or incorrect.
If it is correct, mark **A**.
If it is incorrect, mark **B**.

1 The Adventure Race takes place in different countries at the same time.
2 Unless you succeed in a special test, you won't be able to do the race.
3 You should bring all the equipment on the list you're sent.
4 Everyone in your team should have the same nationality.
5 Teams need to have their routes planned at least one day before the race begins.
6 There's a limit on the time allowed between each checkpoint.
7 It won't matter if you miss one checkpoint.
8 If someone in your team can't continue, you'll have to stop too.
9 All four members of a team must cross the finishing line at the same time.
10 You'll receive £500 to spend on whatever you choose if your team wins.

The Adventure Race

The Adventure Race takes place in a different part of the world every year. This year, the race is in Canada and covers 300 miles. If you take part, you'll see some of the most beautiful scenery in the world. The race begins on 14 July. Part of the race is by horse, part by mountain bike and part by boat. You also walk and run so you need to have a wide range of outdoor skills.

Everyone must pass a skills test before they're allowed to start the race. You'll receive an equipment list when you apply for the race. This changes from year to year and you need to remember that everything on that list is essential. You supply your own food and drink so make sure you bring enough. If you don't bring plenty of food, you'll be hungry! Each team consists of four members, men and women and you must all come from one country. You need to be very fit but you also need to be able to work as part of a team.

The starting and finishing points of the race remain secret to all those taking part until approximately 24 hours before the start. Teams can then choose their route as long as they pass certain checkpoints. The race takes between six and twelve days to complete. You won't be allowed to continue if you fail to reach each checkpoint by a certain time. Each team has a 'passport' which will be stamped at each checkpoint with the date and time of arrival. If one person is injured or decides not to carry on, the rest of the team won't be allowed to either.

The first team to cross the finishing line are the winners. You can't win as an individual, only as one member of the team you start with. There must be no more than 150 metres between the first and the last member of the team reaching the finishing line. All four members receive a plane ticket worth £500 to the place of their choice anywhere in the world. The second team to cross the line receive climbing equipment.

The race usually attracts the attention of the local press so you should be willing to be photographed and possibly interviewed. This is all good publicity for next year! If you're interested, we'll send you an application form as soon as we hear from you. Write to the address at the bottom of this page or look at our website on www.adventurerace.com.

Grammar focus task

Here are some sentences from the exam text and questions. Match the two halves and fill in the gaps with the correct tense of the verb in brackets.

1 If you _take_ (take) part,

2 When you .... (apply) for the race,

3 If you .... (not bring) plenty of food,

4 You .... (not be) allowed to continue

5 If one person .... (decide) not to carry on,

6 If you .... (be) interested,

7 Unless you .... (succeed) in a special test,

8 You .... (receive) £500

a you .... (not be) able to do the race.

b if your team .... (win).

c you .... (receive) an equipment list.

d you _'ll see_ (see) some of the most beautiful scenery in the world.

e the rest of the team .... (not be) allowed to either.

f we .... (send) you an application form.

g if you .... (fail) to reach each checkpoint by a certain time.

h you .... (be) hungry.

A Context listening

Carl

Patti

A1 Patti works for a radio station. She is talking to Carl Ryder, a well-known songwriter. What things do you think he will tell her about?

> his new house   his last holiday   his university studies
> life in the music business   his family   the clothes he likes

A2 🎧 23 Listen and check if you were right.

A3 23◀◀ Listen again and complete the sentences below.

1 I wish I ....*had*........ more free time.

2 I wish I .... so busy.

3 If I .... away now, I'd choose somewhere warm and sunny.

4 I wouldn't want to talk to people if I .... songs to write.

5 If I .... a songwriter, I'd be a fashion designer.

A4 Look at your answers to A3 and answer these questions.

1 What tense did you use to complete the sentences? ....

2 Are Patti and Carl talking about the past? ....

B Grammar

B1 Conditional sentences

Conditional sentences have two parts, a condition and a result:

    condition   **result**

If I didn't have a lot of work, my evenings would be free.

The condition part usually starts with *if*. Different kinds of conditional sentences use different tenses. (See B2, and Unit 22.)

B2 Second conditional

We use this for imaginary situations, which we believe are nearly or completely impossible:

if + past   **would + infinitive**

*If I **had** time, I'd **(would)** go to more concerts.* (But I haven't got time, so I can't go to more concerts.)
*If she **liked** me, she'd **(would)** phone me.* (But I believe she doesn't like me, so she probably won't phone me.)
*If I **didn't have** an exam next week, I **would go** clubbing at the weekend.* (But I have an exam next week, so I won't go clubbing this weekend.)

or we can put the condition **after** the result:

would + infinitive   **if + past**

*I'd **go** somewhere lively **if** I **didn't have** any work to do.* (But I have work to do so I won't go somewhere lively!)
*I **wouldn't be** late for work **if** I **had** a car.* (But I don't have a car so I'm often late for work!)
***Would** I **fail** the exam next week **if** I **went** clubbing at the weekend?* (I probably won't go clubbing, but I'm thinking about the possible result.)

⚠ The verb in the *if* part of the sentence is in the past tense although its meaning is present or future.

⚠ We often use *were* instead of *was* after *If I/he/she/it*:

*If he **weren't** (**wasn't**) a songwriter he'd be a fashion designer.*
*If I **were** (**was**) you, I would write to him.*

➡C1, C2

B3 *I wish*

We use *I wish* + past for a wish about a present situation:

*I **wish** I **had** more free time.* (but I don't)
*I **wish** I **wasn't** so busy.* (but I am)
*I **wish** I **could** speak Spanish.* (but I can't)

⚠ We use a past tense, although we are talking about now.

⚠ We often use *were* instead of *was* after *I/he/she/it*:

*I wish I **were** (**was**) clever.* (but I'm not)

➡C3, C4, C5

C Grammar exercises

C1 Read the first sentence in each pair, then complete the advice in the second sentence.

1 You don't talk to people at parties.

You would enjoy parties if you ...._talked_........ to people.

2 You should practise dancing.

You'd be a good dancer if you ....

3 You eat too much cheese.

You wouldn't have spots if you .... too much cheese.

4 You wear your school shirt at weekends.

If you .... your school shirt at weekends, you'd look better.

5 You never give presents to your friends.

You would be more popular if you .... presents to your friends.

6 You make jokes about your classmates.

If you .... jokes about your classmates, they would like you better.

C2 Read the first sentence in each pair, then complete the advice in the second sentence.

1 You don't revise before exams so you don't get good marks.

You ...._'d get_........ good marks if you revised before exams.

2 You drink coffee after supper and then you can't sleep well.

You .... well if you didn't drink coffee after supper.

3 You don't wear a warm coat and you often catch colds.

If you wore a warm coat, you .... colds so often.

4 You spend all your money on clothes so you don't have any for books.

You .... enough money for books if you didn't spend it all on clothes.

5 You lose things because you never tidy your room.

You .... things if you tidied your room.

6 You're late every morning because you spend hours in the shower.

If you didn't spend hours in the shower, you .... late every morning.

C3 Noel is Danny's older brother. Danny is jealous of Noel. Read what Danny says and then complete the sentences below.

Noel is handsome, but I'm not. He has straight dark hair, but mine is light brown and curly. He works in a sports club. He earns lots of money and owns a motorbike. He lives in the city centre, but I live in a village with our parents. He's twenty-two and I'm only thirteen and a half. When I'm twenty-two I want to be like Noel.

1 I wish I ....was........ handsome.

2 I wish I .... curly hair.

3 I wish I .... in a sports club.

4 I wish I .... lots of money.

5 I wish I .... a motorbike.

6 I wish I .... in a village.

7 I wish I .... thirteen and a half.

C4 Complete this email with the correct form of the verbs in brackets.

Hi Suzanne

How are you? It's very boring here. I wish there 1 ....were.......... (be) some clubs and good shops. We spend every holiday in the Highlands because my father likes it. If my father 2 .... (not want) to go climbing we 3 .... (stay) in Edinburgh with my uncle's family. I wish we 4 .... (not come) to the same place every year. I don't think my mother likes it here either. She 5 .... (enjoy) going to museums if we 6 .... (go) to Edinburgh. And I 7 .... (meet) new people if I 8 ....(go) clubbing with my cousins. If I 9..................... (have) more money I 10 .... (not go) on holiday with my parents.

Email me soon.
LOL Victoria

C5 Complete these sentences with your own ideas.

1 If I won the lottery, ...I'd travel round the world.

2 If I were a fashion model, ...

3 If everyone liked pop music, ...

4 If exams were always easy, ...

5 If I lived in Hawaii, ...

6 If I spoke perfect English, ...

7 If politicians told the truth, ...

8 I wish I had ....

D Exam practice

Reading Part 4

Read the text and questions below.
For each question, mark the correct letter – **A**, **B**, **C** or **D**.

Visit to the Arctic Circle

I was the only person to get off the train at 4pm at Abisko in the Arctic Circle. The train disappeared into the night. I was alone, in the dark, with the temperature at minus 20, as cold as I'd expected it. At that point I thought about giving up this trip and wished I were on my way back home but the train had gone and I could see a hotel ahead.

The girl at reception gave me the key to a 'cabin' as the rest of the hotel was closed. I went back outside. I could see by the light from the hotel and found the cabin easily. My hands were frozen as I turned the key in the lock and pushed the door which refused to move. I pushed it harder. I was thinking of breaking a window to prevent myself from freezing to death when I took my hand off the handle and the door opened gently towards me.

After recovering in the warmth of the cabin, which was actually very comfortable, I went outside again. I realised I wasn't completely alone as I saw car headlights on the road nearby. It was a clear evening full of red, green and blue light in the frozen air. It was so beautiful I wanted to write a poem about it but I had no paper. I could only spend ten minutes outside at a time so I went in and out of the cabin to watch the amazing Northern Lights. I only spent three days there. I was sorry I'd booked a ticket on the train to continue my journey so soon.

1 What is the writer trying to do?

   A persuade other people to visit the Arctic Circle

   B describe his own experiences in the Arctic Circle

   C give advice on travelling to the Arctic Circle

   D explain why he decided to go to the Arctic Circle

2 When he got off the train, the writer felt

   A confused about what to do next.

   B surprised at how cold it was.

   C worried about finding a hotel.

   D sorry he was not still on it.

3 What was the problem when the writer got to the cabin?

   A He pushed the door instead of pulling it.

   B The key didn't turn because of the frozen lock.

   C He couldn't see what he was doing.

   D He had to break a window to get in.

4 How did the writer spend the evening?

   A He stayed inside the cabin and looked out at the stars.

   B He tried to write about what he could see.

   C He walked along the road towards a light.

   D He went outside for short periods of time.

5 What did the writer put in his diary that day?

A

> I'm sorry I came here as there's nothing to do in the dark.

B

> If I had a car, I could drive around and see more of the area.

C

> The best thing about being here is seeing the night sky.

D

> It's a pity this is the only room the hotel could offer me.

Grammar focus task

What did the writer think? Complete these sentences.

1 I wish I ...._was_........ on the train again.

2 If it .... summer, it .... dark.

3 If the hotel .... open, I .... there.

4 I wish this door .... open.

5 If it .... warmer, I .... more time outside.

6 I .... a poem if I .... some paper.

7 I wish I .... stay here longer.

A Context listening

A1 Alan is talking to his friend Maria about a series of science fiction films. Underline the words you think you'll hear.

alien   army   earth   experiment
flower   garage   human   planet
scientist   spaceship

NORMAN STARMAN III

A2 🎧 24 Listen and check if you were right. Tick the words you hear. Does Maria decide to see the film?

A3 24◀◀ Listen again and complete the sentences below.

1 The first two Starman films ....*were made*....... about three years ago.

2 The main part .... to a different actor.

3 He .... to their planet.

4 But the spaceship .... when they land although they .... , luckily.

5 Norman .... by the army.

6 The aliens .... , I guess, and then they'll go back their planet again.

A4 Look at your answers to A3. They are all passive verbs.

How do we make the passive in the present? ....
the past? ....
the future? ....

B Grammar

B1 The passive

I *deliver the* letters in the morning.

I *empty the* rubbish bins once a week.

The rubbish bins **are emptied** once a week.

The letters **are delivered** in the morning.

Active   **Passive**

We use the correct form of *to be* + past participle to make the passive. (See Unit 6 and p.viii for past participles.)

Active		Passive
I/you/we/they **catch**	→	I **am caught**/You/we/they **are caught**
He/she/it **catches**	→	He/she/it **is caught**
I/you/he/she/it/we/they **will catch**	→	I/you/he/she/it/we/they **will be caught**
I/you/he/she/it/we/they **caught**	→	I/you/he/she/it/we/they **were caught**
to catch	→	**to be caught**

We often use the passive when
♦ we don't know who or what does something:
*My car **was stolen**.*
*The spaceship **is damaged**.*
♦ it is obvious or unimportant who does something:
*My train **was cancelled**.*
*The aliens are waiting **to be rescued**.*
***Was** anyone **hurt** in the accident?*
*Letters **aren't delivered** on bank holidays.*

If the person who did something is important we use *by* + person:
Active   **Passive**
*Aliens **caught** Norman*. = *Norman **was caught** by aliens.*

➡C1, C2, C3, C4

B2 To have something done

When other people do a job for us, we can say we *have something done*. We do not usually say who did it.
We use the correct form of *have* + noun + past participle:
*She **has** the spaceship **repaired**. (= The garage repairs the spaceship.)*
*I **had** my hair **coloured**. (= The hairdresser coloured my hair.)*
*We'll **have** a new house **designed**. (= An architect will design a new house for us.)*

➡C5

C Grammar exercises

C1 Look at the <u>underlined</u> verbs in these sentences. Label each one A for active or P for passive.

1 I'<u>m not allowed</u> ^P <u>to drive</u> ^A my parents' car.
2 Our test <u>was marked</u> by the head teacher but our class teacher <u>told</u> us the results.
3 My brother <u>is having</u> a party tonight and you'<u>re invited</u>.
4 The letters <u>were sent</u> to the wrong address and we never <u>saw</u> them.
5 This painting <u>will be finished</u> at the weekend and I <u>think</u> it'<u>ll be</u> good.
6 I <u>paid</u> the taxi driver before I <u>opened</u> the door.
7 Important visitors <u>expect</u> <u>to be met</u> at the airport.
8 We <u>want</u> <u>to find</u> a cheap hotel.
9 If the house needs <u>to be cleaned</u>, I'<u>ll help</u> you.

C2 What happens when a singer does a tour? There's lots of work to be done. Look at these notes and write sentences using the present passive.

1	plan the tour	The tour is planned.
2	book the plane tickets	
3	send contracts to concert hall managers	
4	reserve hotel rooms	
5	design posters	
6	hire musicians	

C3 Fill in the gaps in this magazine article using the past passive.

The singer Hywel Evans 1 ..was educated.. (*educate*) in Wales. He 2 .... (*give*) the main part in a school play when he was ten. He 3 .... (*see*) by a theatre director and he and another boy 4 .... (*ask*) to sing in a TV advert. They 5 .... (*not pay*) much but they 6 .... (*hear*) by a record producer. Hywel's friend 7 .... (*ask*) to be in a musical. Hywel 8 .... (*not give*) a part in the musical, but he 9 .... (*invite*) to star in a film.

C4 Complete the second sentence so it means the the same as the first, using no more than three words.

1 This shop is owned by my uncle.

   My uncle ...._owns_........ this shop.

2 That birthday card was made by my little sister.

   My little sister .... that birthday card.

3 Charles Dickens wrote this letter.

   This letter .... by Charles Dickens.

4 This lunch will be enjoyed by all our guests.

   All our guests .... this lunch.

5 Teenagers don't visit the museum.

   The museum .... by teenagers.

6 Those emails were read by my boss!

   My boss .... those emails!

7 That text wasn't received by my mother.

   My mother .... that text.

8 This match will be watched by five million football fans.

   Five million football fans .... this match.

9 Bono wore these jeans.

   These jeans .... by Bono.

10 This music won't be played by disc jockeys.

   Disc jockeys .... this music.

C5 Read this pop singer's web page about preparing for a concert. Fill in the gaps with the correct form of *to have something done* and the words in brackets.

Before a concert my manager 1 _has the dressing-room painted_ (*dressing-room/paint*) pink, because that's my favourite colour.

He 2 .... (*the furniture/change*) too, if I don't like it. When I arrive I 3 .... (*nails/paint*) and I 4 .... (*my hair/wash*). I also 5 .... (*my clothes/iron*). Then the musicians come in for a chat. If we're hungry, we 6 .... (*a meal/deliver*). Then we do the show.

D Exam practice

Reading Part 2

The people below all want to do a sports course.
On the next page there are eight sports courses.
Decide which course would be the most suitable for the following people.
For questions **1–5**, mark the correct letter (**A–H**).

---

1  Joe wants to go horse-riding every day and also do some other sports. He wants to do a course which provides organised social activities in the evening.

2  Rob wants to have some fun and meet people while he does a sports course for a few days. He'd like to learn to swim and have the chance to play football and rugby.

3  Claudia is looking for a tennis course in the mornings only so she has the rest of the day to relax and explore on her own.

4  Norman is keen on surfing and wants a chance to improve his skills. He would also like to play some tennis.

5  Ellen wants to go mountain-biking or climbing. She doesn't want any other sports and hates cooking. She would like to spend her evenings with other people.

Sports courses

A The Sports Institute runs courses in squash, tennis, dancing and gymnastics. Choose between a morning or an afternoon course. Visits to places of interest are also arranged for anyone interested. All students are given a free ticket to use at the local swimming pool.

B Courses in climbing and horse-riding are available at the **Hillside Centre**. Groups are also taken on mountain-bikes into the hills by guides. Everyone helps to make the meals and transport is provided into the town in the evenings for entertainment.

C Action Sport was started twenty-five years ago and offers several courses. Choose from mountain-biking, climbing and horse-riding in the mornings and in the afternoons everyone is expected to take part in a team sport like basketball, volleyball, football or rugby. A different event is organised every evening such as a theatre visit, a quiz night or a disco.

D At **Brookside** there are watersports courses on the lake and swimming lessons in the indoor pool. Horse-riding lessons are also available. They don't provide food but the accommodation has modern kitchens.

E Sports for All offers courses during which you can learn new skills and make new friends at the organised social events. Lessons are offered in swimming, diving, or athletics. There are several free hours every afternoon when everyone is encouraged to play football, hockey, rugby or tennis together.

F If you want to get away from the city for a week, the **Activity Centre** is the place for you. Groups go climbing, walking, mountain-biking or running in the surrounding mountains. You stay in a hostel where you have all your meals cooked for you. In the evenings social events are organised.

G Sun Sports is based in a large hotel on the coast. Book for one day or several days up to one week. A wide range of watersports is offered at the beach centre, both for beginners and those who are more experienced. Golf, tennis, swimming and volleyball are also available in the hotel.

H At the **Carlton Centre** you can have personal training in the sport of your choice. It is well-known for its football and rugby but also offers courses in sailing and water-skiing. It is close to nightclubs and restaurants for evening entertainment.

Grammar focus task

Complete these sentences with an active verb. For each one, there is a passive sentence in the exam task with the same meaning.

1 The Sports Institute ....._arranges_..... visits to places of interest.

2 The local swimming pool .... a free entry ticket to all students.

3 Guides .... groups into the hills on mountain-bikes.

4 The Hillside Centre .... transport into the town.

5 In the afternoons Action Sport .... everyone to take part in a team sport.

6 Action Sport .... a different event every evening.

7 Sports for All .... lessons in swimming, diving or athletics.

8 Sports for All .... everyone to play football, hockey, rugby or tennis together.

A Context listening

A1 Look at the picture. What do you think the woman is saying?

A2 🎧 **25** You are going to hear Nick telling his friend Will about what happened. Answer these questions.

1 How did Nick's mother feel when she got home?
2 What hadn't Nick done?
3 What did Nick offer to do?
4 What had Nick's mother paid him to do?
5 Why can't Nick go out tonight?
6 What does Will offer to do?

A3 **25**◄◄ Listen again and write the words Nick uses when he reports his conversation with his mother.

1 She said I ......*couldn't*...... go out because I .... tidied the house.
2 She said she .... visitors and the house .... dirty and untidy.
3 I said I .... wash up.
4 She said my friends .... help too.
5 I said I .... washed the car the week before.
6 She said she .... going to keep my pocket money.

A4 Here are the words Nick and his mother actually said. Match them to the reported sentences above. <u>Underline</u> the words which change.

Nick: I'll wash up. **a** ....3....

Mum: You can't go out because you haven't tidied the house. **b** ....

Nick: I washed the car last week. **c** ....

Mum: I'm expecting visitors and the house is dirty and untidy. **d** ....

Mum: Your friends should help too. **e** ....

Mum: I'm going to keep your pocket money. **f** ....

Look at the verbs you have underlined. Which verb doesn't change? ....

B Grammar

B1 Reporting what someone said

After a reporting verb like *said*, we usually change the tenses.

present simple → past simple	
The house is dirty.	*She said (that) the house **was** dirty.*

present continuous → past continuous	
I'm expecting visitors.	*She said (that) she **was expecting** visitors.*

past simple → past perfect	
I washed the car.	*I said (that) I'**d** /**had** washed the car.*

present perfect → past perfect	
You haven't tidied the house.	*She said I **hadn't tidied** the house.*

am going to → was going to	
I'm / I am going to keep your pocket money.	*She said (that) she **was going to** keep my pocket money.*

will → would	
I'll / I will wash up.	*I said (that) I'**d** / **would** wash up.*

can → could	
You can't go out.	*She said I **couldn't** go out.*

⚠ *could/would/should/might* don't change:

*I **couldn't** understand.* → *He said that he **couldn't** understand.*

*Your friends **should** help.* → *She said my friends **should** help.*

The past perfect doesn't change:

*I **hadn't expected** her to come home early.* → *He said that he **hadn't expected** her to come home early.*

When we report *must*

+ We change *must* to *had to*:

*You **must** stay at home.* → *She said I **had to** stay at home.*

− We don't change *mustn't*:

*You **mustn't** do that again.* → *She said I **mustn't** do that again.*

➡ C1, C2

B2 Words which change

We often need to change pronouns when we report what someone said:

I → he or *she, you → them* or *us, my → his* or *her, we → they, our → their*

I can't go out with you because my mother's kept my money. → ***He** said **he** couldn't go out with **them** because **his** mother had kept **his** money.*

Words about time and place also change:

today → that day	*tonight → that night*
tomorrow → the next day	*yesterday → the day before*
next week → the following week	*last week → the week before*
now → then	*this → that*
here → there	

*I often buy bread **here** in **this** shop* → *She said she often bought bread **there** in **that** shop.* ➡ C3, C4

C Grammar exercises

C1 Complete each sentence so that it means the same as the first.

1 He said he was hungry. (I 'm .... hungry.

2 They said they were going to be late. (We .... late.

3 She said she had never flown in a helicopter before. (I .... in a helicopter before.

4 She said they had to get a taxi home. (You .... get a taxi home.

5 They said they'd bought a new computer the day before. (We .... a new computer yesterday.

6 He said she should try harder. (You .... try harder.

7 She said she was waiting for her friend. (I .... for my friend.

8 He said he loved cheese. (I .... cheese.

9 She said she would send me an email the next day. (I .... you an email tomorrow.

10 He said his brother was looking for a new job. (My brother .... for a new job.

C2 A queue of people are waiting outside a new restaurant. Report what they said.

1 'I'll come back later.' He said he ...._would_......... come back later.

2 'We can't get a table.' They said they .... a table.

3 'We arrived at 6 pm.' They said they .... at 6 pm.

4 'We're going to wait.' They said they ....

5 'I've never eaten Thai food before.' He said he .... Thai food before.

6 'The restaurant is too small.' She said the restaurant .... too small.

7 'There won't be a free table for at least an hour.' They said there .... a free table for at least an hour.

8 'We'd expected to get a table.' They said they .... to get a table.

9 'We didn't reserve a table.' They said they .... a table.

10 'We're going home.' They said they .... home.

C3 Look at a policeman's report and then fill in the gaps in the conversation below. Change the underlined words.

♥POLICE

A woman called the police station about a car parked near her flat. I went to the street to talk to her.

She told me that <u>she</u> had seen the car several times before. She said <u>she</u>'d seen it <u>there</u> <u>the week before</u> for the first time. But <u>the day before</u> two men had got out. They'd looked at all the houses in <u>that</u> street. I asked her if I could phone <u>her</u> <u>that evening</u> or <u>the next day</u> to ask some more questions. She agreed.

Policeman: Can **(1)** ......*you*...... tell me about the car please?

Woman: **(2)** .... 've seen it several times before. **(3)** .... saw it **(4)** .... **(5)** .... for the first time. But **(6)** .... two men got out. They looked at all the houses in **(7)** .... street.

Policeman: Can I phone **(8)** .... **(9)** .... or **(10)** .... to ask some more questions?

Woman: Of course.

C4 Read what Sally said to Anne-Marie on the phone, then complete the email which Anne-Marie sent to her brother later.

'I was at a Coldplay concert yesterday. I climbed onto the stage at the end. Chris Martin kissed my hand so I'll never wash it again! I'm going to get their new CD tomorrow. I can't think about anything except their music! I've read everything on their website. Perhaps I might write them a letter.'

Hi
Sally phoned me last weekend and said 1 ......*she'd been*...... at a Coldplay concert
2 .... She said that 3 .... onto the stage at the end and
Chris Martin 4 .... hand so 5 .... it again. She said
6 .... their new CD 7 .... because 8 ....
about anything except their music. She said 9 .... everything on their
website. and perhaps 10 .... them a letter.
Isn't she crazy?!
CU
Anne-Marie

D Exam practice

⚠ This task tests grammar from the rest of the book as well as the grammar in this unit.

Writing Part 1

Here are some sentences about a flat.

For each question, complete the second sentence so that it means the same as the first. **Use no more than three words.**

Example:

0 I moved to this flat one week ago.

I've lived in this flat .... _for_ .... **one week.**

---

1 My cousin lived here before.

My cousin used .... **here.**

2 He said he wanted to live in a bigger flat.

He said ' .... **to live in a bigger flat.'**

3 It's nicer than my friend's flat.

My friend's flat isn't .... **this flat.**

4 It's got a lovely view over the river.

There .... **a lovely view over the river.**

5 My friend said she'd never seen a view like it.

My friend said 'I .... **a view like it.'**

Here are some more things people said about the flat. Report them.

1 My father said 'I don't like the colour of the walls.'

My father said he .... the colour of the walls.

2 My boyfriend said 'I can help you paint them.'

My boyfriend said he .... me paint them.

3 My mother said 'I'll lend you some curtains.'

My mother said she .... me some curtains.

4 My brother said 'I'm going to visit you soon.'

My brother said he .... visit me soon.

A Context listening

A1 A journalist called Tim has written a newspaper report about a footballer, Joe Chapman. His boss wrote the headline. Does the report match the headline?

CHAPMAN: THE GIRLFRIENDS, THE TV CAREER, THE MONEY

Tim Donnelly finds out about Joe Chapman's life away from the football field.

Last season Joe Chapman scored more goals than any other player and he's become one of our star players. But where were the goals on Saturday in the away match? There weren't any. This is because he hurt his knee in training and isn't fully fit. So what plans does Joe have? He's had offers to join other teams but isn't interested. He wants to see United win the cup this year for the third time.

A2 🎧 26 You are going to hear Tim talking about the report. Why is his boss angry?

A3 26◀◀ Listen again and tick the questions Tim asked.

1 Have you got a new girlfriend?
2 Why didn't you score any goals on Saturday? ✓
3 Who were you with at that nightclub?
4 Does your mother always watch your games?
5 Did you argue with the new manager?
6 How long are you going to stay with the team?
7 What do you do in your free time?
8 When will we see your TV programme?
9 How much do you earn from adverts?
10 Will your team win the cup?

A4 Look at the recording script on page 194. Find these sentences and fill in the gaps.

1 I asked him .... he .... any goals on Saturday.

2 I asked him .... his mother always .... his games.

A5 Look at the questions you ticked in A3.

1 Which questions can we answer with *Yes* or *No*? ....

2 Which questions begin with a question word? ....

Look at your answers to A4.

3 When do we use *if* to report questions? ....

4 What do you notice about the word order when we report a question? ....

B Grammar

B1 *said* and *told*

When we report what someone said we often use *said* or *told*.

said: He **said** (that) they would win.	***told***: **not** ~~He told (that) they would win.~~	⚠ Remember the tense changes too (see Unit 25).
He **said** to me (that) they would win.	**not** ~~He told to me (that) they would win.~~	
not ~~He said me (that) they would win.~~	He **told** me (that) they would win.	

➡C1

B2 Other verbs used for reporting

We sometimes use the infinitive (*to* ...) after *tell* and *ask*:

Be careful. → *I **told** him **to be** careful.*
Please don't take any photographs. → *He **asked** us **not to** take any photographs.*

and also after some other reporting verbs:

Would you like to have lunch with me? → *I **invited** him **to have** lunch with me.*
Write a new article! → *He **ordered** me **to write** a new article.*
Remember to watch the match. → *He **reminded** me **to watch** the match.*

➡C2, C3

B3 Reporting questions

There are two kinds of question:

◆ questions which begin with a question word (*how, which, when, what, who, why, where, how long*)
◆ questions we can answer with *Yes* or *No*

Q-word question	**Reporting verb + Q-word + statement**
How's your knee?	→ Tim asked Joe how his knee was. (**not** ~~how was his knee~~)
Where **will** you play?	→ Tim asked Joe where he would play. (**not** ~~where would he play~~)
Why **didn't** you **score**?	→ Tim asked Joe why he hadn't scored. (**not** ~~why hadn't he scored~~)

Yes/No question	**Reporting verb + *if/whether* + statement**
Are you happy?	→ Tim asked Joe **if/whether** he was happy. (**not** ~~if/whether was he happy~~)
Does your mother always **watch**?	→ Tim asked Joe **if/whether** she always watched. (**not** ~~if/whether did she always watch~~)

⚠ Remember the tense changes too (see Unit 25).

We sometimes use a different verb instead of *asked:*

How much do you earn? → *I **wanted to know** how much he earned.*
Will they win? → *I **wondered** if they would win.*

➡C4

B4 Polite questions

When we ask politely for information we use the same word order as in reported questions:

Can you tell me when the match starts? (**not** ~~Can you tell me when does the match start?~~)
I'd like to know if there are any tickets left. (**not** ~~I'd like to know are there any tickets left?~~)
⚠ We don't change the tense.

➡C5

C   Grammar exercises

C1   Underline the correct word, *said* or *told*.

1   My cousin <u>said</u>/told he'd like to come and stay with us.

2   Sarah *said/told* us she'd enjoyed her holiday.

3   Craig *said/told* goodbye to us and left the room.

4   When I invited them they *said/told* they were busy.

5   I *said/told* Frances that I was going to watch television all evening.

6   The shop assistant *said/told* that the shop was closed on Wednesdays.

7   She *said/told* she hated cooking.

8   The bus driver *said/told* the passengers the bus had broken down.

C2   Some students are going on a sailing trip. Their teacher tells them to do these things. Complete the sentences.

1   Get up early.   He told them *to get up early.*

2   Have breakfast.   He told them ....

3   Don't be late.   He told them ....

4   Wear a hat.   He told them ....

5   Don't wear leather shoes.   He told them ....

6   Bring a packed lunch.   He told them ....

7   Don't bring expensive cameras.   He told them ....

8   Don't fall in!   He told them ....

C3   Read what people said on the left. Then complete each sentence on the right with a word from the box. You can use some of the words twice.

asked   advised   invited   ordered   reminded

1   Could you fill in a form please?   → He ....*asked*.... me to fill in a form.

2   Remember to take your keys.   → She .... them to take their keys.

3   Tidy your room immediately!   → She .... them to tidy their room.

4   Would you like to watch a DVD with me?   → She .... him to watch a DVD with her.

5   Don't forget to phone Jim.   → She .... him to phone Jim.

6   Would you walk more slowly please?   → He .... her to walk more slowly.

7   Don't move.   → He .... them not to move.

C4 On a TV programme, the audience asks a singer called Dina some questions. Here is the report on the programme's website.

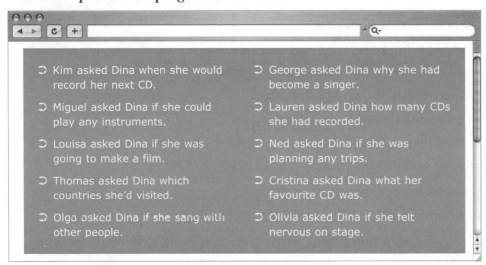

- Kim asked Dina when she would record her next CD.
- George asked Dina why she had become a singer.
- Miguel asked Dina if she could play any instruments.
- Lauren asked Dina how many CDs she had recorded.
- Louisa asked Dina if she was going to make a film.
- Ned asked Dina if she was planning any trips.
- Thomas asked Dina which countries she'd visited.
- Cristina asked Dina what her favourite CD was.
- Olga asked Dina if she sang with other people.
- Olivia asked Dina if she felt nervous on stage.

Write the questions the audience asked.

1 Kim: 'When will you record your next CD ?'

2 Miguel: '...?'

3 Louisa: '...?'

4 Thomas: '...?'

5 Olga: '...?'

6 George: '...?'

7 Lauren: '...?'

8 Ned: '...?'

9 Cristina: '...?'

10 Olivia: '...?'

C5 Some tourists are asking a tourist guide some questions. They aren't very polite. Rewrite their questions politely.

1 What will we eat tonight?   I'd like to know _what we'll eat tonight._

2 Is there a swimming pool?   Can you tell me ....

3 Does this city have underground trains?   Can you tell me ....

4 How long are we staying here?   I'd like to know ....

5 Are we going on a river trip?   I'd like to know ....

6 Where is the nearest bank?   Can you tell me ....

7 Can the hotel change my room?   I'd like to know ....

8 When does it get dark?   Can you tell me ....

D Exam practice

Reading Part 4

Read the text and questions below.
For each question, mark the correct letter **A**, **B**, **C** or **D**.

My problem

My name's Jade, I'm fifteen and an only child living with my parents in Porchester. I've always got on very well with them and I've always felt happy at home.

Last autumn my cousin Bettina came to live our house. She's nineteen, and very pretty and funny. She's staying with us while she's a student at the university in Porchester. At first, I was very pleased to have another teenager in our house, because most of my friends don't live near me, but recently my feelings have changed.

I have lots of homework because I'm studying for school exams, but I have to clean my room and help with the washing-up. Bettina doesn't have exams this year so she doesn't have to work so hard. She has more money than me. She earns a bit because my dad helped her get a part-time job, and because it's at the local leisure centre she doesn't pay the full price for tickets to see films there or go bowling with her friends. And although she doesn't pay rent to my parents they don't make her help in the house like I have to.

When I mentioned this to my parents they reminded me that we have to be kind to Bettina because her dad hasn't been well for a long time. I agree with that but there is a problem: I know Bettina tells lies to my parents. Last week, she told my dad that she was going to the library but she went to meet her boyfriend. Two days ago she asked my mum to lend her some money. She said she needed to buy some books, but I think she spent it all on CDs.

I asked my parents if they knew what she had done, but they didn't believe me. They said I was jealous of her and refused to listen to me.

I'd like to know what I should do now.

1 What is Jade trying to do?

   A describe her older cousin

   B explain why she has problems with school work

   C say why she doesn't like being an only child

   D explain a problem she has at home

2 When Bettina arrived, how did Jade feel?

   A She was jealous of Bettina's good looks.

   B She hoped Bettina could help her with homework.

   C She was happy to have her to stay.

   D She wanted Bettina to meet her friends.

3 What does the writer say about Bettina's job?

   A She earns a lot of money.

   B She gets cheap tickets because of it.

   C She hasn't told Jade's parents about it.

   D She works when she should be studying.

4 Jade's parents asked her to remember

   A that Bettina's family has problems.

   B that she isn't as old as Bettina.

   C that Bettina has many responsibilities.

   D that Jade's father is ill.

5 Which of these things did Jade say to her parents?

A

I want to get a job so that I can earn money like Bettina.

B

It's not fair that I have to help in the house and Bettina doesn't.

C

Bettina's father should pay you more for her accommodation.

D

Bettina gets cheap cinema tickets her friends but not for me.

Grammar focus task

Look at the parts of the text which report these sentences and <u>underline</u> any changes which you find.

1 I'm going to the library. <u>She told my dad that she was</u> going to the library.

2 Could you lend me some money?

3 I need to buy some books.

4 Do you know what she's done?

5 We don't believe you.

6 You're jealous of her.

7 We won't listen to you.

8 What should I do now?

A Context listening

A1 Look at the names of the TV programmes below. Match three of them with the pictures.

> documentary   news   sports programme
> quiz   soap opera   cookery programme

A2 🎧 27 You are going to hear a guide giving some students a tour of the television studios.

1 Which studio do they visit first, second and third? ....

2 Who do the students meet on their tour? ....

A3 27◄◄ Listen again and complete these sentences.

1 We may meet some other people ....*who*............ you can talk to.

2 The news team choose the stories .... will be in the news.

3 Here's a man .... face you'll recognise.

4 That's the soap opera .... you can see every evening at seven on TBC.

5 This is the room .... Mark asked Jill to marry him.

6 We report on all the sports events .... take place around the world.

7 For instance, people like Sally Ravenna .... were stars.

8 Jack's the man .... old boots were sold recently for £10,000.

A4 Look at the words you have written.

1 Can you take out any of the words and keep the same meaning? ....

2 Which of the words can you replace with *that*? ....

B Grammar

B1 Relative clauses

We can give information about someone, something or somewhere by adding a relative clause.
We use a relative pronoun: *who, which, whose, where* or *that*:

relative pronoun

This is the sitting room **which belongs to the Baxter family**.

relative clause

B2 *Which, who* and *that*

We use *which* to join two ideas about a thing or things:
Here's a photo. It shows them on their wedding day.
Here's a photo **which** *shows them on their wedding day.*
not *Here's a photo which* ~~it~~ *shows them on their wedding day.* (it = a photo)

We use *who* to join two ideas about a person or people:
We have different presenters. They're experts.
We have different presenters **who** *are experts.*
not *We have different presenters who* ~~they~~ *are experts.* (they = presenters)

We can use *that* instead of *who* or *which*:
Here's a photo **that** *shows them on their wedding day.*
We have different presenters **that** *are experts.*

➡ C1

B3 No relative pronoun

Sometimes the verb in the relative clause has a new subject:
You can see the café which <u>Mark</u> *owns.* (*the café* is not the subject of *owns*)

We don't need to use *who* or *that* in the sentence above:
You can see the café <u>Mark</u> *owns.*

but we need *who* or *that* when there is no new subject.
Compare:
They choose the headline (**which/that**) <u>the newsreader</u> *will read first.* (new subject: *the newsreader*)
They choose the stories **which** *will be in the news.* (no new subject)
Here's a footballer (**who**) <u>you</u>*'ll recognise.* (new subject: *you*)
Here's a footballer **who** *played for England.* (no new subject)

➡ C2

B4 *Where* and *whose*

We use *where* to join two ideas about a place. It means *at/in* which. It cannot be left out or
replaced by *that*:
Here's the desk **where** *the newsreader sits.* (**not** ~~where the newsreader sits at~~)
(= *Here's the desk. The newsreader sits at that desk.*)

We use *whose* with a noun to mean *his/her/their/its*. It cannot be left out or replaced by *that*:
Jack's the man **whose** *old boots were sold.* (= Jack's the man. + His old boots were sold.) ➡ C3, C4

C Grammar exercises

C1 Join these pairs of sentences with *who* or *which*.

1 I've got a ring. It belonged to my grandmother.

   I've got a ring <u>which belonged to my grandmother.</u>

2 My sister has a beautiful leather jacket. It cost £200.

   My sister has a beautiful leather jacket ....

3 I have a penfriend. He lives in Australia.

   I have a penfriend ....

4 This is the computer. It doesn't work.

   This is the computer ....

5 Those are the singers. They won a music competition on television last night.

   Those are the singers ....

6 My brother told me about his friend. She worked for a film company.

   My brother told me about his friend ....

C2 Read these sentences. Decide which ones don't need *who*, *which* or *that* and cross it out.

1 Sandra is the teacher ~~who~~ we invited to tea.

2 Here's the book which I promised to lend you.

3 Why did you change the plan that we made?

4 That's the hotel which has a swimming pool on the roof.

5 Where's the bunch of flowers that you bought yesterday?

6 Elaine wrote to the university that had offered her a place.

7 This is the letter that caused all our problems.

8 I emailed all the people who my boss wanted to see.

9 Andrew is the man who won the science prize.

10 When will you finish the work which I asked you to do?

C3 Complete these sentences with *who*, *which*, *whose* or *where*.

1 I met a man ....<u>who</u>........... plays football for Germany.

2 This is the library .... I usually study.

3 That's the woman .... daughter won the chess prize.

4 That's the girl .... my brother is going to marry.

5 We lost the map .... you drew for us.

6 Please show me the cupboard .... you keep your cleaning materials.

7 Mungo opened the present .... his friends gave him.

8 Can you tell me the name of the man .... car you borrowed?

9 Gabrielle painted the picture .... hangs in our sitting-room.

10 I have a friend .... lives in Barcelona.

Look at sentences 1–10 again. In which sentences can you cross out the relative pronoun?

C4 **Read this conversation between Emily and her father. Fill in the gaps in the conversation with relative clauses using the information in the box.**

1 May plays in Emily's volleyball team.
2 Alec lived next door when Emily was small.
3 Bernard gave Emily guitar lessons last year.
4 Emily met Ailsha at Spanish lessons.
5 They are staying at a guesthouse called Sunny Villa.
6 The party will be at a club called the Beach House.
7 Emily has bought a present for Herman.
8 They're going to Herman's party.

Emily: Dad, I want to go away with some friends for Herman's birthday party.

Dad: Who are these friends?

Emily: May, Alec, Bernard, Ailsa and Herman. The party's at the Beach House.

Dad: But I don't know these people. Who's May?

Emily: She's a girl 1 who plays in my volleyball team .

Dad: And who's Alec?

Emily: Dad, you know Alec. He's the boy 2 ....

Dad: Oh, yes. Well, who's Bernard? I don't know him.

Emily: No, but, Mum knows him. He's the boy 3 ....

Dad: I see. And Ailsa, who's Ailsa?

Emily: She's the girl 4 .... We're sharing a room at Sunny Villa.
Sunny Villa's the guesthouse 5 ....

Dad: And what's this Beach House?

Emily: The Beach House is the club 6 ....

Dad: What's that parcel?

Emily: It's the present 7 ....

Dad: And who's Herman?

Emily: Oh Dad! He's the boy 8 ....

Dad: Oh, I see. I suppose it's all right if your mother agrees.

D Exam practice

Reading Part 2

The people below all want to go out to have a meal.
On the next page there are eight places to eat.
Decide which place would be the most suitable for the following people.
For questions 1–5 mark the correct letter (**A–H**).

1

Mark is going out with some friends on Wednesday evening. They'd like to have an Indian meal. They want to go to a restaurant which they can drive to and park at easily.

2

Ulla is meeting a friend for lunch on Friday in the town centre. She wants to eat a salad and would like to be able to sit outside.

3

Heidi and her boyfriend are going to the cinema in the town centre at 8.15 on Sunday evening. They want to have a quick meal nearby before they see the film.

4

Will is going out with his father for a meal on Monday evening. They both like fish and want to go to a restaurant which has a pleasant view.

5

Ian's grandparents are celebrating their wedding anniversary and the whole family are going out on Saturday evening. They need a restaurant which serves a range of dishes to suit everyone. It must have a car park.

A **Martin's** is in the town centre and is very popular with people who work in the local offices. It is open Monday–Friday lunchtime from 12–2 and in the evening from 5–10. It offers simple dishes and a fast service. Choose from hot dishes, soup or sandwiches.

B **The Roma Restaurant** is a new restaurant by the river, owned by an Italian family. It serves pizza and pasta which the family make themselves. There is a terrace which overlooks the river so you can sit and watch the boats go by. It is open every day from 11 until 5.30 and is very close to the shops and main car parks.

C **The Taj Mahal** is an excellent Indian restaurant which is about 2 km from the town centre. It is on one of the main roads out of the town and has a large car park. It is open lunchtimes at weekends and every evening.

D **The Corner House** is 50 years old and still owned by the same family. It's in the industrial part of the town. The menu offers fish or vegetarian dishes but no meat. It is open every evening from 7.30–11.30 and parking is easy as it has its own large car park at the back.

E **The Rainbow** is in the town centre and has a very nice terrace where you can sit and watch what's happening in the market square. It is open every day from 11–5 except Wednesday. It serves salads and sandwiches which are all specially made to order but service is fast.

F **The Star** is a small Indian restaurant in the town centre. They won't take large groups and it's worth booking a table as it's very popular. It's ideal for a relaxed evening meal. There's no car park. It's open all day every day except Tuesdays.

G If you enjoy a good view, **the Fountain** is the place to go. It's the only restaurant whose windows look over a lake. It's in the middle of the park so you need to allow 15 minutes to walk there from the road where you can park. It serves a wide range of food from fish to salads to vegetarian dishes.

H **Bertie's Kitchen** is a large restaurant just outside the town which has a wonderful selection of home-cooked dishes on the menu. It's open every evening. There's no need to book during the week as there's plenty of room but at weekends it gets busy. There's a large car park.

Grammar focus task

Complete these sentences from the exam task with *who*, *which*, *where* or *whose*.

1 They want to go to a restaurant ...which.. they can drive to.

2 They need a restaurant .... serves a range of dishes to suit everyone.

3 Martin's is very popular with people .... work in the local offices.

4 It serves pizza and pasta .... the family make themselves.

5 There is a terrace .... overlooks the river.

6 The Taj Mahal is an excellent Indian restaurant .... is about 2 km from the town centre.

7 The Rainbow has a very nice terrace .... you can sit.

8 It serves salads and sandwiches .... are all specially made to order.

9 It's the only restaurant .... windows look over a lake.

In which sentences can you put *that*? ....

In which sentence can you put nothing in the gap? ....

So/such; too/enough

28

so/such (+ that); enough and too (+ to infinitive and for)

A Context listening

A1 Holly and Max are sister and brother. They are getting ready to go out. Where are they going and what is Max's problem?

A2 🎧 28 Listen and check if you were right.
What does Holly think Max should do?

A3 28◄◄ Listen again and complete the sentences below about Holly and Max.

1 He says his blue shirt isn't smart ....*enough*.......... .

2 It's .... small for me.

3 She tells Max not to be .... silly.

4 He says Holly loses weight .... easily.

5 She says Max is .... a lazy person.

6 She says he never walks quickly ....

7 She says he has .... much ice cream and .... many burgers.

8 She says he doesn't eat .... fruit.

A4 Look at your answers to A3.

1 Write the words which follow *so*: ...*silly*......................

2 Write the three words which follow *such*: ....

3 Write the word which follows *enough*: ....

4 Write the words in sentences 1 and 6 which go before *enough*: ....

5 Write the words which follow *too*: ....

B Grammar

B1 *So* and *such*

So and *such* make the words that follow stronger:

so + adjective or adverb	*such* + (*a*) + (adjective) + noun
*You're **so lazy**.* (adjective) *You're **so lucky**.* (adjective) *You lose weight **so easily**.* (adverb)	*You're **such a lazy** person.* (countable noun) *You say **such unkind things**.* (plural countable noun) *You talk **such nonsense**.* (uncountable noun)
so + *many/few* + (adj) + countable noun:	*such* + *a lot of* + countable or + uncountable noun
*You make **so many excuses**.* *I've got **so few nice clothes**.*	*You make **such a lot of excuses**.*
so + *much/little* + (adj) + uncountable noun	
*They cost **so much money**.* *I have **so little time**.*	*They cost **such a lot of money**.*

➡C1

B2 *So* and *such* + (*that*) ...

We use *so* and *such* + (*that*) to say why something happens.

Action/event etc.	*so/such*	+ (*that*) result
I'm	**so busy**	(***that***) *I can't think about keeping fit.*
= I can't think about keeping fit because I'm extremely busy.		
He walked	**so slowly**	(***that***) *we arrived late.*
= We arrived late because he walked extremely slowly.		
It was	**such an untidy office**	(***that***) *we couldn't find our books.*
= We couldn't find our books because the office was extremely untidy.		
The news was	**such a shock**	(***that***) *they didn't know what to say.*
= They didn't know what to say because the news was a big shock.		
Max ate	**so many sweets**	(***that***) *he felt ill.*
= Max felt ill because he ate a lot of sweets.		
Max lost	**so much weight**	(***that***) *he had to buy new clothes.*
= Max had to buy new clothes because he'd lost a lot of weight.		

➡C2

B3 *Enough* and *too*

Enough means the right quantity. *Too* means more than enough.

Enough goes:
- before a noun:

*We've got **enough sandwiches**.*

*We haven't got **enough sandwiches**.*

Too goes:
- before *many/much* + noun:

*We've got **too many sandwiches**.*

*We've got **too much food**.*

- after an adjective/adverb:

*This room is **warm enough**.*

*This room isn't **warm enough**.*

*Am I speaking **loudly enough**?*

- before an adjective/adverb:

*This room is **too warm**.*

*This room is **too cold**.*

*Am I speaking **too loudly**?*

➡C3

B4 *enough* and *too* + *to* infinitive or *for*

If we want to add information we use:
- *enough/too* + to infinitive.
  *It's **too far to walk**.*
  *It's not **near enough to walk**.*
  *Have you got **enough work to do**?*
  *He wasn't running **quickly enough to catch us**.*
- *enough/too* + for something/someone.
  *This shirt is **too small for me**.*
  *I don't have **enough money for gym membership**.*

➡C4

C Grammar exercises

C1 Fill in the gaps with *so* or *such*.

1 Everyone likes her because she's ....*so*........... funny.

2 That was .... an unkind thing to say.

3 He has .... few good friends.

4 Our team lost because they played .... badly.

5 My brother's .... handsome all my friends want to meet him.

6 We had .... fun at the seaside.

7 I saw .... many wonderful places when I was on holiday.

8 It was .... a lovely surprise to see my cousin at the meeting.

9 I'm sorry I have .... little time for sightseeing on my business trips.

10 It's .... a pity you can't come with us to the theatre.

C2 Fill in each gap in this email with one of the phrases a–g.

> a they had no time for a break
> b I got there in ten minutes
> c they were selling very quickly
> d I could hardly get in the door
> e ~~I had to come home in a taxi~~
> f everyone wants them
> g nobody believes him

Hi Suzi

How are you?

Yesterday I bought so many new clothes 1 ....*c*....... ! My brother Ricky told me there was a half-price sale on at Gabrielle's, you know, that expensive shop in town. It sells such beautiful clothes that 2 ....

Well, at first, I wasn't sure because Ricky usually talks such nonsense 3 .... Anyway, Mum said it was true. I ran so fast 4 .... The shop already had so many customers 5 .... The clothes were so cheap 6 .... I did find some good things. I felt sorry for the staff, though. They were working so hard all day that 7 .... When can you come and see what I bought?

Love

Frances

C3 Complete the second sentence so that it means the same as the first. Use the word in brackets.

1 This coffee is very sweet. I can't drink it.

This coffee <u>is too sweet.</u> .... (*too*)

2 You can't put all your clothes in your leather suitcase.

Your leather suitcase .... (*enough*)

3 I've got a lot of work to do. I can't finish it all.

I've got .... (*too*)

4 The weather's cold and this jacket is too light.

This jacket .... (*enough*)

5 You don't need any more CDs.

You've got .... (*enough*)

6 You should eat more slowly.

You eat .... (*too*)

7 I need to have my hair cut.

My hair .... (*too*)

8 We've got lots of extra glasses, we don't need them all.

We've got .... (*too*)

9 I don't play games on my computer because it has very little memory.

I don't play games on my computer because it .... (*enough*)

10 She got up late so she missed the bus.

She missed the bus because she .... (*enough*)

C4 Read this conversation and <u>underline</u> the correct word, *to* or *for*.

Landlady: This is your bedroom. I hope it's big enough **1** *to/for* you and this cupboard is
for clothes. Is there enough room **2** *to/for* all your things?

Student: Yes, I think so.

Landlady: We can put your big suitcase in the basement if it's too big **3** *to/for* go on top
of the cupboard.

Student: Thank you.

Landlady: The bathroom is next door. Switch the water heater on in the morning so
there's enough hot water **4** *to/for* have a shower. Can you understand
everything? Do I speak slowly enough **5** *to/for* you?

Student: Yes, I can understand you. But my English isn't good enough **6** *to/for* say
everything I want to.

Landlady: Oh, don't worry, I'm sure you'll soon learn.

D Exam practice

⚠ This task tests grammar from the rest of the book as well as the grammar in this unit.

Writing Part 1

Here are some sentences about a motorbike.
For each question, complete the second sentence so that it means the same as the first.
Use no more than three words.

Example:
0 I was given a motorbike by my uncle.

   My uncle ....*gave*........................... **me a motorbike.**

---

1 It was such a surprise I didn't know what to say.

   I was so .... **I didn't know what to say.**

2 I have such a lot of friends who would like a motorbike.

   I have so .... **friends who would like a motorbike.**

3 My father said I was too young to ride it.

   My father said I wasn't .... **to ride it.**

4 I told him not to worry.

   I said to him: '... **worry.'**

5 If he won't let me ride it, I'll be angry.

   Unless he .... **me ride it, I'll be angry.**

Grammar focus task

Look at the sentences below. Write similar sentences with the same meaning.
Use sentences 1, 2 and 3 above to help you.

1 I had such a shock I didn't know what to say.

....

2 I have such a lot of money I don't know what to spend it on.

....

3 My father said I was too small to be a firefighter.

....

A Context listening

A1 Nancy is talking to Steve about a TV programme she watched last night. Before you listen, look at the pictures and try to put them in the correct order to tell the story of the programme.

A   B   C   D

A2 🎧 **29** Listen and check if you were right.
What happened to Orville?

A3 **29◀◀** Listen again and complete the sentences below.

1 Claudia went to an evening class ....*to*........................ learn Greek.
2 He put on a false beard .... he didn't want her to recognise him.
3 Damian was there .... he was waiting for his brother.
4 Claudia knew Damian .... her job.
5 Orville was making a terrible noise .... the college receptionist called the police.
6 No-one helped him .... he was taken to the police station.

A4 Look again at A3. Do all the sentences below mean the same as the ones in A3? Tick the ones that mean the same.

1 Claudia wanted to learn Greek so she went to an evening class. ✓
2 Orville put on a false beard because he didn't want Claudia to recognise him.
3 Damian was waiting in the entrance hall to meet his brother.
4 Claudia knew Damian because she'd met him when she was working.
5 Orville was making a terrible noise because the college receptionist called the police.
6 Orville was taken to the police station because no-one helped him.

B Grammar

Linking words connect different ideas.

B1 *Because (of)*, *as* and *since*

We say *because (of)*, *as* or *since* when we give a reason for something.
Because is more common than *as* and *since*.

action	linking word	reason
She said nothing	*because* *as* *since*	she didn't recognise him.

We use *because of* when the reason is a noun, not a sentence:
*Claudia knew Damian **because of** her job.*
*She didn't recognise him **because of** the beard.* (**not** because of he was wearing a beard.)

⚠ When we answer a question beginning *Why ...*, we use *Because* (not *as* or *since*).
*Why was he there? **Because** he was waiting for his brother.*
(**not** As/since he was waiting for his brother.)

➡C1

B2 *So* and *therefore*

We say *so* and *therefore* when we give the result of something.
So is usually in the middle of a sentence.
Therefore is at the beginning of a new sentence and is mainly used in writing.

action	linking word	result
Orville was making a terrible noise	*so*	the receptionist called the police.
Orville was making a terrible noise.	*Therefore*	the receptionist called the police.

Compare the meaning of these sentences:
*He didn't believe her **so** he followed her.*
*= He followed her **as/since/because** he didn't believe her.*
*The teachers were on strike. **Therefore** the school was closed.*
*= The school was closed **as/since/because** the teachers were on strike.*

➡C2, C3

B3 *To* and *in order to*

We say *to* or *in order to* when we explain why we do something (our purpose).
(In order) to is always followed by the infinitive.

action	linking word	purpose
She was going to an evening class	*to*	learn Greek.
He followed her	*in order to*	see where she went.

(In order) to can answer a question beginning with *Why ... ?*
*Why did he follow her? **To** see where she went.*

➡C4, C5 and C6

C Grammar exercises

C1 Fill each gap with *because* or *because of*.

We chose this flat **1** ...*because of*... the
balcony. We had to move **2** .... our
old flat was too small. The rent is quite high
3 .... this block is in the city
centre, but we like it **4** .... the view
over the park. And it's good **5** ....
we can get to work in only ten minutes.

C2 Match the beginnings and endings of these sentences.

1 I finished my lunch quickly since ....*d*.....   **a** a traffic jam.

2 I bought a new umbrella as ....   **b** I didn't hear my phone.

3 I gave my friend a present because ....   **c** I couldn't contact her.

4 I lost my friend's phone number so ....   ~~**d** I had to go out.~~

5 I got home very late because of ....   **e** I'd lost my old one.

6 I was listening to music so ....   **f** it was her birthday.

C3 Complete the second sentence so that it means the same as the first.

1 Peter missed his station because he fell asleep on the train.
   Peter fell asleep on the train *so he missed his station.* ....

2 Hannah goes to lots of concerts because she likes music.
   Hannah likes music ....

3 Thieves steal from parked cars. Therefore it is important to lock your vehicle.
   It is important to lock your vehicle ....

4 Parissa was feeling sick so she didn't eat her ice cream.
   Parissa didn't eat her ice cream ....

5 Sam got a job because he needed money.
   Sam needed money ....

6 Theresa enjoyed sport so she joined the tennis club.
   Theresa joined the tennis club ....

7 Sheila went for a walk as she had a headache.
   Sheila had a headache ....

8 Philip opened the parcel since he believed it was for him.
   Philip believed the parcel was for him ....

171

C4 Complete each sentence with the *to* infinitive of a verb from the box.

1 We phoned the cinema ....*to check*........ the time of the film.

2 They hired a car .... the mountains.

3 We joined the swimming club .... the pool.

4 He went on a diet .... weight.

5 She went into the kitchen .... some coffee.

6 Did you come here .... my computer?

~~check~~	lose
make	mend
tour	use

C5 Underline the correct words in this email.

○○○ ⊖

Hi Lizzie – I need your help, quickly.

I went to the airport this morning 1 *because / in order to* meet my friend Adam. I wanted to drive him to his house 2 *so/as* I borrowed my father's car. I usually go to the airport by bus 3 *because/so* the airport car park is so expensive. However, I knew he'd be tired 4 *so/since* it was a long flight.

The traffic was very heavy 5 *as/so* I was nearly late. I went to the machine for a ticket when I parked. I pressed the button 6 *so/to* get a ticket but it didn't give me one, but I pressed it again and this time it gave me a ticket. I put in my purse without looking at it and ran into the airport.

When we came out, I went to the kiosk 7 *to / because of* pay. The car park man said I had to pay three hundred pounds 8 *so/because* the car had been there for two weeks! The ticket machine had printed the wrong date. He didn't believe there was anything wrong with the ticket 9 *since/so* we had to leave the car and come home on the bus. I don't know what I'm going to tell my father 10 *therefore/as* I borrowed the car without asking him. What am I going to do??? — Lisa

C6 For each pair, mark S for sentences which mean the same and D for the ones with different meanings.

1 I've bought a computer as I work at home.

I've bought a computer since I work at home. ....*S*....

2 I chose it because of the low price.

I chose it as it was cheap. ....

3 A friend helped me to set up my email as I don't know much about it.

A friend helped me to set up my email. Therefore I don't know much about it. ....

4 I'm working at home in order to save money on train fares.

I'm working at home to save money on train fares. ....

5 I've sold my car because I don't drive to work.

I've sold my car so I don't drive to work. ....

6 I wear old clothes since I stay at home all day.

I stay at home all day as I wear old clothes. ....

D Exam practice

Reading Part 3

Look at the sentences about a football club called Wickton City.
Read the text to decide if each sentence is correct or incorrect.
If it is correct, mark **A**.
If it is incorrect, mark **B**.

---

1 Tony's dream was to be a football coach.

2 Tony is doing his second job since going back to Wickton.

3 One part of Tony's job takes up the most time.

4 A few teenagers on the 'Football Skills' courses are offered jobs with Wickton City.

5 Equipment on the courses is provided free for everyone.

6 The aim of the Saturday club is for young people to practise playing matches.

7 The number of different football teams for young people in Wickton has increased recently.

8 In the past young people in Wickton were fans of teams from outside the area.

9 Tony thinks the club may have to close in the future.

10 The fact that most of the Wickton City players are from the area is positive.

Wickton City
Football Club

Tony Connor has been Wickton City's youth officer for 18 months. At the age of 16 he went from Wickton to Ipswich Town to train to be a professional footballer. This had always been his ambition but he had to return home because he was injured and that's where he's stayed. He was then a football coach for over 7 years. Now, as youth officer, he has three parts to his job - to run the mini-soccer centre on a Saturday morning, to teach football to local teenagers, and to help look after the football club's Academy for players who are training in order to play in the first team. He says 'Everything I do is important but I spend longer teaching local teenagers than I do on the other parts of the job.'

He wants teenagers to get football qualifications, therefore he's developed a programme to help them. 'These 'Football Skills' courses are for young people who have no qualifications. We obviously can't give them jobs at the end but, by doing our courses, I hope they'll find a job in the future and a few of them might actually work for a football club. There's no charge for most of the courses we run. We usually charge a small fee for the equipment but we sometimes provide that free as well.'

On Saturday mornings, the mini-soccer centre offers opportunities for local children at the club. 'There are no competitions. They don't win or lose. They come in order to have a chance to train at the football club.'

In addition, for the first time in the club's history, there are now three children's teams. 'Since last year, we've got under-twelves, under-fourteens, under-sixteens, and also the Academy teams, which contain the best players in the town.'

As well as forming football stars of the future, the club is also trying to encourage younger fans. 'We hope to attract more of the young kids here, to make them feel part of the club, in order to save them travelling miles to Manchester United or Liverpool every week.'

Tony says the club went through a bad period. 'A few years ago we nearly lost our team altogether as the club had very little money so we're making sure that doesn't happen again. For about fifteen years, the club couldn't get well-known players since the money wasn't available. Therefore a lot of local players have played in the first team over the last two years and that's helped the level of football in the area. So that's a good thing.'

Grammar focus task

Answer these questions about the text. Begin your answers with *because*, *(in order) to* or *so (that)*. Look back at the text if you need to.

1 Why did Tony go to Ipswich Town? _To train to be a professional footballer._
2 Why did he return home? ....
3 Why do players train at the Academy? ....
4 Why has Tony developed a programme for teenagers? ....
5 Why do children come to the mini-soccer centre? ....
6 Why does the club want to attract more young fans? ....
7 Why did the club nearly lose its team? ....
8 Why couldn't the club get well-known players in the first team? ....

A Context listening

A1 Selina has phoned Mr Smart to ask him about his holiday. Look at this brochure and the photo Mr Smart took. What was Mr Smart's problem?

Hotel Concordia

A2 🎧 30 **Listen and check if you were right.**
Which hotel did Mr Smart and his wife prefer?

A3 30◄◄ **Listen again and complete the sentences below.**

1 I enjoyed most of the holiday, ...*but*............ I didn't enjoy the first night.

2 .... I asked for a quiet hotel, your company put me in the Concordia.

3 My wife and I .... work very hard.

4 Unfortunately .... the manager .... his assistant were out.

5 .... I left several messages, he didn't phone me back until the second day.

6 .... the bad start, we had a good holiday.

7 I'm going to tell our bookings manager about your problems .... she comes into the office.

8 Will you phone me .... you find out what went wrong?

9 I'll .... phone .... email you.

A4 **Look at your answers to A3 and mark these sentences T for True or F for False.**

1 In sentences 1, 2 and 5 *but* and *although* are used when the same idea is repeated. ....

2 In sentences 3 and 4 *both* is used before a noun and before a verb. ....

3 In sentence 6 *in spite of* is used before a noun. ....

4 In sentences 7 and 8 the *will*-future tense is used after *as soon as* and *when*. ....

5 In sentence 9 *either* and *or* are used before verbs. ....

B Grammar

Linking words connect different ideas.

B1 *But, although* and *though*

But and *although* (or *though*) contrast two ideas and are followed by noun + verb:

idea A	linking word	idea B
The hotel was excellent	**but**	*the food was boring.*
The hotel was excellent	**although/though**	*the food was boring.*

linking word	idea B	idea A
Although/though	*the food was boring,*	*the hotel was excellent.*

⚠ We can't use *although* (or *though*) and *but* in the same sentence:
not ~~Although the food was boring, but the hotel was excellent.~~

Although (or *though*) is stronger than *but*.
But is always in the middle of a sentence. *Although* (or *though*) is sometimes at the beginning of a sentence and sometimes in the middle.

➡C1

B2 *In spite of / despite*

In spite of / despite + noun contrasts two ideas.

idea A	linking word	idea B
The hotel was excellent	**in spite of/despite**	*the boring food.*

linking word	idea B	idea A
In spite of/despite	*the boring food,*	*the hotel was excellent.*

⚠ We can't use noun + verb after *in spite of / despite*:
not ~~The hotel was excellent in spite of the food was boring.~~

B3 *Both ... and, ... and ... both, either .... or*

We use *both ... and* and *either ... or* to connect two people or things:
Both *my wife* **and** *I work very hard.*
Either *the bookings manager* **or** *her secretary made a mistake.*

We often use noun *and* noun + *both* + verb:
Mr Smart and Mrs Smart **both** *work very hard.*

We often use *either ... or* to connect two verbs:
Either *phone me* **or** *send me an email.*
You can **either** *eat out* **or** *have dinner in your hotel.*

⚠ *Both* goes after the verb *to be* and auxiliary verbs:
My wife and I **were both** *looking forward to a rest.*

➡C2

B4 *When, until, before, after, as soon as, while*

We use *when, until, before, after, as soon as* and *while* to connect two actions in time:
When *we arrived in Florida, we hired a car.*
We waited with our friends **until** *their bus arrived.*

⚠ When we talk about the future, we use a present tense after these words:
We'll hire a car, **when** *we* **arrive** *in Florida.* (**not** ~~will arrive~~)

➡C3, C4, C5

C Grammar exercises

C1 Rewrite these sentences using *although/though.*

1 I don't often eat ice cream but I really like it.
   Although *I really like ice cream, I don't often eat it.*

2 Elena speaks Polish but she's never been to Poland.
   .... though ....

3 Zach didn't want to go to the disco but he enjoyed it when he got there.
   Although ....

4 No-one eats fruit but Mum still buys it.
   .... though ....

5 Dennis didn't get good marks in his exams but he went to university.
   Though ....

6 Mahmoud is the shop manager but he's only nineteen.
   .... although ....

C2 Make each pair of sentences into one sentence using the words in brackets.

1 I travelled to New York. There was a strike. (*in spite of*)
   I travelled to New York in spite of the strike.

2 Nigel bought some CDs. Anthony bought some CDs. (*both ... and*)
   Both Nigel and Anthony bought some CDs. or Nigel and Anthony both bought some CDs.

3 Tom sent that email. Martin sent that email. (*either ... or*)
   ....

4 Dolores was working in the garden. The sun was hot. (*despite*)
   ....

5 Her dress is new. Her jacket is new. (*and ... both*)
   ....

6 Michael wasn't late. There was a traffic jam. (*in spite of*)
   ....

7 My father gave me some money. My mother gave me some money. (*and ... both*)
   ....

8 Do your homework now. Get up early and do it tomorrow. (*either ... or*)
   ....

9 You can go on your bike. You can come with me in the car. (*either ... or*)
   ....

177

C3 Greta is talking about leaving school. <u>Underline</u> the correct words.

Although we enjoyed school sometimes, because we were
with our friends, we were happy **1** *when/while* we left. We all
walked out of the gate together **2** *after/before* we took the final
exam. We wanted to go on holiday **3** *while / as soon as* the
school term finished, but we had to wait **4** *after/until* we had
our marks.

I got a job **5** *while/before* I waited to get my exam results. I
needed to earn some money **6** *before/when* I went away.

We all phoned our friends **7** *until/when* the results arrived. Everyone had passed! I was so
happy **8** *after/when* I knew that. We could all enjoy our holiday.

C4 Read this email and put the verbs in brackets into the present simple or *will* future.

Hi Andreas
You asked about my plans for this summer. You'll be jealous when I 1 ....tell............. (*tell*) you!
I'm going to fly to Argentina as soon as I my holiday 2 .... (*begin*). My uncle will meet
me when I 3 .... (*arrive*) and take me to his house. I expect I 4 ....
(*stay*) with his family for about a month. My cousins will show me around the city before we
5 .... (*go*) to their holiday house. After I 6 .... (*leave*) Buenos Aires, I'm
going to fly to Ecuador. I 7 .... (*tour*) around until my money 8 .... (*run*)
out. I don't have fixed plans, but I'm definitely going to take a river trip while I 9 ....
(*be*) in Ecuador. I'm really excited.
What about you? What are you going to do after your exams 10 .... (*be*) over?
All the best
Euan

C5 There are mistakes in five of these sentences. Find them and correct them.

1   Although the film was quite exciting at the beginning, ~~but~~ the last part was so boring I fell asleep.

2   Both university students and school teachers can use this library.

3   We had a good time at the beach in spite of the weather was windy.

4   Maggie isn't really friendly though she is very polite.

5   We'll leave the restaurant as soon as the waiter will bring our bill.

6   This room is terribly untidy! Or help me to tidy it or go away.

7   In spite of our hard work, we didn't win the prize.

8   I don't play an instrument although my father and my mother both are musicians.

9   We're going to change our car before we start our tour of Scandinavia.

D Exam practice

Reading Part 1

Look at the text in each question.
What does it say?
Mark the letter next to the correct explanation – **A**, **B** or **C**.

1

> James
>
> Sally can't get tickets for the film tonight. Can you go either tomorrow afternoon or evening? Ring her as soon as you get home or by 5 at the latest.
>
> Mum

A James should tell Sally before 5 today whether he can go to the cinema tomorrow.

B James should try to buy the cinema tickets as Sally can't get them.

C James should phone Sally before 5 tomorrow about going to the cinema.

2

> This shop is closed while owner is away. Take all enquiries to bookshop across the road.

A This shop has closed and is moving opposite.

B This shop has a new owner who lives opposite.

C If you need something, go to the shop opposite.

3

> Hi Annie
> Although I'd like to lend you my camera for your holiday, I won't be able to because I've promised to take photos at Peter's wedding.
> Sorry. Love Ruth

Ruth is apologising for

A not lending Annie her camera because she needs it herself.

B promising to lend Annie her camera and then changing her mind.

C not being able to take photos at Peter's wedding.

4

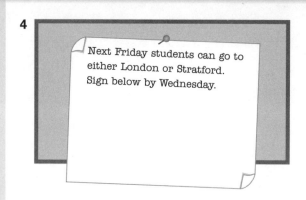

Next Friday students can go to either London or Stratford. Sign below by Wednesday.

A Put your name here before Friday if you want to join a trip.

B You can go to either London or Stratford on Friday if you put your name here.

C The people whose names appear below are going to either London or Stratford on Wednesday.

5

Dear Julia, I'm enjoying myself in spite of the noisy road outside the hotel. You said it was quiet when you came. Everything else is perfect – exactly as you said.
Carmen

A Carmen is pleased that the road is not as noisy as she had expected.

B Everything about the hotel is as Julia described it except the traffic outside.

C Carmen is sorry she took Julia's advice when choosing her hotel.

Grammar focus task

Correct these signs and messages. Look at the task above to help you.

1

Ring Tomas as soon as you ~~will~~ get home.

2

This CLINIC IS closed while DOCTOR WILL BE ON HOLIDAY.

3

Although I'd like to come out with you, but I won't be able to because I'm babysitting.

4

Hotel guests can either eat in the dining-room and beside the pool.

5

I enjoyed the film in spite of the actors were very bad.

Recording scripts

Recording 1

Emily: Come on Callum. Let's try this shop now.

Callum: Oh, not another clothes shop. I'm tired.

Emily: But I still need to find something to wear for my birthday party. I'm really excited about it. You are coming, aren't you?

Callum: Yes, of course ... But can't we have a rest? Shopping's so tiring. And clothes shops are always boring and crowded, especially on Saturdays.

Emily: I suppose you're not really interested in clothes. That's why you're tired.

Callum: And bored.

Emily: Well, do you want to get anything in town today?

Callum: I'd like to go to the computer shop over there. Now that shop is interesting.

Emily: But you don't need a new computer.

Callum: No, but there's a new computer game I want. It's really exciting. I played it at Jack's last week.

Emily: Look, I promise we'll go to the computer shop afterwards. Come on please. I want to look good at the party and I haven't got anything yet. I want you to help me.

Callum: Oh, ... all right then.

Callum: Where shall we go now then?

Emily: Well, last week I saw a lovely short black wool skirt, with a black and white belt, in that new shop that's just opened. I tried it on but I wasn't sure. It was quite expensive.

Callum: Well, your mum gave you some money. So why don't we go and see if they still have it? You can try it on again.

Emily: I hope it's still there. I did like it. And the material felt really soft. I can wear my favourite long black boots with it. I bought them a long time ago but they're comfortable and they'll look good with the skirt. And I can wear ...

Callum: Come on, then. Oh just a minute. Can we go in this shop first? Look at those white leather trainers. They're really cool. They're just what I want, and they're in the sale.

Emily: I thought you were tired ...

Recording 2

1

Mum: Hello.

Josh: Hi, Mum.

Mum: Oh, hello Josh. Are you at the station?

Josh: No. I'm outside my office but I'm getting on my bike now to cycle there. The boss said I could leave at lunchtime so I can catch the 1.30 train.

Mum: That was nice of him.

Josh: Yeah. He's a good boss. He treats us well.

Mum: Well, hurry now so you don't miss the train. It's already one o'clock.

Josh: Don't worry. I cycle very quickly and it's not far anyway. I know a quick route.

Mum: Oh, but ride carefully, won't you?

Josh: Of course I will.

Mum: You won't be late today, will you Josh?

Josh: No. I know I'm usually late for everything but I won't be late today.

Mum: OK. I don't want you to spoil the surprise for Sophie. Everyone's coming here by six o'clock.

Josh: Yes I know. You've arranged everything perfectly Mum and I'll be there.

Mum: Good.

Josh: You know I don't want to miss my little sister's 16th birthday.

Mum: Yeah, I know. Sorry.

Josh: I need to go now or I will miss the train.

Mum: Of course. Bye then. See you later.

Josh: Bye.

2

Josh: Hello?

Sophie: Hi Josh. It's Sophie.

Josh: Hi. How are you? Happy birthday by the way.

Sophie: Oh thanks.

Josh: What's the matter? You sound miserable.

Sophie: Why can't you come home Josh? It's going to be extremely boring with just me and mum and dad. And I never see you.

Josh: I know. I'm sorry. I've got a new boss. We have to work very hard and I can't have time off this week.

Sophie: That's so unfair.

Josh: But I posted your present on Wednesday. I wrapped it really well so I hope it didn't get broken. Do you like it?

Sophie: I don't know. It hasn't come.

Josh: And I sent you a card as well.

Sophie: What's that noise? It sounds like a train.

Josh: Oh that. It's ... a motorbike outside. It's rather noisy here.

Sophie: Where are you then?

Josh:	Err ... I'm in a café. I often come here on Friday lunchtimes. I'll ring you later. Sophie? Oh you've gone.

3

Dad:	Josh? Where are you?
Josh:	I'm still at the station. I've just arrived. It was a fast train so it got in at 5.30.
Dad:	Well I can't come to the station now because people are arriving.
Josh:	OK. I'll get a taxi then.
Dad:	Good. They always stop round the corner. So hurry and try to get near the front of the queue. I hope it doesn't take you too long to get here. The traffic's moving very slowly outside our house.
Josh:	It'll be OK Dad. Where's Sophie?
Dad:	She's waiting patiently at her friend's house I hope. You know. Er Natasha. She often goes there after school. We told her we had a surprise for her but she doesn't know it's a party. She'll be really pleased to see you.
Josh:	Yeah. I'm glad I could come. See you soon then.
Dad:	Bye.

Recording 3

Peter:	And finally, with new music magazine *Smash* launching this month, we thought we'd look at how it compares with some of the other music magazines which are on sale. Here to tell us all about them is Jessie Crawford.
Jessie:	Thank you Peter. I've got three magazines in front of me – *Hits!*, *Buzz* and *Smash*. *Hits!* and *Buzz* have both been around for a while and they're very popular.
Peter:	*Hits!* seems more colourful than *Buzz*. Does it sell more copies?
Jessie:	No, *Buzz* is as popular as *Hits!* – probably because of its free posters. *Hits!* doesn't usually have any posters or other extras. That's why it's less expensive than *Buzz*. And it's smaller than *Buzz* too. I think people like it because you can read it more easily. They're very similar magazines really.
Peter:	So which one do you prefer?
Jessie:	In my opinion *Buzz* isn't as good as *Hits!*
Peter:	And what about this magazine – *Smash*?
Jessie:	*Smash* is the newest – as you said, this is its first month – and they're advertising it as the country's best music guide.
Peter:	Really?
Jessie:	Yeah. It's got the most reviews and contains the most information.
Peter:	And do the journalists write well? That's sometimes a problem with these kinds of magazines.

Jessie:	Yes, in fact they write much better than some of the journalists on the national newspapers.
Peter:	So if you want something interesting to read, buy *Smash*.
Jessie:	Yes, I think so.
Peter:	What about price Jessie? How much is *Smash*?
Jessie:	It's £2.50. *Hits!* is the cheapest at £1.50.
Peter:	And *Buzz* is the most expensive?
Jessie:	That's right. It costs £3.20.
Peter:	And does *Smash* have any disadvantages?
Jessie:	It has a lot of adverts – all three of them do – but *Hits!* has the most adverts.
Peter:	Let's see what our listeners think. Do you agree with Jessie? Do write in and tell us - send us an email or go to our website and leave us a message – that's www.musicplace ...

Recording 4

Welcome everybody to this Cititours Bus. I hope you're having a good time here in the West of England? I'm Anna and I'm your guide today here in Durrington. Our tours usually last about one hour but this week they're taking a little longer because some roads are closed in the centre of town. I'm here to tell you about some of the most interesting sights in Durrington. Has everyone got a map and can you all hear me? Good, I've got a sore throat and I can't shout.

The bus is now turning into Queens Road. From this road we can see a very modern building. This is the town's new sports stadium. All the big matches happen there but at the moment, an international company is using it for a conference, I think.

OK, so, please look to your left. We're now passing the City Theatre. This building is one hundred years old. It's very pretty, as you see, but it doesn't have enough seats for big shows. We've got a new entertainment centre in Victoria Park. We don't pass it on the bus, but you may be interested to know it's got a cinema and a concert hall. Most people prefer it because it's got air-conditioning but I still enjoy an evening at the old theatre. The theatre's got a very good café if you want somewhere to have lunch.

Now, on your right, is the High Street. This takes you to the Market Place. This Cititour bus normally goes along the High Street into the Market Place. But, um, at the moment some musicians are practising for an outdoor concert there. So we're driving round a slightly different route because the roads into the Market Place are closed. The market was an important local trade centre until about 1970. Farmers bought and sold their cows and sheep there. However, we don't see animals in the city centre these days. The market area's got some good shops round it now. I go there most weekends. Why don't you have a walk round there later on, and then you can have lunch in one of the cafés?

Recording 5

Donny:	Hi.
Mum:	Hello Donny, where are you?
Donny:	Oh, hi Mum. I'm on the bus.
Mum:	But it's nearly eleven o'clock.
Donny:	I'll be home in half an hour. I've got something to tell you.
Mum:	Well, I've phoned you three times this evening. You went out and I didn't know where you were. You didn't say goodbye.
Donny:	Oh, sorry. You were having a shower when I went out. I wanted to see the new film at the Arts Cinema and I was late.
Mum:	Well, you didn't say anything to me. I phoned you at eight o'clock. Your phone was on but you didn't answer.
Donny:	Oh, yeah. Sorry.
Mum:	So? Why didn't you answer?
Donny:	I didn't answer my phone because I was listening to an argument. You see, I was having a coffee in the cinema café while I was waiting for the film to begin. I was sitting near the ticket desk and the manager was shouting at a woman. She was one of the ticket sellers. Then she ran out of the cinema. She was almost crying. It was quite exciting.
Mum:	I see. Well, I texted you at nine o'clock. Your phone wasn't on.
Donny:	No, at nine o'clock I was watching the film. Of course my phone wasn't on.
Mum:	And I tried to contact you again at ten o'clock. You didn't answer again.
Donny:	I was talking to the manager when you rang me.
Mum:	What about?
Donny:	Well, I was leaving the cinema when I saw a notice about the ticket seller's job. I went to the manager's office and I applied for it.
Mum:	And?
Donny:	He offered me the job! Three nights a week. And cheap tickets.
Mum:	Oh. We'll talk about that later. You have homework every night.
Donny:	Oh, but Mum ...
Mum:	See you in half an hour. Bye.
Donny:	OK. Bye.

Recording 6

Annie:	James, answer the door. Our first guests have arrived!
James:	Oh, Annie, no, I'm not ready. I haven't put all the balloons up yet.
Annie:	Well, I still haven't dried my hair.
James:	OK, OK, I'll get the door.

Leah:	Hi James, happy birthday. I've brought a pizza. I made it this morning.
James:	Oh, thanks Leah. You make the best pizza I've ever eaten. Come in, both of you. Have you met my sister Annie? Annie, this is Leah and Garry.
Leah:	Hello Annie. It's nice to meet you.
Annie:	Hello, Leah. Hello Garry. What are you doing here?
Leah:	Oh, have you two already met?
Garry:	Er, yeah, actually, we have.
Leah:	Oh, really? When did you meet then?
Garry:	Um ... I've seen Annie at the cinema.
Annie:	Yes, I've got an evening job there. I've worked there for two months. But, Garry ...
Garry:	Yes, um, well, happy birthday, James.
Leah:	Yes, happy birthday.

Leah:	Garry, how long have you known Annie?
Garry:	Leah, really, that's the second time you've asked me. I met Annie last week at the cinema.
Leah:	I don't believe you. She's worked there since April.
Garry:	So?
Leah:	You haven't taken me to that cinema for weeks. And you're always busy. Now I'm beginning to understand.
Garry:	But, Leah ...

Garry:	Annie, where were you last weekend? I waited in the cinema for you on Saturday. I was there for an hour.
Annie:	I didn't work last weekend.
Garry:	Oh, I didn't know.
Annie:	And I didn't know about your girlfriend. But I've just met her!
Garry:	Look, I explained last week. She's just a friend, not a girlfriend.
Annie:	She doesn't think so.
Garry:	Just let me explain. Come outside for a minute.

James:	Annie, I need some help in the kitchen. Leah, have you seen Annie?
Leah:	She's gone out.
James:	What? When?
Leah:	She left an hour ago ... with Garry.
James:	Oh, no! But this is my birthday. And she promised to help.
Leah:	I'll help you if you want. It's better than sitting here feeling miserable.

Dan: Hi. I'm Dan Savery and this week in our series 'Going Back' I'm talking to Peter, a young engineer who has lived in Britain for – is it seven years?

Peter: Yes, seven.

Dan: Seven years. And where did you go last week, Peter?

Peter: Well, last week I visited my home city.

Dan: This was your first visit in seven years?

Peter: That's right. And it had changed a lot. I also wanted to see my friend Stefan from high school.

Dan: I'm sure it was great to see him and look round.

Peter: Oh, yeah. When I arrived, Stefan had finished his work for the day but he hadn't had lunch, so we went to a café. It was in a smart new building. When we'd eaten lunch, we walked by the river.

Dan: Nice?

Peter: Yeah, the riverside used to be the factory area, but now there are gardens and a fantastic new sports centre.

Dan: That sounds great.

Peter: Definitely. There didn't use to be a sports centre in the city.

Dan: What else did you see?

Peter: We walked across an interesting modern road bridge. The engineers had just started it the year I left. I used to watch them on my way home from school. I had already decided to become an engineer and I was excited because I'd never seen anything like it. But now it's finished and it's so busy.

Dan: Did there use to be less traffic?

Peter: Yes. We used to see a lot of big lorries in the city, but most people didn't use to go to work by car, so the roads weren't so busy. We used to get pollution from factories, now it comes from cars!

Dan: So, not so good, then?

Peter: No.

Dan: So, any other surprises?

Peter: Well, in the evening, we went for a meal in a restaurant. That was the best surprise of the day.

Dan: Oh?

Peter: I walked into the restaurant and I saw all my old friends. Stefan had invited them to join us. We had a brilliant evening.

1

Are you tired of sitting on the beach? How about a holiday with some action? With Appleby Adventures you can go climbing in the Alps or the Andes. We're not suggesting sailing across the Atlantic Ocean but you can sail around the coast of Greece or on Lake Garda. Or you can watch the sun set over the Sahara Desert. And if you've only got a few days, go on one of our city breaks to Rome or New York. We have ten free holidays to give away. Just phone 0845 765298 for a brochure and you might be one of those ten lucky people. All you need is a passport. Don't forget the number 0845 765298.

2

Make sure you don't miss the Sandersons Sale. For this weekend only we've got some unbelievable prices – our women's jeans are just £6 a pair. And just in time for the summer, our shorts are on special offer. For men, Sandersons have the best selection of trousers you'll find anywhere in Oldcastle. If it's shoes you're looking for, people travel from all over the area to Sandersons and this weekend they're all half price. Yeah! So hurry before they're all gone. Sandersons, everyone's favourite store.

3

You're listening to 555FM – the station which brings you more music. The music on 555FM is perfect for a Friday afternoon. We've got our road report after the news. Are you sitting in your car in the traffic? If you are, ring us and tell us what the traffic is like where you are. We bring you the latest information every hour. Next this evening it's the news and we've got the weather – yes, it's still raining! Then it's your chance to phone us and ask us a question about money. I haven't got any so it's not a problem for me. But I'm sure you have. Our expert, Mark Sherlock, is here to give you advice and answer your questions. So ring us on 0700 707007. The phone lines are open now. And it's now five o'clock so here's Tracey Scarlett with the news.

You will hear a tour guide talking to some tourists about the town of Medbury. For each question, fill in the missing information in the numbered space. You will hear the recording twice.

As you can see from the signs, this was Medbury's old cheese market. It's been a market since 1540. Country people used to bring cheese and butter and things here to sell but since 1970 we've had the supermarkets of course, and so this has been a craft market since 1982.

If you want to take presents home, there are plenty of things to choose from like these hand-painted T-shirts or those traditional baskets, but personally, I'd advise you to look first at the stall over there selling jewellery. You really won't find anything like it anywhere else.

Now this town was also well-known for its leather goods, especially shoes. That long building over there was the factory where they were made. It's become a museum because most of the shoes we buy now are made abroad. There'll be time to go and look round it if you want to, and it's quite interesting, actually.

If you need to change some money before you go shopping, you'll find a bank over there beside the cinema. If that one's busy there's another one but it's a few minutes' walk - it's opposite the park.

We'll meet at 4.30. We're taking the coach back to London today as we want to visit somewhere else on the way back but if you come here again from London, the quickest way to get here is by train. The station is just down the road. You can just see the taxi rank outside.

There's a kiosk in the centre of the market here where you can get information about the town. Do go and ask some questions. If you want a map there's a newsagent over there and just behind the town hall is a very nice café.

OK then. Have a good afternoon and I'll see you here at half past four.

Now listen again. (*The recording is repeated.*)

Recording 9

Hi, Mia. It's me, Tom. I'm on my way and I arrive at seven oh five. I don't need a taxi as I haven't got much luggage – I've only got a few small bags so I can walk from the station. I'll be there about twenty past seven. Shall I buy some food – there's a shop just outside the station. Let me know.

Mia. It's Giorgio. Where are you? I'm in the Central Café in town. I'm really surprised because there isn't anybody here. I was sure we all agreed to meet in the café before going to the cinema but there's nobody here. The café's completely empty. Where is everyone? Have I got the wrong day? I've already rung everybody and no-one's answered and now you're not in. Ring me back if you get this message.

Oh Mia hi. It's Chloe. You know I'm looking for a job. I really need some money urgently for our holiday. Well, I've just bought the paper because it has all the job ads today but I've found nothing. Well I haven't found anything I can apply for. So I wondered about the shop where you work. I'm a bit worried because I've got no experience but I do work hard. Do they need anyone? Will it matter that I haven't got any experience? Ring me back. Please!

Mia. This is Roseanne. It's about the picnic tomorrow. Everything is organised. Lots of people are coming and everyone's bringing something. Can you bring some bread? Oh, and can you buy some crisps? We'll need several packets. Have I forgotten anything? Oh, I bought a couple of cakes. Because it's your birthday tomorrow and

mine on Tuesday, I got two cakes. There'll be a lot of people so I'm sure we'll eat them both. See you at 12 by the river. We'll find somewhere quiet. Talk to you later. Don't forget to ring me.

Recording 10

Presenter:	And now we're going to talk to Kirsty who recently appeared on the TV programme 'New Rooms'.
Kirsty:	Yes. Hi.
Presenter:	You're going to talk about your bedroom I believe. Can you tell us what happened?
Kirsty:	Yes. Well, my mum wrote into the show and she asked them to do a makeover on my bedroom for my birthday. You know, they go to a different place every week and change someone's room.
Presenter:	Sounds great.
Kirsty:	Well, there were three people who came – two men and a woman – and each of them had a different job to do. They spent all week in my bedroom.
Presenter:	Did they ask you what you wanted?
Kirsty:	Yeah. They showed me some paint and we tried each colour on the wall. In the end I had to choose between blue and orange.
Presenter:	So what did you choose?
Kirsty:	Well, either colour was OK with me so they did two walls blue and two walls orange. But now they've finished, neither of the colours looks very nice.
Presenter:	And what about the furniture?
Kirsty:	I like my bed so I've kept that. They didn't really want me to have much furniture at all but I said I needed a desk and a chair and a TV. Well, all teenagers watch TV and most people have a TV in their room, don't they? In fact, every room in our house has a TV.
Presenter:	So you've got a TV?
Kirsty:	Yes and an armchair. It's red and it's really ugly. And I've got a fridge. I was a bit surprised. I didn't expect that.
Presenter:	No bedrooms have fridges in them, do they? But I suppose you can keep drinks cold in the summer. Is there anything in the room you like?
Kirsty:	There are two new lights and both of them are really nice but they've put some old-fashioned pictures on the wall. I like modern art and none of them are modern. I do like the one of a sunset, though. I had some posters on the wall before but most of them were very old. And they broke my mirror so they bought a new one. It's cool. It's got stars round it and each star has a light in it.

Presenter: So that's good. Your bedroom sounds different anyway but you don't really like it.

Kirsty: No, but most of my friends like it. Some of them want to copy it.

Presenter: So what do you think of designers?

Kirsty: I think they're all mad! I'm going to be a scientist.

Presenter: OK. Well good luck with that and bad luck with the room, Kirsty. Now our next guest is here to tell us ...

Recording 11a

Boy: Have you seen 'Market Street' this week? I missed last night's programme. Did anything exciting happen?

Girl: It was about Cara. (*Who?*) You know. Cara is Sally's sister and they share a flat. Well, Sally went on holiday but she lent her key to their cousin Tony. He doesn't have his own flat and he wants to leave his parents' house because he isn't happy living with them.

Boy: Now who's Tony?

Girl: He's that good-looking one. You know, he works in the newsagent's. Do you remember he broke his leg a few months ago? Oh yeah. Carry on. The problem was that Sally forgot to tell Cara about the key. And she didn't know that Tony and Cara had had a big argument two weeks before and they were still angry with each other. So when Tony arrived at the flat, Cara was furious and refused to let him in. She was really rude to him because she was looking forward to being in the flat on her own.

Boy: So what did Tony do?

Girl: Well, later on when Cara was at work he used Sally's key and went into the flat. He was sitting there by himself when he had an idea.

Boy: Yes ...

Girl: He invited some friends of Cara's to the flat. So when Cara arrived home in the evening, there were lots of people there. They'd cooked a meal and they were all waiting for her.

Boy: So did she get angry again?

Girl: They were friends of hers so she couldn't. She came in and had some nice food. She really enjoyed herself. They all went home about midnight.

Boy: And what about Tony?

Girl: Oh, she let him stay. She decided he wasn't so bad after all. But I don't know what her boyfriend will think. He's been away but he's coming back soon.

Boy: He's that huge guy, isn't he? Could be interesting.

Recording 11b

You will hear an interview with Helen who is a basketball player. For each question put a tick in the correct box. You will hear the recording twice.

Interviewer: Welcome to 'Sport People', the programme where we talk to people interested in different sports. Today we have in the studio Helen who plays basketball and lives in the United States with her twin sister. She's back in Britain for a holiday. Welcome Helen. Tell us, where are you living in the States?

Helen: In North Carolina. Our hobby was playing basketball and a friend of ours told us about colleges in the United States which train people in particular sports. We were both really excited at the idea so we applied and we got places because we're good at basketball.

Interviewer: So you went to the United States straight from school?

Helen: No, we had started at college in England. The lectures and everything were free there but we had to pay for our training which was really expensive. At the American college everything is free except for our accommodation. We don't pay for our courses and we get free basketball training. We actually have our own trainer.

Interviewer: And in return you play in their college team. And what about the rest of the team? What are they like?

Helen: Fine. We get on well. We're lucky we've never had to stop playing because of injuries. Quite a few in the team have had to stop playing because they hurt themselves. We aren't very tall in comparison to the rest of the team – in fact we're the smallest, but we're just as strong as them, maybe even stronger.

Interviewer: And what's it like being a sports student?

Helen: Well, some people think because we're training and playing matches we don't have to study hard but that's not true. We study sports science and medicine as well as all the other subjects so we study harder in fact. And if we miss any of our classes we're not allowed to play in the team.

Interviewer: Oh, I nearly forgot to ask. When did you first start playing basketball?

Helen: We've been in the United States since last August and we'll be there for at least four years. But we started playing six years ago after watching our brother in matches. He still plays and he started playing more than ten years ago. His team isn't as good as ours of course!

Interviewer: And what about your free time?

Helen: Er, I spend most of my time studying and training. I'm not really interested in shopping like most of my friends. My sister and I get quite tired so when we have free time we usually sit in our room by ourselves watching TV. We share a room and we look after each other as we are so far from home.

Now listen again. (*The recording is repeated.*)

Recording 12

Kelly: Hi Elliot.

Elliot: Hi Kelly.

Kelly: What are you doing tonight?

Elliot: Well ...

Kelly: We've got tickets for a film. We're going to see the new James Bond film. It starts at nine o'clock.

Elliot: Oh, that would be great but I can't.

Kelly: But why? We've finished our exams.

Elliot: I'm not studying for exams tonight. You know my company?

Kelly: No I don't know what you're talking about.

Elliot: I've started an internet company.

Kelly: You've what?

Elliot: I sell books and CDs online and there are articles and things written by teenagers for teenagers.

Kelly: Wow.

Elliot: So you can sit at home, have fun and do your shopping on the screen without leaving the house. All you need is a mouse and a keyboard.

Kelly: And a computer of course.

Elliot: Yeah, yeah. Everybody will do shopping by computer in a few years' time.

Kelly: Oh, I'm sure you're right. But, anyway, what about Saturday and Sunday? We're going to spend the weekend at the seaside. My brother's going to drive us there.

Elliot: I'm flying to Rome tomorrow.

Kelly: No!

Elliot: I'm meeting a designer at 10.30 on Saturday.

Kelly: Well, come on Sunday then.

Elliot: My flight leaves Rome at 11 pm on Saturday and it arrives in London at 1 am. I won't get much sleep on Saturday night so I expect I'll be asleep all day on Sunday. I'll probably feel really tired.

Kelly: OK then. Don't worry about your friends. I'm sure your company is more interesting.

Elliot: Don't be annoyed. Look, I've got half an hour free. Let's do something now. What about a coffee?

Kelly: OK. I'll have a coffee with you.

Elliot: And I'll pay. Come on, Kelly. I'll be 17 next week and I hope that in three years' time I'll be really rich, I'll have a fast car and I'll drive you all to the seaside or wherever you want ...

Recording 13a

1

Alex: Excuse me. I've come for an interview. The waiter's job. My name's Alex.

Maria: Oh yes. Mr Kent's expecting you. He's the boss. I'm Maria.

Alex: Hi Maria. Can I sit here for a minute?

Maria: Yes of course you can. Have you come a long way?

Alex: Not far but I walked quickly. May I get a drink of water? I'm really thirsty.

Maria: Yes, of course. Over there look.

Alex: Could I use the phone? I just want to ring my girlfriend.

Maria: I'm afraid not. We're not allowed to. Oh look, here's Mr Kent.

2

Alex: Morning Maria.

Maria: Morning Alex. Are you looking forward to your first day here? [*Mm*] I'm getting everything ready.

Alex: OK.

Maria: Can you help me? Can you do those tables over there? Knives, forks and glasses.

Alex: Of course I can.

Maria: When you've finished the tables, will you help me put out today's menus?

Alex: Yes I will.

Maria: And would you check the salt and pepper? Each table has one of each.

Alex: OK.

Maria: Then could you sweep the floor?

Alex: Is that my job? I'm a waiter not a cleaner.

Maria: Yes, it is part of your job you know.

3

Mr Kent: Well Alex. How was your first day?

Alex: Great. I've enjoyed it. But shall we move some tables outside? People like sitting outside. And we could serve more interesting food perhaps. I mean, some of it's really boring.

Mr Kent: Now, just a minute.

Alex: Let's go into the kitchen now. I've got some ideas. I can make one of my special recipes if you like.

Mr Kent: That won't be necessary Alex. I don't think being a waiter is the right job for you.

Maria: Shall I put the advert back in the window Mr Kent?

Recording 13b

There are seven questions in this part. For each question, there are three pictures and a short recording. Choose the correct picture and put a tick in the box below it. You will hear each recording twice.

1 What does the woman order?

Woman: Excuse me. I want to buy one of those jackets over there. The one with a belt and a collar but you don't have my size – 36.

Shop assistant: You'll have to order it. Shall I have a look on the computer for you? It's got a zip up the front, hasn't it? Well, I'm afraid we haven't got any more but we have one exactly like it but without the belt.

Woman: I don't really like belts anyway so that's fine. I'll order it. Now, may I try on that skirt – the one in the window.

Shop assistant: Of course.

Now listen again. (*The recording is repeated.*)

2 Where is the boy?

Jack: Hi, Mum.

Mum: Hello, Jack. I expected you home half an hour ago. Where are you?

Jack: Well I got on the wrong bus. I've walked back to the bus station. It took a long time but there isn't a bus now for two hours. So would you come and pick me up? I'll wait for you here.

Mum: I'm sorry Jack. I'm afraid I can't. I'm finishing some work. Why don't you call a taxi?

Now listen again. (*The recording is repeated.*)

3 When will the man see Dr Browning?

Receptionist: Good morning. Dr Browning's surgery.

Man: Oh, hello. I've got an appointment tomorrow afternoon at a quarter to six. Could I change it please? I need to come earlier.

Receptionist: OK. Just a minute. Er ... we've got one at ten to three and one at five past four.

Man: Thanks. I'll take the earlier one.

Now listen again. (*The recording is repeated.*)

4 Where will the man park his car?

Man: Excuse me, can I leave my car here?

Woman: No, I'm afraid not. This is just for people who live in the flats. But if you carry on down this street and take the first road on the left, you'll come to a crossroads. Go straight over and then take the first turning on the right. There's a car park at the end of that street. It's never busy and it's not far.

Man: Oh, thank you so much.

Now listen again. (*The recording is repeated.*)

5 What do they decide to do?

Man: Do you want to go out tonight? What about going to see a film at the cinema?

Woman: There's nothing good on. Shall we go to that new restaurant?

Man: It's quite expensive. Let's rent a DVD. We'll have more choice than at the cinema.

Woman: All right. I can't really afford the restaurant either.

Now listen again. (*The recording is repeated.*)

6 What does Jane want Maria to do?

Hi Maria. It's me. Jane. Could you help me please? I know you're looking after your little brother today. Well, my mum's ill and there's nobody to look after my sister. I've got to go to work in the shop. They'll be really annoyed if I don't go. So can you do it? My sister can play with your brother. I'll borrow my friend's car and drive her to your flat before I go to work. Ring me back as soon as you can.

Now listen again. (*The recording is repeated.*)

7 How will the woman travel to the city centre?

Receptionist: Good morning madam.

Woman: Good morning. I want to go into the city centre. I'm thinking of walking there. Is it far?

Receptionist: It'll take you about half an hour. Shall I book you a taxi? That would be quicker. Or you could take the underground. That's the fastest way.

Woman: I'm not in a hurry so I'll go on foot. And I'll see more that way. Thank you for your help.

Now listen again. (*The recording is repeated.*)

Recording 14

Rosie: Mum ... Mum ... You'll never guess. I'm going to be on TV.

Mum: Really?

Rosie: Yes. A few weeks ago the local TV station had a big advert outside for people to appear on a programme called 'Life in The Castle'.

Mum: What castle?

Rosie: Oh, it's in Scotland somewhere. The idea is that a group of people go and live together there for a week and they're filmed. You know ...

Mum: You mean it's one of these reality TV programmes?

Rosie: Yes. That's right. We live together in the castle and pretend it's hundreds of years ago. We have to look after the animals and things like that.

Mum:	Well, I'm not sure about this. Who are the other people?
Rosie:	Oh, we're all ordinary people. We don't have to be good at acting or anything like that.
Mum:	I see, but how were you chosen?
Rosie:	Well, when I saw the advert I went in and talked to them and then I forgot about it. But I've just had a letter.
Mum:	So you're going to live in the castle ...
Rosie:	... for a week. Oh, I'm so excited. But there are lots of rules about what we must and mustn't do.
Mum:	Are you allowed to phone me?
Rosie:	No we mustn't use mobile phones.
Mum:	That'll be difficult for you.
Rosie:	I know. And we mustn't take modern equipment with us like CD players. There's no electricity anyway. But we have to wear a microphone all the time for the TV programme.
Mum:	So, no mobile you said. You ought to take a diary so you can write down what happens.
Rosie:	That's not allowed either.
Mum:	Well, it'll be boring. You could take some books.
Rosie:	No books. And we don't have to take our own clothes because they give us those. I expect they'll be horrible.
Mum:	Do you need to take any food with you?
Rosie:	They give us food because we can't grow it all like they did hundreds of years ago but we have to cook the meals.
Mum:	Why don't you cook me a meal tonight as practice?
Rosie:	OK. I should learn to cook I suppose.
Mum:	Well, you must read the letter carefully and check the details. You shouldn't sign anything until you've done that.
Rosie:	I have read it Mum.
Mum:	And if you don't like it there?
Rosie:	We needn't stay there if we don't like it. But I will like it!
Mum:	And I suppose ... I shouldn't worry so much.
Rosie:	No, I'll be fine. You really needn't worry. I must phone my friends and tell them.
Mum:	Just a minute.

Questioner:	And let's see how we're doing so far. Team A, you have six points. For the last round of our quiz, we have our 'guess what's in the photo' question. Team A, it's your turn first. Can you say what's in the photo?
Team A man:	Mmm ... It might be an insect. I think it could be a butterfly because those are its wings.

Team A woman:	It can't be a butterfly because it hasn't got a body.
Team A man:	It could be a hairbursh.
Team A woman:	A strange hairbrush! What about a flower?
Team A man:	But it's got a hole in it.
Team A woman:	Mmm, you're right. It can't be a flower ... I know, that's paper, so it must be a book – it's an open book.
Questioner:	Is that your answer?
Man and woman:	Yes
Questioner:	OK. Team B. Here's your photo. Are you able to say what the object is?
Team B man:	Let's see. I think it may be a headlight ... of a car.
Team B woman:	Mmm. I don't think so. I think it's something very small.
Team B man:	Mmm. It could be a needle. That's the hole at the end of the needle.
Team B woman:	No it's the wrong shape, it can't be a needle. Oh dear, I can't decide what it is.
Team B man:	Oh. It might be a pencil.
Team B woman:	Oh yes. Wait a minute. It must be a pen because that looks like ink.
Team B man:	Oh, yes.
Questioner:	Is that your answer?
Team B woman:	Yes. It's a pen.
Questioner:	Both teams have answered correctly. Picture A is the top of an open book and Picture B is the end of a pen. Now, Team A, will you be able to come back next week? (*yes*) Team B, will you be able to come back next week? (*yes*) Good, because next week ...

DJ:	Hi everybody and welcome to our very special phone-in. I have one of my favourite singers here with me. Della Dombey, we're so excited to have you here in Manchester with us all the way from the USA!
Della:	And I'm excited to be here. Thank you for inviting me.
DJ:	Thank you for agreeing to answer listeners' questions.
Della:	It's my pleasure.
DJ:	Well, we've got lots of people waiting to speak to you, so let's hear our first one. And it's Chrissie. Chrissie, what's your question?
Chrissie:	Hi Della.
Della:	Hi.
Chrissie:	Um, do you like Manchester?
Della:	Yes, I do. It's a great city.
Chrissie:	How long are you going to stay here?

Della:	Only four days. I know that's not long enough. But I have to go to London after the concert here at the weekend.	Mum:	But just a minute. You said we. Who's going with you?
DJ:	I'm looking forward to that concert very much.	Amy:	Ricky.
Della:	So am I!	Mum:	Ricky ... Now, is he that boy who you used to see on the bus? The one you talked about all the time? Does his mum work in the library?
DJ:	Now let's hear our next caller. This is Sabrina.		
Della:	Hi, Sabrina.	Amy:	No, Mum, not him! I'm talking about my cousin Ricky.
Sabrina:	Uh, hello Della. Um. Where did you sing in public for the first time?	Mum:	Oh. But I haven't seen him since he was about 15.
Della:	Umm, at my high school concert. I was terrible!	Amy:	No, neither have I. But he sent me an email on my birthday last year and I replied and he's phoned and emailed me several times since then.
DJ:	We don't believe that! And now here's Matt with his question.		
Matt:	Della, have you been to any clubs in Manchester?	Mum:	But are you sure you'll get on all right? You don't really know him. I always liked him when he was little.
Della:	No, I haven't. But my boyfriend and I are going out tonight. We know Manchester has some fantastic clubs.		
		Amy:	So did I. And it's not the first time he's been to Asia so that'll be helpful.
DJ:	Who is your boyfriend now, Della?	Mum:	But do you like doing the same kinds of things?
Della:	Dean Bradley. We're still together. I know the newspapers say we're not, but they're wrong!	Amy:	Yes, we do. I like sports and adventure and so does Ricky.
DJ:	I'm happy to hear that, Della. Now we've just time for one more question. And it's from Sassy.	Mum:	OK. So when is all this going to happen?
		Amy:	Next month.
Sassy:	My question is about music, Della. We all love your music, but whose music do you like best?	Mum:	Well, that's not very long to make all the arrangements.
Della:	Ah. My boyfriend Dean's! He's really talented and I know he's going to be famous soon.	Amy:	No, it isn't so we've already started but I think we ought to get together before we set off.
DJ:	Well, I'm afraid we've run out of time. Sorry to everyone who didn't ask their question and a big thank you to Della Dombey. And if you ...	Mum:	So do I. You don't even know what he looks like now. All right then, let's get a map ...

Now listen again. (*The recording is repeated.*)

Recording 16b

Look at the six sentences for this part. You will hear a conversation between a teenager, Amy, and her mother about a trip. Decide if each sentence is correct or incorrect. If it is correct put a tick in the box under A for YES. If it is not correct put a tick in the box under B for NO. You will hear the recording twice.

Amy:	Mum ... I've just given up my job in the café.
Mum:	What?
Amy:	I decided to leave. I've got plans.
Mum:	I'm sure they'll understand if you say you made a mistake. You can't leave a job after such a short time. Give them a ring in the morning and explain.
Amy:	No, I'm not going to do that. It's not that I didn't like the job or anything. In fact I'm sorry to leave. But I've got other plans now.
Mum:	What plans have you got?
Amy:	We're going to travel.
Mum:	Where are you going to go?
Amy:	Round the world.
Mum:	And how long is this trip going to take?
Amy:	At least six months.
Mum:	Well, which countries are you going to visit?
Amy:	First of all Thailand and India and then maybe China.

Recording 17

Hello, welcome to Forest Adventure! I'm Isobel and I'd like to tell you a few things before you go to your cottage so you can find everything easily. We have so many facilities, and I don't want you to miss anything.

If you look at this map beside me, you can see that the cottages are all across the lake from this building. You can reach your cottage by car over the bridge or you can walk or cycle round the lake on the paths. Cars aren't allowed on these paths, so they're very safe. You can hire bikes in the bicycle store, which is the building next to this one. You can cycle anywhere in the park, except on the road and in the square. The swimming pools are at the east end of the lake, with three restaurants above them. The square and café are in front of the swimming pool building. The shops are opposite, with a hairdresser, a chemist and so on. At the other end of the lake we have the gym with the tennis courts and skateboarding area behind it. You can borrow rackets and other equipment from the kiosk between the courts and the skateboarding area. The disco is under the gym. Can you see the island in the lake? There's a barbecue on the island twice a week. When you arrive at your cottage you'll find details of all our special events. And of course we have paths through the forest where you can get away from everything for a quiet walk. But I'll leave you to enjoy exploring those. If you have any questions, please do call in here. We're here to make your stay as much fun as we possibly can. Now, let me give you your cottage keys.

Recording 18

Simon: And now, what about the sports events we can look forward to in the next few months?

Dea: Well, in ten days there's one of my favourite events, the London Marathon.

Simon: And are you taking part this year?

Dea: Yes, I love it. I run every day for one or two hours. So I'm nearly ready for it, I hope.

Simon: That's great, we'll all watch you on the day of the race. And now, what else?

Dea: Well, we've got some great football very soon. Next month there's the Cup Final in London of course.

Simon: That's on the 18th, right?

Dea: OK, so that's in your diary now. But don't forget the rugby final in Paris. That's what I'm going to watch. That's the same weekend, but on Sunday.

Simon: Yeah, and there's more great football, at the European Champions' final, which is at the end of the month in Dublin.

Dea: Then if you're a motor racing fan, don't forget the British Grand Prix in July. But don't wait till July to get your tickets.

Simon: And talking of tickets that sell out, this summer, as usual, fans will arrive at sunrise and queue for hours to see their favourite tennis stars play at Wimbledon.

Dea: I think, if you want to go during the first week, it's worth waiting until five o'clock. You can get in more cheaply then and still see some wonderful tennis.

Simon: That's true. I did that on my birthday last year and saw several big name players.

Dea: Of course, if it rains during a match, you don't get your money back, but that's a chance you have to take.

Simon: Yeah, well that's sport in the summer in England, isn't it?

Dea: And that's all. We haven't got any more time at the moment, but we'll be back tomorrow with more music and chat. So bye from me.

Simon: And bye from me!

Recording 19

Mr Orwell: OK everyone. That's all for today. Don't forget your homework for Thursday. Katie, can I talk to you for a minute?

Katie: Yes?

Mr Orwell: Katie, why haven't you asked me for a university application form?

Katie: Oh, well. Umm, you see, well, I mean. I've changed my mind. I don't feel like going to university.

Mr Orwell: But you're a very good student.

Katie: Well, my sisters, you know, Emma and Olivia insist on applying for the same university as me.

Mr Orwell: Mm. Well I approve of that plan.

Katie: Do you?

Mr Orwell: You're interested in studying different subjects, and it'll be good to have people you know at university, so I don't think there's a problem.

Katie: Sorry, but there is. They're both so good at their subjects and if I'm not good enough, what will I do?

Mr Orwell: You mean you think your sisters may succeed in getting places at university, but not you?

Katie: Yes, I'm really worried about it. They've already started to fill in the forms.

Mr Orwell: So talk to them. Explain your feelings. You usually get on well with your sisters. And you may find that they're also worried about getting places at university.

Katie: I don't think so. They're really excited about going away to study.

Mr Orwell: Shall I tell you a secret?

Katie: Er ... OK.

Mr Orwell: Last week Emma came to me in private. She said she didn't want to go to university because ...

Katie: She was worried she'd be the only one who didn't get a place?

Mr Orwell: Exactly! And yesterday, Olivia told me the same thing. So stop worrying about it. I'm sure you'll all do well. I'm looking forward to congratulating you all on your exam results.

Katie: Oh, thank you. And thank you for listening to me. And to my sisters.

Mr Orwell: Now take this application form. Give it back to me by Friday and I'll look through it with you.

Katie: Yes, I will. OK. Bye. Thanks.

Mr Orwell: Bye Katie.

Recording 20

Mickey: Hi, Cristina.

Cristina: Hi, Mickey.

Mickey: How was work?

Cristina: Horrible as usual. The manager has put up a notice today. It says 'No talking except on business'. He's not human!

Mickey: Oh, dear. Well, you'll soon have enough money for the big trip to New Zealand, then you can leave.

Cristina:	Yes, I don't enjoy working there. I haven't had a pleasant day since joining that company!
Mickey:	Well, I've been busy too. I've been on the Internet since finishing my essay. We need to get plenty of information before planning our holiday. I found this website while looking for ideas about South Island.
Cristina:	Yeah?
Mickey:	It's about this place called Doubtful Sound.
Cristina:	Funny name!
Mickey:	Yeah, it's like a kind of lake in the National Park. It's brilliant for natural beauty.
Cristina:	Can we go walking there? You promised to go walking with me on holiday.
Mickey:	Well, we probably can, but, um, actually this website is about a company that does boat trips.
Cristina:	Is it a good place to take photos?
Mickey:	Oh, yeah, we'll see some fantastic scenery, so taking photographs is one of the main attractions of the trip.
Cristina:	What about animals?
Mickey:	It says here, 'Seeing dolphins and seals is almost certain, seeing penguins is a possibility.'
Cristina:	Really? It's one of my dreams to see some penguins.
Mickey:	Anyway, we'll look at the website again before booking. You can see what the accommodation's like, too.
Cristina	Good.
Mickey:	It sounds quite comfortable, and they provide food of course. In fact it says 'When booking, please tell us if you are vegetarians.' So that's OK for you.
Cristina:	Yeah. It does sound good.
Mickey:	We can book by filling in this form online. We can do it without leaving the house. I'll make some coffee and then we can look at it together.
Cristina:	Thanks, that's a good idea. I need a good coffee after working in that office all day!

Recording 21

Jeff:	In a few minutes I'm going to teach you to make necklaces, but before we start I'd like to share some ideas with you. When you decide to make something, think about what you intend to do with it. Can you imagine wearing it yourself? Do you hope to sell it? At first it may not be perfect …
Mary:	But I just want to make interesting jewellery for myself. I don't mind wearing something which isn't completely perfect, if I've made it.
Garth:	I want to sell mine if I can. It needs to be really good or nobody will want to buy it.

Jeff:	Well, I advise students to make several things before they consider selling anything. You need to practise using different materials and making different designs. I can help you.
Garth:	But I can't afford to buy a lot of materials. People like expensive stones.
Jeff:	Sure. But for now, I suggest practising with simple things.
Garth:	OK. Will you help us to choose the best beads to start with?
Jeff:	Of course. I've got some coloured, plastic beads, or some stones here if you feel like making something heavier.
Mary:	Oh, beads for me. I hate wearing heavy jewellery.
Garth:	But I don't mind.
Jeff:	OK, but remember to check the weight of your materials before you begin. Avoid making jewellery which is so heavy you can't wear it! I remember making some earrings for a customer. They were beautiful, but she only wore them once. She made me use lots of heavy stones and they hurt her ears so much she couldn't wear them! OK. Let's look at the other things you need. I've got some nylon or leather here. I'll let you decide. Which do you prefer to use?
Mary:	Nylon for me.
Garth:	Well, I plan to wear this one myself, so leather for me.
Jeff:	And here are the stones and beads. Try to find some which look good together.
Mary:	Oh, they're beautiful.
Garth:	Yeah. I'd like to use these square black ones.
Jeff:	Don't forget. Design something simple this time.
Mary:	Oh, yes.
Jeff:	Right, let's begin.

Recording 22

Mrs Scott:	Good morning Edina, please have a seat.
Edina:	Thank you, Mrs Scott.
Mrs Scott:	OK, so you'd like a job in my souvenir shop for six months.
Edina:	Yes. I've finished school and I want to work and travel before I go to university next year. When I finish working here, I'll probably travel abroad. That's why I want to earn some money.
Mrs Scott:	I see. Well, you know the wages aren't very high, but if you work here on Sundays, you'll earn extra money. And we close at six, so your evenings will be free if you work here. Have you worked in a shop before?
Edina:	Yes, well, the camera shop. Do you know it? The one near the park.

Mrs Scott: Oh, right. Yes, I know the owner. Simon Brown, isn't it? So, Edina, what's the most important thing about working in a shop?

Edina: You have to serve people quickly. Customers get annoyed if they have to wait.

Mrs Scott: That's quite right.

Edina: And you must also smile and be friendly.

Mrs Scott: Mm. If the shop assistants aren't friendly, the shop loses customers.

Edina: Yes.

Mrs Scott: If I phone the camera shop, will Simon recommend you?

Edina: Yes, I think so.

Mrs Scott: OK. You'll start work on Monday unless I phone you. I just want to have a quick chat with Simon first, but I'm sure everything will be fine. You can start on Monday?

Edina: Oh, yes. What time do I need to be here?

Mrs Scott: If I don't phone you tomorrow, you'll start at nine o'clock.

Edina: OK. Thanks very much.

Mrs Scott: So, what about this trip you want the money for? Where do you plan to go?

Edina: Well, if I save two thousand pounds, I'll go to South America. But if not, I mean, if I don't save as much as that, I'll go round Europe.

Mrs Scott: Oh, that sounds very exciting.

Edina: I hope it will be.

Mrs Scott: I'm sure it will. So, OK, that's it for now.

Edina: Thanks, goodbye.

Mrs Scott: Bye.

Recording 23

Patti: Welcome to Music World. I'm Patti and our guest this week is every band's favourite songwriter, Carl Ryder.

Carl: Hi, Patti.

Patti: Thanks for coming to the studio, Carl. We know you've had a lot of success in the past few years, but is life in the music business all fun, or are there any disadvantages?

Carl: Well, it is fun, yes, but if you want to be successful it's hard work. That can cause problems. (*Mm?*) For example, I wish I had more free time.

Patti: What would you do, if you didn't have so much work?

Carl: Well, if I had time, I'd go to more concerts. It's good for me to hear new bands.

Patti: I hope you'll get a break soon. But what about new songs? Are you writing any at the moment?

Carl: Oh yeah, I am. But it's tiring, because I'm trying to write new songs in the evening and in the day I'm going to meetings, working with singers and so on. I wish I wasn't so busy. It would be good if I could spend a few weeks somewhere just writing songs.

Patti: Well, I know you can't go away now, but if you could go anywhere in the world, where would you go?

Carl: If I went away now, I'd choose somewhere warm and sunny, but quiet.

Patti: Mmm. But wouldn't you be bored if it was a quiet place?

Carl: No, because I'd write songs. I wouldn't want to talk to people if I had songs to write. (*Yeah, right.*) Of course I'd go somewhere lively if I didn't have any work to do at all, somewhere with lots of clubs and good shops!

Patti: Uh-huh. I know you have many interests apart from your songwriting. You've had a lot of success with that of course, but if you weren't a songwriter, what would you be?

Carl: Mm. If I wasn't a songwriter, I'd be a fashion designer.

Patti: Really?

Carl: Yeah, I studied design at university for a year before I had my first successful song. I really like unusual clothes. But I never have enough time to look for them.

Patti: Maybe when you're not so busy. On that holiday you're going to have one day.

Carl: Yeah, maybe.

Patti: Well, Carl. I hope that'll be soon. And thank you for giving us your time today.

Carl: You're welcome.

Recording 24

Alan: Hi, Maria. I'm going to the cinema this afternoon. Do you want to come?

Maria: Well, what are you going to see?

Alan: 'Norman Starman III.'

Maria: Norman what?

Alan: Where have you been? This is the third Norman Starman film. The first two Starman films were made about three years ago.

Maria: I never saw them.

Alan: They're just brilliant. Really funny. In the second one the main part was given to a different actor, but he was just as good as the first one.

Maria: So what are they about?

Alan: Well, they're all about this guy Norman. He's a space traveller. (*Oh, yeah.*) And, um, in the first film Norman is caught by aliens and he is taken to their planet.

Maria: So what happens?

Alan: He's taught to speak their language and he's changed by their scientists so he looks like them. But he still feels like a fifteen-year-old human. It's really funny.

Maria: Is that how it ends?

Alan:	No, at the end of the film he escapes. He flies away in one of their spaceships but he doesn't realise that two of the aliens are hiding in the spaceship. So these aliens go to earth with him.
Maria:	It sounds quite funny.
Alan:	Yeah, it is. They get on well together on the journey and various things happen, you know. But the spaceship is damaged when they land, although they aren't hurt, luckily. And that's how it ends.
Maria:	What happens in the second film, then?
Alan:	Well, he's on earth, but he's got these two aliens with him. Norman is arrested by the army and he's put in a special kind of prison with the aliens.
Maria:	Why?
Alan:	The humans think he's an alien too because he looks like them now. The soldiers don't believe him when he tries to explain. Anyway, one of them, a woman, believes him in the end and she helps him escape. She has the spaceship repaired at a friend's garage. But the aliens are waiting to be rescued and that's what the third film will be about.
Maria:	Yeah, I'd like to see it. I wonder what will happen.
Alan:	Mm. The aliens will be rescued, I guess, and then they'll go back to their planet again. But I don't know how it'll be done. I'm sure Norman will get into trouble somehow.
Maria:	Well, let's go. It'll be nice to do something silly for a change.

Recording 25

Nick:	Hi Will. It's Nick here.
Will:	Hi. Hey, where were you on Friday night?
Nick:	I'm sorry I didn't meet you. That's why I'm ringing. I had an argument with my mum.
Will:	What was it about?
Nick:	Well, I didn't have to go to college on Friday so I asked a few friends round. I hadn't expected mum to come home early. So when she arrived she was really angry.
Will:	Why?
Nick:	Oh, you know, because there were some dirty plates and a few saucepans.
Will:	Why? Were you cooking?
Nick:	Yeah. We had some spaghetti. Anyway she said I couldn't go out because I hadn't tidied the house and I hadn't washed up.
Will:	That's so unfair.
Nick:	She said she was expecting visitors and the house was dirty and untidy.
Will:	Was it?
Nick:	Not really. But she said I had to stay at home. But I did feel a bit guilty so I said I would wash up.

Will:	Yeah? And what about the others?
Nick:	She said my friends should help too but they'd disappeared by then. All that shouting frightened them I think.
Will:	So you washed up?
Nick:	Yeah. But she was still angry. She seems to forget all the things I do to help. So I said that I had washed the car the week before but that seemed to make her angrier because I forgot that she paid me to do that.
Will:	So what did she say then?
Nick:	She said she was going to keep my pocket money this week.
Will:	No way!
Nick:	So I can't go out tonight either because I haven't got any money.
Will:	I can lend you some. I'll see you at the bus stop at 8 then?
Nick:	Great. See you there.

Recording 26

Boss:	Tim. I've just read this article. I wrote the headline for you and we found a good photo but you've written about football. That's not what our readers want. They want to know the interesting things about Joe Chapman. Did you ask him the questions I gave you? Did you ask him about his new girlfriend?
Tim:	No, but I asked him why he hadn't scored any goals on Saturday – he usually scores at least one.
Boss:	Yes ...
Tim:	I asked him how his knee was because he'd hurt it in training. He said it was getting better.
Boss:	I'm delighted.
Tim:	I told him to be careful the next time.
Boss:	Great. But did you ask him who he was with at that nightclub last week?
Tim:	No, but I asked him if his mother always watched his games.
Boss:	Very interesting I'm sure. And does she?
Tim:	Yes, every single one.
Boss:	Did you ask him about the argument with the new manager?
Tim:	No, but I asked him how long he was going to stay with the team. I asked him if he was happy. He said that he had no plans to move to another club.
Boss:	I'm very pleased for him. But surely you asked him about his free time? We want to know where he goes, what he does.
Tim:	No, but I invited him to have lunch with me after the interview.
Boss:	And he agreed?
Tim:	Yes.

Boss:	So then you asked him about the TV programme he's going to do?
Tim:	No, but he reminded me to watch the match next Saturday as it's a really important one.
Boss:	But not very interesting information for our readers.
Tim:	I asked him where he would play next Saturday – which position. He said that he'd play his normal position - Centre forward.
Boss:	What about those fashion adverts he's in – for men's clothes? Did you ask him how much he earns from those?
Tim:	No, but I asked him if his team would win the cup. He said he expected them to win for the third time. Oh and we didn't get a photograph of him because he asked us not to take any.
Boss:	Oh, next time I'll do it myself. And I advise you not to do any more interviews with Joe Chapman.

Recording 27

Welcome to the TBC studios. My name is Rob and I'm going to show you round. I know some of you are interested in working in television so please ask me any questions. We may meet some other people who you can talk to while we're walking round. OK. So follow me please. This way.

This is the news studio. Here's the desk where the newsreader sits to read the news. Behind the studio is the newsroom where the news team choose the stories which will be in the news. Every morning they choose the headline the newsreader will read first. We call that the lead story. But by the evening, the headlines will probably change.

And here's a man whose face you'll recognise. Hello, Gavin. Gavin presents the lunchtime news every day. Gavin, have you got time to answer a few questions? Anyone like to ask ...

I'm sure you know where we are now – this is the sitting room which belongs to the Baxter family. They live in Solomon Street – that's the soap opera which you can see every evening at 7 on TBC. Well, some of you seem to recognise it. Lots of things have happened here. This is the room where Mark asked Jill to marry him and here's a photo which shows them on their wedding day. Ten million people watched that. And through the window you can see the café which Mark owns. It's only the front of the café of course. The inside is in a different studio.

Anyone keen on sport? OK. Well this is the sports room where we report on all the sports events which take place around the world. We have different presenters who are all experts in their sport. For instance, people who were stars like Sally Ravenna, the tennis champion and Peter Davenport, the international rugby player. And it looks as though we're lucky today. Here's a footballer you'll

recognise. He played for England over 50 times. Hello Jack. Now Jack's the man whose old boots were sold recently for £10,000. Well, Jack, there's an important football match tonight. I believe ...

Recording 28

Holly:	Max?
Max:	Hi, Holly.
Holly:	Are you ready to go to the party?
Max:	No, I don't know what to wear. I've got so few nice clothes.
Holly:	Well, what about your blue shirt?
Max:	It isn't smart enough. And it's too small for me.
Holly:	What?
Max:	I think I've grown.
Holly:	Don't be so silly. You're twenty-three. You haven't grown, you're just too fat.
Max:	You say such unkind things to me. You don't understand because you're so lucky.
Holly:	What do you mean?
Max:	You lose weight so easily.
Holly:	You talk such nonsense! I'm slim because I walk everywhere. Your problem is that you don't take enough exercise.
Max:	But I have so little time. You don't know what my job's like. I'm so busy that I can't think about keeping fit.
Holly:	But you could walk to work.
Max:	It's too far to walk.
Holly:	You're such a lazy person! You never walk anywhere.
Max:	I walk around in my lunch break.
Holly:	But you just look in the shop windows. You never walk quickly enough. Anyway, if you really want to get fit, you could join a gym, like me.
Max:	They cost such a lot of money! I don't have enough money for gym membership.
Holly:	My gym isn't too expensive.
Max:	I'm sure it is.
Holly:	Well you can start by thinking about what you eat. I know you eat the wrong food. You have too much ice cream and too many burgers. And you don't eat enough fruit.
Max:	I sometimes have a salad with my burger, but it costs extra.
Holly:	You make so many excuses. How can anyone help you!

Recording 29

Nancy:	Did you watch TV last night?
Steve:	No, I was out. Was there anything good on?
Nancy:	Well there's this new cartoon series, it's very funny.
Steve:	Yeah?

Nancy: It's called Orville. What happened last night. Well, there was this man, Orville, OK, and he had a beautiful girlfriend, Claudia, who was a model and she loved him, but he was extremely jealous. And, um, Claudia went to an evening class to learn Greek. (*Yeah.*) Well, he asked Claudia about the evening class, but he didn't believe her so he followed her to see where she went. He put on a false beard as he didn't want her to recognise him. (*OK.*) Anyway, when she arrived at the college for her class, there was another young man, um Damian, in the entrance hall.

Steve: And why was Damian there?

Nancy: Because he was waiting for his girlfriend, a teacher, I think.

Steve: Oh.

Nancy: But Claudia knew Damian because of her job. He was a fashion photographer. Damian said "Hi!" and they began talking, so Orville started shouting at him. He thought Claudia was lying about the Greek lessons and that she had a date with Damian. (*Mm*) Orville was making a terrible noise so the college receptionist called the police. And the police came and Orville didn't know what to do. He'd forgotten that he was still wearing the false beard.

Steve: Oh, right.

Nancy: He said to Claudia, 'Tell them who I am!' She said nothing since she didn't recognise him.

Steve: Really?

Nancy: Yes, because of the beard. Well, it was a very big beard. No-one helped him so he was taken to the police station. It was so funny.

Steve: But why was it funny?

Nancy: Because of the beard and Orville's face and, oh, I don't know. Watch it next week and see.

Steve: OK, well, perhaps.

Recording 30

Mr Smart: 377203.

Selina: Hallo, Mr Smart?

Mr Smart: Yes.

Selina: Hi, I'm Selina and I'm phoning from Bestways Tours Holiday Company.

Mr Smart: Yes?

Selina: I believe you've just returned from a holiday with our company.

Mr Smart: Yes.

Selina: We always phone our customers when they return home. May I take a few minutes of your time to ask you how it was?

Mr Smart: Oh, OK, if it doesn't take too long.

Selina: Thank you. Well, first, did you enjoy your holiday?

Mr Smart: Well, I enjoyed most of the holiday, but I didn't enjoy the first night.

Selina: Oh, why was that?

Mr Smart: Because of the noise. Although I asked for a quiet hotel, your company put me in the Concordia, on the main road along the beach. My wife and I both work very hard and we need to relax when we're on holiday. The first night, we couldn't sleep until the clubs and restaurants closed. That was four o'clock in the the morning!

Selina: Oh, dear. I hope our local staff were able to help you.

Mr Smart: Not at first. I phoned your local office in the morning, but unfortunately both the manager and his assistant were out.

Selina: I'm sure the manager phoned you as soon as he could.

Mr Smart: Although I left several messages, he didn't phone me back until the second day. I couldn't change my hotel until then.

Selina: But was the second hotel all right?

Mr Smart: Oh, yes, he offered us either the San Francisco or the Cristina and we moved to the San Francisco after I spoke to him, and that was lovely. Well, the hotel was excellent but the food was boring. Anyway, we didn't mind that very much, we ate out most nights. In spite of the bad start, we had a good holiday.

Selina: I'm so pleased. Well, I'm going to tell our bookings manager about your problems as soon as she comes into the office. I think someone made a mistake with your hotel reservation.

Mr Smart: Thank you. Will you phone me when you find out what went wrong? I'd really like to know.

Selina: Yes, of course, I understand. I'll either phone or email you.

Mr Smart: Good, thank you.

Selina: My pleasure. Goodbye.

Mr Smart: Goodbye.

Unit 1

A1

Sample answer:
B beautiful grey silk   C grey cotton
D short black wool   E white leather

A2

They're shopping. They talk about A, D and E.

A3

2 Emily   3 shopping   4 Callum   5 Callum
6 (the) computer shop
7 (a) computer game

We use adjectives ending in *-ed* to talk about feelings.
We use adjectives ending in *-ing* to talk about things.

A4

1 short black wool
2 favourite long black
3 white leather

Lovely and *favourite* describe someone's opinion.
Short and *long* describe size or shape.
Grey, *black* and *white* describe colour.
Wool and *leather* describe the material.
Opinion adjectives usually go first.
Material adjectives usually go last.

C1

2 g   3 e   4 f   5 c   6 a   7 b
(Grammar B1)

C2

2 I wore my dirty old blue jeans when I painted the ceiling.
3 I borrowed my sister's lovely long silk dress to wear to the party.
4 I was surprised that Mike wore that white cotton jacket.
5 He bought some expensive new shoes yesterday.
6 Jenny's father gave her a beautiful long gold necklace for her 18th birthday.
(Grammar B2)

C3

2 tired   3 bored   4 tiring   5 surprised   6 excited   7 boring
8 amazing   9 annoyed   10 interested
(Grammar B3)

C4

bus stop   city centre   credit card   football boots
evening performance   film star   fire engine   police car
traffic jam   wedding invitation

2 film star   3 credit card   4 football boots
5 evening performance   6 traffic jam
(Grammar B4)

C5

There is a lovely ~~and~~ sandy beach and the sea is blue and warm.
          beautiful old
The town has lots of old beautiful buildings. My parents like
      art galleries   *bored*
going to the galleries art but I get boring so I go to the shops. You

can buy cheaps clothes there.
          favourite restaurant
I hope we'll go to my restaurant favourite. Write back and tell
       exciting
me all your excited news.
(Grammar B1, B2, B3, B4)

Exam task

1 G   2 E   3 F   4 D   5 A

Grammar focus

2 beautiful old   3 pleasant flat   4 pretty little
5 active young   6 popular new

Unit 2

A1

A He's working in an office.
B She's at school.
C They're preparing for a party.

A2

1 Josh is outside his office. He's going home because there's a party for his sister's 16th birthday.
2 Josh is on a train. His sister's unhappy because she wants him to be there on her birthday (and she hasn't had his present).
3 Josh is in the station. His sister is at her friend's house because the party is a surprise.

A3

1 quickly   2 carefully   3 usually   4 perfectly
We add -ly to the adjective. quick, careful, usual, perfect

A4

extremely   very   really   rather
They make the meaning stronger.

A5

to the station; now
always; round the corner
very slowly; outside our house
patiently; at her friend's house
often; there; after school

how often?	how?	where?	when?
always often	very slowly patiently	to the station round the corner outside our house at her friend's house there	now after school

C1

2 suitable 3 unhappily 4 honest 5 politely 6 angry
7 calmly 8 differently 9 sensibly 10 slowly
(Grammar B1 and B2)

C2

2 good 3 hard 4 correct 5 badly 6 correct 7 late
8 correct 9 well; clearly 10 correct
(Grammar B1, B2 and B3)

C3

2 I missed the train yesterday. *or* Yesterday I missed the train.
3 I enjoyed that television programme very much.
4 correct
5 I have never been to Spain.
6 correct
7 They were still waiting when we arrived.
8 This shop is always open on Sundays.
9 correct
10 My friends and I went to a nightclub last night. *or* Last night
   my friends and I went to a nightclub.
(Grammar B4)

C4

Sample answers:
2 My best friend is really tall/pretty/clever.
3 Some sports are extremely dangerous/exciting.
4 In my country the people are fairly friendly/tall/serious.
5 When I come home from holiday I usually feel rather
   sad/lazy/relaxed.
6 In winter in Britain the weather is quite cold/wet/cloudy.
(Grammar B5)

C5

2 but I went to a theme park near London on Saturday.
  or but on Saturday I went to a theme park near London.
3 I wanted to go on the big wheel but other people had the same
  idea as well
4 so I had to wait very patiently in the queue but it was a great
  ride.
5 I also went on the water slide.
6 I had lunch in a café at midday
  or At midday I had lunch in a café
7 I'll never forget it.
8 I had a really wonderful day there.
(Grammar B4 and B5)

Exam task

1B 2A 3B 4D 5C 6C 7B 8A 9B 10D

Grammar focus

1

1 carefully 2 locally 3 usually 4 regularly 5 healthily
6 separately 7 privately

2

1 careful 2 local 3 usual 4 regular 5 healthy
6 separate 7 private

Unit 3

A2

music   posters   reviews   journalists   adverts

A3

2 popular 3 expensive 4 smaller 5 good

A4

Which magazine	HITS!	BUZZ	SMASH
is the newest?			✓
has the most reviews?			✓
is the most expensive?		✓	
has the most adverts?	✓		

A5

A3 is about comparing two things; A4 is about comparing more
than two things.

C1

2 bigger 3 nicer 4 more interesting 5 more nervous
6 richer 7 easier 8 hotter
(Grammar B1)

C2

2 Golf is safer than horse-riding.
3 Water-skiing is more difficult than swimming.
4 Motorcycling is noisier than cycling.
5 Rugby balls are heavier than tennis balls.

7 Horse-riding isn't as safe as golf.
  Horse-riding is less safe than golf.
8 Swimming isn't as difficult as water-skiing.
  Swimming is less difficult than water-skiing.
9 Cycling isn't as noisy as motorcycling.
  Cycling is less noisy than motorcycling.
10 Tennis balls aren't as heavy as rugby balls.
   Tennis balls are less heavy than rugby balls.
(Grammar B1)

C3

2 She coloured the drawings neatly.
3 She explained her designs well.
4 She sewed her clothes beautifully.
6 more neatly; the most neatly
7 better; the best
8 more beautifully; the most beautifully
(Grammar B2)

C4

old–new; tidy–untidy; small–big; near–far; expensive–cheap
  2 the oldest house.
  3 the tidiest garden.
  4 the cheapest house.
  5 the furthest from the city centre.
  6 more
  7 most
  8 fewer
  9 fewest
10 more
(Grammar B1 and B3)

Exam practice

1 more 2 funniest 3 am interested 4 as popular as
5 'm/am not

Grammar focus

0 as/so good as 1 most 2 as/so funny as 4 more popular

Unit 4

A1

1 a theatre 2 a sports stadium 3 a cinema 4 a market

A2

They saw the sports stadium and the theatre.

A3

2 is now turning 3 're now passing 4 normally goes
5 are practising

A4

1 1 and 4
2 2, 3 and 5
3 1 and 4
4 2, 3 and 5

A5

have: a good time, a walk, lunch
have got: a map, a sore throat, a new entertainment centre, a cinema, air-conditioning, some good shops

C1

2 arrives 3 has 4 prepares 5 does 6 works
7 doesn't have 8 has 9 orders 10 doesn't leave
(Grammar B1.)

C2

Follow model in C1. (Grammar B1)

C3

2 Are you coming 3 am/'m sitting 4 're waiting
5 are shouting 6 Is he talking 7 is/'s reading
8 am/'m getting 9 is leaving 10 am/'m coming
(Grammar B2.)

C4

2 I'm working 3 I come 4 I get 5 I'm sharing
6 It's not/It isn't 7 I prefer 8 I don't want 9 I'm saving
10 I'm/I am getting
(Grammar B1,B2,B3.)

C5

2 I've got a headache.
3 She's got long straight hair.
4 Has your hotel got a swimming pool?
5 I haven't got much/any money.
6 Have these suitcases got locks (on them)?
7 The doctor hasn't got time to see you today.
(Grammar B4.)

C6

2 has 3 go 4 is staying; am sleeping 5 Do you understand
6 are having 7 belong 8 is having
(Grammar B1, B2, B3, B4.)

Grammar focus

1 See B2 2 See B4 3 See B1, B3

Exam task

Sample answer:
Dear Sven
I'm staying at a campsite near the sea. It's a beautiful place with a good beach. The town's got restaurants and a sports hall but no nightclubs. In the evenings we have a barbecue on the beach.
love Pia

Unit 5

A1

1 in a café 2 in a cinema 3 in an office

A2

He has a job (at the cinema).

A3

1 She phoned Donny.
2 Because he was listening to an argument.
3 She texted him.
4 He was watching the film.
5 She tried to contact him again.
6 Because he was talking to the manager.

A4

1 1, 3, 5
2 2, 4, 6
3 2, 4, 6
4 1, 3, 5

C1

2 visited   3 saw   4 didn't work   5 was   6 had   7 went
8 ate   9 spent   10 found   11 bought   12 Did you go
(Grammar B1, B2.)

C2

2 Tanya was buying the drinks and Tony was choosing the music.
3 Tanya was tidying the house and Tony was preparing the food.
4 Tanya was blowing up the balloons and Tony was decorating the rooms.
5 Tanya was ironing her dress and Tony was having a shower.
(Grammar B3)

C3

2 were working   met
3 was studying   fell
4 was cooking   burnt
5 was staying   painted
6 was tidying   discovered
7 were climbing   saw
(Grammar B1, B2, B3, B4)

C4

2 went   3 met   4 invited   5 didn't go   6 didn't get
7 was watching   8 was having   9 was reading   10 rang
11 looked   12 was standing   13 went   14 didn't open
15 got   16 had
(Grammar B2, B3 (State verbs: have), B4)

C5

2 wanted   3 was   4 was counting   5 chose   6 wrapped
7 was waiting   8 decided   9 found   10 ran   11 looked
12 was searching   13 were looking   14 knocked   15 waved
(Grammar, B1, B2, B3, B4)

Grammar focus

2 was carrying   3 stopped   4 looked   5 was following
6 dropped   7 ran

Exam task

Sample answer:

... The sun was shining and I was eating an ice cream. Two girls were standing in the middle of the square. They were looking at some photos. Their handbags were on the ground beside them.

Suddenly, a boy ran across the square and took their handbags. When he came near me, I stood up and pushed my chair in front of him. He fell over and dropped the handbags. I took them to the girls. The café owner phoned the police and they took the thief away.

The girls thanked me and we had lunch together.

A2

Garry met Annie at the cinema.
Garry and Annie leave the party together.

A3

1 haven't put   2 haven't dried   3 made   4 Have ... met
5 I've worked   6 met   7 's worked   8 waited   9 've ... met
10 left

A4

1 Sentences 3, 6, 8 and 10. Simple past.
2 Sentences 1, 2, 4 and 9. Present perfect.
3 Sentences 5 and 7. Present perfect.

C1

2 've/have collected
3 've/have bought
4 haven't checked
5 've/have chosen
6 haven't packed
7 've/have phoned
8 've/have seen
9 said
10 haven't found
11 Have you looked
12 haven't got
(Grammar B1)

C2

2 met   3 did you decide   4 began   5 ran   6 had
7 haven't paid   8 has won   9 have disappeared
10 have you planned   11 haven't chosen   12 have helped
(Grammar B2)

C3

2 for   3 never   4 ago   5 How long   6 since   7 When
8 already   9 ever   10 still   11 yet
(Grammar B2, B3)

C4

2 D   3 D   4 S   5 D   6 S   7 S   8 S
(Grammar B2, B3, B4)

Exam practice

1 bigger than   2 got   3 haven't   4 has worked   5 enjoys

Grammar focus

1 D   2 D   3 D

A1

1 seven years ago   2 last week

A2

He wanted to see his friend Stefan.
He saw new gardens and a new sports centre.

A3

2 arrived; had finished
3 had eaten; walked
4 used to be
5 use to be
6 had just started; left
7 had already decided
8 walked; saw

A4

1 used to
2 2 3 6 8 yes

C1

2 'd asked 3 had just left 4 had already gone
5 hadn't brought 6 hadn't shut 7 'd gone 8 'd realised
9 hadn't seen 10 'd booked
(Grammar B1)

C2

2 had started 3 had/'d never seen 4 hadn't finished
5 had/'d never been 6 had already studied 7 had/'d just visited
(Grammar B2, B3)

C3

2 used to walk 3 Did you use to know 4 used to be
5 didn't use to have 6 Did they use to travel 7 didn't use to
go 8 used to have
(Grammar B4)

C4

Sample answers:
  2 used to be lazy
  3 didn't use to be slim
  4 used to ride a bike
  5 didn't use to like my brother
  6 didn't use to go to the cinema very often
  7 used to be shy
  8 didn't use to enjoy sport
  9 used to be a vegetarian
10 used to live in the city centre
(Grammar B4)

C5

Follow models in C4.

Exam practice

1 C 2 B 3 D 4 A 5 B 6 D 7 C 8 B 9 A 10 D

Grammar focus

1 They'd already started planning the baths.
2 They used to wash and meet their friends.
3 They'd built towns, roads and bridges.

A1

1 B 2 C 3 A

A2

1 the Andes
2 the Atlantic Ocean; Greece; Lake Garda
3 the Sahara Desert
4 Rome New York
We use *the* before the names of mountain ranges, deserts and
oceans.

A3

jeans, shorts, shoes, trousers
You can use *jeans*, *shorts* and *trousers* only in the plural.
Sock, *shoe* and *shirt* can be singular.

A4

1 music 2 traffic 3 information 4 money 5 advice
You can't make these nouns plural because they are uncountable.

C1

boot, bracelet, earring, glove, shoe, sock
(Grammar B1)

C2

3 euros 4 money 5 bread 6 vegetables 7 food
8 shops 9 information 10 travel 11 traffic 12 music
13 chairs 14 furniture 15 sand 16 stones
(Grammar B2)

C3

1
2 a 3 – 4 the 5 a 6 The 7 The 8 the
2
1 a 2 the 3 the 4 the 5 the 6 – 7 the 8 a
3
1 a 2 – 3 the 4 a 5 a 6 the 7 the 8 the 9 The 10 –
(Grammar B3, B4)

C4

  2 Tom Cruise was wearing a black jacket, black jeans and black
    shoes.
  3 I'm happy with ~~a~~ the furniture in my room, but I want to
    change the curtains.
  4 I'm sending this card to wish you a good luck for your driving
    test.
  5 My cousin's just been on a ~~travel~~ trip/journey round France.
  6 I listen to music~~s~~ when I'm working so I feel more relaxed.
  7 The weather was marvellous so we went to the beach and
    swam in the sea.
  8 I'll go to the swimming-pool for some information~~s~~ about
    diving lessons.
  9 If I send you ~~a~~ money, will you buy me some earrings like
    yours?
10 We saw some lovely old towns in the Czech Republic on our
    last holiday.
(Grammar B1, B2, B3, B4)

201

Exam practice

1 1982 2 jewellery 3 museum 4 cinema 5 train
6 information

Grammar focus

2, 3, 4, 5, 6
3, 4, 5
2, 6
Only one (we say *travel by train*, not ~~by the train~~).

A1

1 On a train. He's ringing to say what time he'll arrive.
2 In a café. He's ringing to ask where his friend is.
3 In a newsagent's. She's looking for a job.
4 At home / in her kitchen. She's planning a birthday party.

A3

2 some food
3 because there isn't anybody in the café.
4 everybody
5 nothing
6 She's got no experience.
7 lots of people
8 some bread and some crisps
9 a couple of cakes

A4

1 much ; few
2 anybody; nobody
3 nothing; anything
4 no; any
5 lots; lot of
6 couple; two

C1

2 an 3 any 4 some 5 some 6 any 7 some 8 some
9 any 10 no
(Grammar B1)

C2

2 somewhere 3 no-one 4 somebody 5 nobody 6 nothing
7 somewhere 8 everybody 9 Nobody 10 No-one
11 anything 12 something
(Grammar B2)

C3

2 S 3 D 4 S 5 D 6 S 7 S 8 D 9 S
(Grammar B1, B2)

C4

Countable: *CDs, magazines, parties, T shirts*
Uncountable: *homework, money, fruit, jewellery*
A couple of / a few / lots can be used with uncountable nouns
A little / lots of / much can be used with uncountable nouns.
(Grammar B3)

Sample anwers:
I read a couple of magazines last weekend.
Isabella has lots of jewellery.
Andy hadn't got much homework he watched TV.

Exam task

1 A 2 A 3 B 4 A 5 A 6 B 7 A 8 B 9 B 10 B

Grammar focus task

1 lots of information
2 lots of entertainment
3 a free programme
4 food
5 because there'll be a lot of traffic

a free programme is countable; *information, entertainment, food* and *traffic* are uncountable. You can say *a few free programmes*; you can say *a little information, entertainment, food* and *traffic*.

A1

Makeover means to change something to make it more attractive. The girl's bedroom was painted and she has a new chair, new pictures, new lights and a new mirror.

A2

No, she doesn't.

A3

2 Either 3 Neither 4 All 5 Most 6 Every 7 No
8 Both 9 None 10 Some

A4

Each, all, most, every, no, none and *some* are about more than two things or people.
Either, neither and *both* are about two things or people.

C1

2 those 3 that 4 these 5 this 6 those 7 the ones
(Grammar B1)

C2

2 All of 3 Some of 4 All of 5 None of 6 Some of
7 Most of
(Grammar B2)

C3

2 Neither **of** these jackets fits me.
3 We stopped for a meal because both of us ~~was~~ were hungry.
4 I was surprised that most **of** the people staying in the hotel were Italian.
5 Either of the restaurants you suggested is fine with me.
6 He's tidied the garden and put away all **the** chairs.
7 I liked both pairs of jeans, but I chose the black ones for the party.
8 ~~This~~ **That** was an awful meal we had yesterday. We won't go to that restaurant again.
9 We're giving a party for my father and we're inviting all of **his** old friends.
10 Some ~~of~~ airports have several restaurants.
(Grammar B1, B2, B3)

C4

2 Both 3 either 4 Both 5 Every 6 all 7 each 8 every 9 all 10 all
(Grammar B3, B4)

Exam task

1 as well 2 of the 3 many 4 no-one/nobody 5 the teachers

Grammar focus task

neither, all
Yes.
All of them except *no*.

Unit 11

A3

1 their 2 his own 3 his 4 her own 5 himself 6 hers 7 herself

A4

2 Cara is Sally's sister.
3 He wants to leave his parents' house.
4 He works in the newsagent's.
5 He used Sally's key.

C1

3 my father
4 are ours
5 belong to us
6 yours
7 you
8 This is my grandparents' car.
9 This car is my grandparents'.
10 Those are their videos.
11 Those videos are theirs.
(Grammar B1 and B2)

C2

2 his/our 3 mine 4 him 5 theirs 6 yours 7 her 8 his 9 her 10 ours
(Grammar B2)

C3

2 yourselves 3 themselves 4 herself 5 myself 6 himself
(Grammar B3)

C4

2 There are 3 It's 4 It's 5 it's 6 There's 7 it's 8 There's 9 it's 10 There's
(Grammar B4)

C5

2 father's 3 their own 4 themselves 5 his 6 It 7 mine 8 me 9 There 10 Alan's
(All grammar sections)

Exam practice

1 A 2 C 3 B 4 C 5 B 6 B

Grammar focus

2 own
3 hurt themselves
4 ours
5 ourselves

Unit 12

A1

Elliot's going catch a plane and go to a meeting. Kelly's going to go to the beach.

A2

Because he's too busy to see his friends.

A3

2 'm not studying 3 're going to spend 4 'm meeting 5 leaves; arrives 6 'll be 7 'll have 8 'll be; 'll have; 'll drive

A4

1 5
2 1, 3
3 2, 4
4 6, 7, 8
5 5
6 6, 8
7 1, 2, 3 4
8 7

C1

2 won't leave
3 will be
4 won't come
5 will become
6 will you need
(Grammar B1)

C2

2 isn't going to win.
3 're going to be
4 Are you going to join
5 'm going to play
6 's not going to rain.
(Grammar B2)

C3

2 We're going to buy
3 I'll think
4 Paula nd Ros are going to come
5 I'll check
6 I'll buy
(Grammar B1, B2)

C4

2 're listening
3 is he doing
4 's giving an interview
5 's he going
6 's going
7 's staying
8 'm spending
9 's presenting
10 are having a meal together
(Grammar B3)

C5

2 going to look   3 leaves   4 returns   5 'll do   6 'll have
7 starts   8 'm meeting   9 'll be   10 Are you going to have
(Grammar B1, B2, B3, B4)

Exam practice

1 A   2 C   3 B   4 C   5 B

Grammar focus task

1
Sale starts
Shop opens/closes

2 (*two of these*)
I'm working late
We're staying
we're going to spend
Paula is travelling
Paula is walking
Paula is staying
Mr Johnson is going to arrange a meeting

3 (*two of these*)
I expect I'll miss
Lewis will probably arrive at the concert after Jack.
Lewis will probably pick up Jack on his way to the concert.
Jack will probably meet Lewis inside the concert hall.
She'll probably bring

Unit 13

A1

They work in a café. Mr Kent is the boss, Maria is a waitress and
Alex is a waiter.

A2

1 Alex makes suggestions and offers to do things in conversation 3.
2 Maria asks Alex to do things in conversation 2.
3 Alex asks for permission to do things in conversation 1.

A3

2 May   3 Could   4 Can   5 Will   6 would   7 could
8 Shall   9 could   10 can

A4

Asking for permission	*Asking someone to do something*	*Making offers or suggestions*
Can I	Would you	We could
Could I	Will you	Shall we
May I	Can you	I can
	Could you	

C1

2 Peter ought to help us.
3 We'll (We will) decorate the flat.
4 We shouldn't (should not) invite too many people.
5 Can you bring your CDs?
6 Could your mother lend us some plates?
7 We mustn't make too much noise.
8 The neighbours might complain.
(Grammar B1)

C2

2 Could/Would/Can/Will you hold the door please?
3 Could/Would/Can/Will you fasten my seat belt please?
4 Could/Would/Can/Will you open my bottle of water please?
5 Could/Would/Can/Will you help me put my coat on please?
6 Could/Would/Can/Will you close the window please
(Grammar B2)

C3

2 I can cook   3 What about having   4 Shall I get
5 Shall I show   6 I can / I could give
(Grammar B3)

C4

2 eat   3 Could   4 Can   5 Shall   6 Will   7 Shall   8 inviting
9 Would   10 meet
(Grammar B2, B3 and B4)

C5

2 May/Could/Can I leave
3 Can/Will/Could/Would you buy
4 Shall I paint
5 Shall I/we / Why don't we leave
6 Shall I do
7 You can use
8 Can/Will/Could/Would you find
9 What/How about buying / Shall I/we / Why don't we
10 May/Could/Can I put
(All grammar sections)

Exam practice

1 B   2 C   3 A   4 C   5 B   6 A   7 B

Grammar focus

2 May I try on that skirt?
3 So would you come and pick me up?
4 Why don't you call a taxi?
5 Could I change it please?
6 Excuse me, can I leave my car here?
7 What about going to see a film at the cinema?
8 Shall we go to that new restaurant?
9 Could you help me please?
10 So can you do it?
11 Shall I book you a taxi?
12 Or you could take the underground.

Unit 14

A1

A reality TV programme where some people live together for a week and they're filmed. In this programme they live in a castle and pretend it is hundreds of years ago.

A3

	We have to	We mustn't	We don't have to	We needn't
be good at acting			✓	
use mobile phones		✓		
take modern equipment		✓		
wear a microphone	✓			
take our own clothes			✓	
cook the meals	✓			
stay there				✓

A4

We don't have to be good at acting.
We mustn't use mobile phones.
We mustn't take modern equipment.
We have to wear a microphone.
We don't have to take our own clothes.
We have to cook the meals.
We needn't stay there.

No, *mustn't* doesn't mean the same as *don't have to*.
Yes, *needn't* means the same as *don't have to*.

C1

2 must   3 will/'ll have to   4 Do we have to   5 had to
6 mustn't   7 don't have to   8 did you have to
(Grammar B1)

C2

2 mustn't   3 doesn't have to   4 mustn't   5 mustn't
6 don't have to   7 don't have to   8 mustn't
(Grammar B2)

C3

1
2 needn't
2
1 need to   2 needn't
3
1 need to   2 needn't   3 needn't
(Grammar B3)

C4

2 needed   3 did you need   4 didn't need
(Grammar B3)

C5

Suggested answers:
2 You could offer to work extra hours.
3 You must arrive at work on time.
4 You ought to look tidy.
5 You shouldn't look bored.
6 You mustn't lose the key to the safe.
(Grammar B4)

C6

2 had   3 didn't have   4 should   5 shouldn't   6 'll have
7 needn't
(All grammar sections)

Exam practice

Sample answer:

There are lots of rules in my school too. We have to be at school by eight and we have to stay there until four. We're not allowed to go to town at lunchtime. We have to do homework every night and we mustn't give it in late. That's probably a good rule because it makes us do it! Other rules are that we have to be polite and we mustn't run in the corridors. We have to wear school uniform but I hate that because the uniform is really old-fashioned. I think there are too many rules in my school.

Unit 15

A2

A a book   B a pen

A3

Photo A: 2 could   3 can't   4 must
Photo B: 5 may   6 can't   7 might   8 must

A4

1 3, 4, 6 and 8.
2 1, 2, 5 and 7.

A5

1 can you
2 are you able to
Yes, they mean the same.

C1

2 must 3 can't 4 might 5 could 6 can't 7 must
8 can't 9 might 10 may
(Grammar B1)

C2

Sample answers:

It must be Sweden.	It can't be Sweden. It might be South Africa. It must be Australia.	It can't be Nepal. It could be Australia. It must be Brazil.

(Grammar B1)

C3

2 could 3 can 4 couldn't 5 Can 6 can't 7 can 8 can't
9 couldn't 10 Could 11 couldn't 12 Can
(Grammar B2)

C4

2 Are 3 Will 4 weren't 5 won't be 6 hasn't been
7 to be 8 wasn't 9 Is 10 be 11 wasn't 12 isn't
(Grammar B2)

Exam practice

1 A 2 A 3 B 4 C 5 C

Grammar focus

1 We can't accept credit cards if you spend £5 or less.
2 It might be too difficult for Tom.
3 Can you take it back?
4 One free concert ticket for students who can serve
refreshments.
5 Gemma's gloves might be in Katie's bedroom.
6 Gemma's gloves must be in Katie's flat.
7 *no change*
8 He can't be on holiday.

Unit 16

A3

2 How long are you going to
3 Where did you sing
4 Have you been to
5 Who is
6 Whose music do you like

A4

b 1 c 4 d 5 e 2 f 3

A5

1 2, 3, 5, 6
2 1, 4
3 The answers for questions words are people or things. The
other answers are Yes or No.

C1

3 Are Sam and Emma getting married?
4 Did Bob drive to Malaga?
5 Has Joanne got lots of CDs?
6 Can you dive very well?
7 Does Eddy watch football every Saturday?
8 Has Adam seen that film?
9 Had Marc dropped his watch?
10 Were you late for school yesterday?
(Grammar B1)

C2

2 h 3 c 4 a 5 j 6 g 7 d 8 i 9 e 10 b
(Grammar B2)

C3

2 Why 3 How 4 Whose 5 Who 6 How long
7 How many 8 What 9 How much 10 What
11 When/What time
(Grammar B3)

C4

2 Where had he been on holiday?
3 What was he wearing?
4 Which island was he on?
5 Why did he have to come home suddenly?
6 Who phoned from London?
7 How did he get/travel to the airport?
8 How long did it take to get there?
9 Where is his brother?
10 When will he change his clothes?
(Grammar B3, B4)

C5

If you agree, you say:
3 So have I. 4 So am I. 5 So was I.
6 Nor did I. *or* Neither did I. 7 So would I.
8 Nor could I. *or* Neither could I.
(Grammar B5)

C6

Sample answers:
1 Why did you decide to become an actor/footballer etc.?
2 How often do you visit Europe?
3 Where were you born?
4 Who helped you when you were young?
5 How long do you practise every day?
6 Do you enjoy your work?
(Grammar B1, B3, B4)

D

Exam practice

1 A 2 B 3 A 4 B 5 A 6 A

Grammar focus

1 have you got
2 is this trip going to take
3 are you going to visit
4 's going
5 Does ... work
6 do you like
7 have
8 did
9 does
10 do

Unit 17

A2

She mentions all of them except the campsite and the Internet café.

A3

YOU ARE HERE

A4

1 T   2 F (you can walk or cycle)   3 F (they are at the east end of the lake)   4 F (it's over the disco)   5 T

C1

2 g 3 b 4 a 5 j 6 c 7 d 8 i 9 e 10 f
(Grammar B1)

C2

2 in 3 onto 4 below 5 in 6 into 7 at 8 on top of
9 above/over   10 off
(Grammar B1, B2)

C3

2 on top of 3 round 4 over 5 along 6 under 7 through
8 above 9 across   10 over
(Grammar B2, B3)

C4

2 on 3 above/over   4 behind   5 above   6 on/on top of
7 beside/by/next to   8 opposite   9 in front of
10 beside/by/next to
(Grammar B1, B2, B4)

C5

Follow models in C4.

C6

2 She watched the children run ~~onto~~ into the park to the bus stop.
3 Timmy saw Mel ~~in~~ at the party but he didn't speak to her.
4 Andy ran ~~through~~ along the beach to the next village and came back by bus.
5 I took the ticket out ~~from~~ of my bag and gave it to the man by the door.
6 Please don't park ~~behind~~ in front of my window – I can't see anything.
7 We were very tired when we arrived ~~at~~ in Paris after a long flight.
8 Jacky hid ~~between~~ behind a car when she saw Lewis because she didn't want to speak to him.
9 I called ~~in~~ at Rebecca's house, but she wasn't at home.
10 The guide held a small flag ~~on top of~~ above her head so that the tourists could follow her easily.
(Grammar B1, B2, B3, B4)

Exam practice

Sample answer:

Bunbury is on the coast. There are lots of factories in the east and south of it, but most people live on the north side of the town, near the beaches. The sports centre is in that part of the town too. It's in a park. My school is behind the sports centre, and I often walk through the park on my way home. Sometimes I play football there.

The town centre has also got a lot of shops and a big art gallery. We can go to them when you visit. There's a good cinema opposite the gallery, too.

Unit 18

A1

A rugby   B football   C basketball   D tennis   E motor-racing
F rock-climbing   G marathon

A2

G, B, A, E, D

A3

2 for 3 – 4 on 5 at 6 in 7 at; for 8 until 9 on
10 during   11 in   12 at

A4

1 July, the summer
2 the end of the month, sunrise, the moment
3 the 18th, my birthday,
4 a match
5 one or two hours, hours
6 five o'clock
7 next month

C1

2 New Year 3 14th June 4 last 5 the nineteenth century
6 their wedding anniversary 7 the moment 8 the 1950s
9 the evening 10 the end of this lesson
(Grammar B1)

C2

2 at 3 in 4 – 5 at 6 in 7 on 8 at 9 – 10 until
11 at 12 on 13 until 14 by
(Grammar B1, B3)

C3

2 during 3 until 4 by 5 In 6 for
(Grammar B2, B3)

C4

2 at 3 on 4 till/until 5 on 6 in 7 during 8 until
9 by 10 in 11 until 12 for
(Grammar B1, B2, B3.)

Exam practice

1 C 2 D 3 A 4 B 5 C

Grammar focus task

2 at 3 in/during 4 in/during 5 for 6 in 7 in

Unit 19

A1

They're triplets.

A2

She's worried about applying to university. She thinks her sisters
might get a place and she won't.

A3

2 of 3 in 4 at 5 in 6 about 7 about 8 on 9 for

A4

1 prepositions
2 the -ing form
3 nouns

A5

1 check = look through
2 complete = fill in
3 have a good relationship = get on well

C1

2 by; on 3 at; at; in 4 by; on 5 by; on 6 in; in 7 at; on
8 by; in 9 in; by
(Grammar B1)

C2

2 the children from coming in. 3 on helping him.
4 Ellen for helping him/for her help. 5 for breaking the jug.
6 Sue for breaking the jug. 7 in passing their exam.
8 the driver to help her.
(Grammar B2, B3)

C3

2 f 3 d 4 b 5 c 6 a
(Grammar B4)

C4

2 The nurses have been very kind to you, you mustn't be rude
~~with~~ to them.
3 There are boats ~~at~~ for hire here, or we can go for a swim.
4 Are you in this country ~~for~~ on holiday or are you working?
5 My parents don't approve ~~on~~ of some of my friends.
6 Did the manager insist ~~in~~ on changing your a day off?
7 My mother's ~~in~~ at work at the moment, but she can phone you
this evening.
(Grammar B1, B2, B4)

C5

arrived – turned up
became – turned into
connected – put through
delayed – held up
entered – got into
refused – turned down
removed – took away
(Grammar B5)

Grammar focus

1 on; for; for 2 I'm sorry

Exam practice

Sample answer:
Hi Gracie
Congratulations on your exam results! That's brilliant news.
Thanks for asking me to your party but I can't come. I have to go
to my cousin's wedding. I'm so sorry. I hope we can meet soon.
I'll phone next week.
Love
Freya

Unit 20

A2

1 Her job 2 Finishing his essay early and looking for
information/planning a holiday

A3

2 F 3 E 4 A 5 B 6 G 7 H 8 I 9 C

A4

The -ing form.

C1

2 smoking 3 No eating or drinking 4 Cycling
5 No talking 6 Playing games
(Grammar B1)

C2

2 Check the address before posting the parcel.
3 Read the instructions before connecting the mouse to the keyboard.
4 Ask the price when booking seats for the concert.
5 Take a holiday after passing your exam.
(Grammar B2)

C3

2 since   3 while   4 before   5 After   6 after   7 when
8 before
(Grammar B2)

C4

2 studying   3 shopping   4 after eating   5 swimming
6 Before going   7 since starting   8 without dieting
9 by emailing   10 for texting
(Grammar B1, B2, B3, B4)

Exam practice

1 B   2 A   3 B   4 C   5 B

Grammar focus task

1 Taking photographs
2 come swimming
3 when leaving
4 without making, without having to make, without checking
5 since joining

Unit 21

A1

1 B   2 A

A2

1 to wear   2 to sell   3 B   4 A

A3

2 wearing   3 practising   4 wearing   5 to check   6 making
7 me use   8 you decide   9 to wear   10 to use

A4

1 intend, remember, plan, (woul)d like
2 don't mind, suggest, hate, remember
3 remember
4 made, let

C1

 3 agreed to help
 4 refused to tell Sally
 5 ordered Euan not to use
 6 asked Zena to open
 7 promised not to forget
 8 intended to read ten books
 9 invited Aziza to stay
10 expected to see
(Grammar B1, B2)

C2

2 d   3 f   4 b   5 a   6 c
(Grammar B2, B3)

C3

3 to go   4 to get   5 going   6 to come   7 seeing   8 talking
9 to be   10 waiting   11 spending   12 wasting
(Grammar B2, B4)

C4

2 to look   3 travelling   4 spending   5 to check   6 changing
7 phoning   8 to contact
(Grammar B5)

C5

2 to fly   3 to save or saving   4 not travelling   5 to come
6 to see   7 to get   8 share   9 to hear   10 to book
(All grammar sections)

Exam practice

1 C   2 B   3 D   4 A   5 D   6 D   7 B   8 C   9 B   10 B

Grammar focus

In 2, the other answers are wrong because they are followed by -ing not the to-infinitive.
In 4, the other answers are wrong because they are followed by the to-infinitive not -ing.
In 5, the other answers are wrong because they aren't followed by like.
In 7, the other answers are wrong because they are followed by the infinitive without to, not the to-infinitive.
In 10, the other answers are wrong because they are followed by the to-infinitive not -ing.

Unit 22

A1

a souvenir shop

A2

1 Because she wants to travel abroad (before she goes to university)
2 a camera shop
3 on Monday (morning)

A3

2 'll earn extra money.
3 they have to wait.
4 the shop loses customers.
5 unless I phone you.
6 'll start at nine o'clock.
7 'll go to South America.
8 'll go round Europe.

A4

1 3, 4
2 1, 2, 5, 6, 7, 8.

A5

if not

A6

No (see B4)

C1

2 If   3 when   4 if   5 if
(Grammar B1.)

C2

Sample answers:
2 the music is good.   3 they're bored.   4 they have no money.
5 my homework is difficult.   6 they tell the truth.
(Grammar B2)

C3

2 will die   3 learn   4 'll/will buy   5 will eat   6 will tell
7 don't enjoy   8 will buy   9 become   10 'll/will take
(Grammar B3)

C4

2 unless   3 unless   4 won't go   5 unless   6 I'm not
(Grammar B2, B3, B4)

C5

3 I come   4 will you be   5 The dog will bark / barks
6 you ring   7 the dog barks   8 it'll disturb   9 he wakes
10 he'll be   11 He won't let   12 he's   13 will you see
14 I wait   15 it rains
(Grammar B3)

Exam practice

1 B   2 A   3 A   4 A   5 B   6 A   7 B   8 A   9 B   10 B

Grammar focus

2 apply; c 'll receive   3 don't bring; h 'll be   4 won't be; g fail
5 decides; e won't be   6 're; f 'll send   7 succeed; a won't be
8 'll receive; b wins

Unit 23

A2

his university studies
life in the music business
the clothes he likes

A3

2 wasn't   3 went   4 had   5 wasn't

A4

1 past simple
2 No, they are talking about the present or the future.

C1

2 practised   3 didn't eat   4 didn't wear   5 gave   6 didn't make
(Grammar B2)

C2

2 would/'d sleep   3 wouldn't catch   4 would/'d have
5 wouldn't lose   6 wouldn't be
(Grammar B2)

C3

2 didn't have   3 worked   4 earned   5 owned   6 didn't live
7 wasn't
(Grammar B3.)

C4

2 didn't want   3 would stay   4 didn't come   5 would enjoy
6 went   7 would meet   8 went   9 had   10 wouldn't go
(Grammar B2, B3)

C5

Sample answers:
2 I'd wear beautiful clothes.   3 teenagers wouldn't argue with
their parents.   4 everyone would pass them.   5 I'd go surfing
every day.   6 I wouldn't need to do this exercise.   7 they
wouldn't win elections.   8 a motorbike.
(Grammar B2, B3)

Exam practice

1 B   2 D   3 A   4 D   5 C

Grammar focus

2 was/were;   wouldn't be
3 was/were;   could stay
4 would
5 was/were;   would spend
6 'd (would) write;   had
7 could

Unit 24

A2

alien army earth garage human planet scientist spaceship
Maria does decide to see the film.

A3

2 was given   3 's/is taken   4 is damaged; aren't hurt
5 is arrested   6 'll/will be rescued

A4

We use the verb *to be* in the correct form:
the present – is
the past – was/were
the future – will be

C1

2 was marked [P]   told [A]
3 is having [A]   're invited. [P]
4 were sent [P]   saw [A]
5 will be finished [P]   think [A]   'll be [A]
6 paid [A]   opened [A]
7 expect [A]   to be met [P]
8 want [A]   to find [A]
9 to be cleaned [P]   'll help [A]
(Grammar B1)

C2

2 The plane tickets are booked.
3 Contracts are sent to concert hall managers.
4 Hotel rooms are reserved.
5 Posters are designed.
6 Musicians are hired.
(Grammar B1)

C3

2 was given   3 was seen   4 were asked   5 weren't paid
6 were heard   7 was asked   8 wasn't given   9 was invited
(Grammar B1)

C4

2 made   3 was written   4 will enjoy   5 isn't visited   6 read
7 didn't receive   8 will watch   9 were worn   10 won't play
(Both grammar sections)

C5

2 has the furniture changed   3 have my nails painted
4 have my hair washed   5 have my clothes ironed
6 have a meal delivered
(Grammar B2)

Exam practice

1 C   2 E   3 A   4 G   5 F

Grammar focus

2 gives   3 take   4 provides   5 expects   6 organises
7 offers   8 encourages

Unit 25

A2

1 She was angry.
2 He hadn't washed up or tidied the house.
3 He offered to wash up.
4 She'd paid him to wash the car.
5 He hasn't got any money.
6 He offers to lend Nick some money.

A3

1 hadn't   2 was expecting; was   3 would   4 should   5 had
6 was

A4

b 1   c 5   d 2   e 4   f 6
should doesn't change

C1

2 're/are going to be   3 've never flown   4 must/have to
5 bought   6 should   7 'm/am waiting   8 love   9 'll/will send
10 's/is looking
(Grammar B1)

C2

2 couldn't get   3 'd/had arrived   4 were going to wait
5 'd/had never eaten   6 was   7 wouldn't be
8 'd/had expected   9 hadn't reserved   10 were going
(Grammar B1)

C3

2 I   3 I   4 here   5 last week   6 yesterday   7 this   8 you
9 this evening   10 tomorrow
(Grammar B2)

C4

2 the day before   3 she'd climbed   4 had kissed her
5 she'd/would never wash   6 she was going to get   7 the next
day   8 she couldn't think   9 she'd read   10 she might write
(All grammar sections)

Exam practice

1 to live   2 I want   3 as nice as   4 is   5 've never seen

Grammar focus

1 didn't like   2 could help   3 'd/would lend
4 was going to visit

Unit 26

A1

The report doesn't match the headline. The headline is about the
footballer's private life - what he does away from the football
field. The article is about his life as a footballer.

A2

Tim's boss is angry because he didn't ask any questions about the
footballer's private life.

A3

2 ✓   4 ✓   6 ✓   10 ✓

A4

1 why; hadn't scored
2 if; watched

A5

1 4; 10
2 2; 6
3 We use if to report questions which we can answer with Yes or
No.
4 The word order doesn't change.

C1

2 told   3 said   4 said   5 told   6 said   7 said   8 told
(Grammar B1)

C2

2 to have breakfast.   3 not to be late.   4 to wear a hat.
5 not to wear leather shoes.   6 to bring a packed lunch.
7 not to bring expensive cameras.   8 not to fall in.
(Grammar B2)

C3

2 reminded   3 ordered   4 invited/asked   5 reminded
6 asked   7 ordered
(Grammar B2)

C4

2 Can you play any instruments
3 Are you going to make a film
4 Which countries have you visited
5 Do you sing with other people
6 Why did you become a singer
7 How many CDs have you recorded
8 Are you planning any trips
9 What is your favourite CD
10 Do you feel nervous on stage
(Grammar B3)

C5

2 if there's a swimming pool?
3 if this city has underground trains?
4 how long we're staying here.
5 if we're going on a river trip.
6 where the nearest bank is?
7 if the hotel can change my room.
8 when it gets dark?
(Grammar B4)

Exam task

1 D   2 C   3 B   4 D   5 B

Grammar focus

2 to lend her some money.
3 She said she needed to buy
4 if they knew what she had done
5 they didn't believe me
6 I was jealous of her
7 refused to listen to me
8 I should do now

Unit 27

A1

a soap opera; the news; a sports programme

A2

1 They visit the studios in this order: news studio; soap opera;
  sports room.
2 a newsreader (Gavin) and a footballer (Jack)

A3

2 which   3 whose   4 which   5 where   6 which   7 who
8 whose

A4

1 Yes, you can take out the relative pronoun in sentences 1 (*who*)
  and 4 (*which*).
2 You can replace the relative pronouns in sentences 1, 2, 4, 6
  and 7 with *that*.

C1

2 which cost £200.
3 who lives in Australia.
4 which doesn't work.
5 who won a music competition on television last night.
6 who worked for a film company.
(Grammar B1 and B2)

C2

2 Here's the book ~~which~~ I promised to lend you.
3 Why did you change the plan ~~that~~ we made?
4 That's the hotel which has a swimming pool on the roof.
5 Where's the bunch of flowers ~~that~~ you bought yesterday?
6 Elaine wrote to the university that had offered her a place.
7 This is the letter that caused all our problems.
8 I emailed all the people ~~who~~ my boss wanted to see.
9 Andrew is the man who won the science prize.
10 When will you finish the work ~~which~~ I asked you to do?
(Grammar B3)

C3

2 where   3 whose   4 who   5 which   6 where   7 which
8 whose   9 which   10 who
(Grammar B2, B3, B4)
You can cross out *who* in 4, *which* in 5 and *which* in 7.

C4

2 who/that lived next door when I was small.
3 who/that gave me guitar lessons last year.
4 (who/that) I met at Spanish lessons.
5 where we're staying (which we're staying at).
6 where the party will be.
7 (which/that) I've bought for Herman.
8 whose party we're going to.
(Grammar B2, B3, B4)

Exam task

1 C   2 E   3 A   4 G   5 H

Grammar focus task

1 which   2 which   3 who   4 which   5 which   6 which
7 where   8 which   9 whose   10 which
a Sentences 1, 2, 3, 4, 5, 6, 8 and 10
b Sentences 1 and 4

Unit 28

A1

They're going to a party. Max isn't ready / doesn't know what to
wear.

A2

He should lose weight / walk to work / walk more quickly / join a
gym / take more exercise.

A3

2 too   3 so   4 so   5 such   6 enough   7 too; too   8 enough

A4

1 silly, easily   2 a lazy person   3 fruit   4 smart, quickly
5 small, much, many

C1

2 such   3 so   4 so   5 so   6 such   7 so   8 such   9 so
10 such
(Grammar B1)

C2

2 f   3 g   4 b   5 d   6 c   7 a
(Grammar B2)

C3

2 isn't big enough (for all your clothes)   3 too much work (to
do / to finish it all)   4 isn't heavy/warm enough   5 enough
CDs   6 too fast/quickly   7 is/'s too long   8 too many glasses
9 hasn't enough memory   10 didn't get up early enough
(Grammar B3)

C4

2 for   3 to   4 to   5 for   6 to
(Grammar B4)

Exam practice

1 surprised   2 many   3 old enough   4 Don't   5 lets

Grammar focus

1 I was so shocked I didn't know what to say.
2 I have so much money I don't know what to spend it on.
3 My father said I wasn't big/tall enough to be a firefighter.

Unit 29

A1

A D B C

A2

Orville is arrested.

A3

2 as   3 because   4 because of   5 so   6 so

A4

They all mean the same except for 5 (see B1 and B2).

C1

2 because   3 because   4 because of   5 because
(Grammar B1)

C2

2 e   3 f   4 c   5 a   6 b
(Grammar B1, B2, B3)

C3

2 so she goes to lots of concerts.   3 because thieves steal from
parked cars.   4 because she was feeling sick.   5 so he got a job.
6 because she enjoyed sport.   7 so she went for a walk.
8 so he opened it.
(Grammar B1,B3)

C4

2 to tour   3 to use   4 to lose   5 to make   6 to mend
(Grammar B3)

C5

2 so   3 because   4 since   5 so   6 to   7 to   8 because
9 so   10 as
(Grammar B1, B2, B3)

C6

2 S   3 D   4 S   5 D   6 D
(Grammar B1, B2, B3)

Exam practice

1 B   2 A   3 A   4 B   5 B   6 B   7 A   8 A   9 B   10 A

Grammar focus

2 because he was injured
3 (in order) to play for the first team
4 so (that) they can get football qualifications
5 (in order) to have a chance to train at the football club
6 so (that) they feel part of the club
7 because the club had very little money
8 because the money wasn't available

Unit 30

A1

The brochure didn't show him that the hotel was on a busy road.

A2

The San Francisco

A3

2 Although   3 both   4 both; and   5 Although   6 In spite of
7 as soon as   8 when   9 either; or

A4

1F We use *but* and *although* when we contrast two different
   ideas. (see B1)
2T
3T
4F We don't use the future tense after *as soon as*. (see B5)
5T

C1

2 Elena speaks Polish though she's never been to Poland.
3 Although Zach didn't want to go to the disco, he enjoyed it when he got there.
4 Mum still buys fruit though no-one eats it.
5 Though Dennis didn't get good marks in his exams, he went to university.
6 Mahmoud is the shop manager, although he's only nineteen.
(Grammar B1)

C2

3 Either Tom or Martin sent that email.
4 Dolores was working in the garden despite the hot sun.
5 Her dress and her jacket are both new. *or* Both her dress and her jacket are new.
6 Michael wasn't late in spite of a/the traffic jam.
7 My father and my mother both gave me some money. *or* Both my father and my mother gave me some money.
8 Either do your homework now or get up early and do it tomorrow.
9 You can either go on your bike or come with me in the car.
(Grammar B2, B3)

C3

2 after 3 as soon as 4 until 5 while 6 before 7 when
8 when
(Grammar B4.)

C4

2 begins 3 arrive 4 'll stay 5 go 6 leave 7 'll tour
8 runs 9 'm 10 are
(Grammar B4)

C5

2 correct
3 We had a good time at the beach in spite of ~~the weather was windy~~ the windy weather.
or ... beach although/though the weather was windy.
4 correct
5 We'll leave the restaurant as soon as the waiter ~~will bring~~ brings our bill.
6 This room is terribly untidy! ~~Or~~ Either help me to tidy it or go away.
7 correct
8 I don't play an instrument although my father and my mother ~~both~~ are both musicians.
9 correct
(Grammar B1, B2, B3, B4, B5)

Exam practice

1 A 2 C 3 A 4 B 5 B

Grammar focus

2 This clinic is closed while the doctor ~~will be~~ is on holiday.
3 Although I'd like to come out with you, ~~but~~ I won't be able to because I'm babysitting.
4 Hotel guests can either eat in the dining-room ~~and~~ or beside the pool.
5 I enjoyed the film in spite of ~~the actors were very bad~~ the bad actors/acting.

Grammar glossary

adjective
A word which tells us about
- a **noun**:
  *a **long** holiday; an **interesting** idea*
- or a **pronoun**:
  *They feel **happy**.*

adverb
A word which tells us
- about a **verb**:
  *The plane landed **safely**.*
  *I met him **yesterday**.*
  *Our team played **well**.*
- or an **adjective**
  *It's a **very** old motorbike.*

auxiliary verb
A **verb** (e.g. *be, do, have*) which we use with a **main verb** in some tenses:
*My friends **are** singing.*
*She **didn't** listen.*
***Has** he written the letter?*

determiner
A short word which goes in front of a **noun**:
***some** bread, **every** customer*

imperative
A **verb** which gives an order:
***Wait** here, please.*
***Be** quiet!*

infinitive
The basic form of a **verb** which we can use after other verbs, often with *to*:
*Maisie wants **to go** home.*
*You could **get** a taxi.*

main verb
The part of a **verb** which gives its meaning (compare **auxiliary**):
*He is **cooking**.*
*We don't **have** any coffee.*
*Did you **enjoy** the film?*

modal verb
A special kind of **verb** which we use with an **infinitive** to give extra meaning:
*He **can** drive.*
*They **shouldn't** talk here.*
***May** we sit here?*

noun
A word for a person or thing:
*A **woman** spoke to the **crowd** of **students**.*
*This is the **café** where we had **lunch**.*
*Can you give me some **information**?*

object
A **noun** or **pronoun** which follows a **verb**:
*Let's play **chess**.*
*We don't like **him**.*
*Has she found **her keys**?*
*Ana sent **me an email**. [2 objects]*

participle
The -*ing* form of the **verb** (e.g. *playing, speaking*) or the past participle (e.g. *played, spoken*) which we use with **auxiliary** verbs to make **tenses**:
*The girls are **playing** tennis.*
*I've **spoken** to my teacher.*
-*ing* can sometimes be a **noun**:
***Studying** is hard work.*
*I enjoy **shopping**.*
A participle can sometimes be an **adjective**:
*a **boring** film; the **tired** child*

preposition
A short word which usually goes in front of a **noun** or **pronoun** and links it to other words:
*Carole's **in** the sitting-room.*
*This parcel is **for** you.*
*We ran **under** the bridge.*
*My train leaves **at** midnight.*

pronoun
A word used in the place of a **noun**:
*Sara took some photos and **she** showed **them** to Robbie.*
*Did **you** speak to **him**?*

sentence
A group of words in which there is usually a **verb** and its **subject** or **object**.
In writing, sentences begin with a capital letter.
A sentence can
- make a **statement**:
  This CD is mine.
- ask a question:
  Is this your CD?
- give an instruction (see **imperative**):
  Listen to this CD.
- be an exclamation:
  This CD is brilliant!

statement
A **sentence** which tells us some information:
Francis is eating ice cream.
His brother doesn't want anything.

subject
The person or thing which does the **verb**:
***Eddie** went to Italy.*
***This photo** is beautiful.*
***Swimming** is fun.*
*Do **you** like this music?*
*Why are **you** here?*

tense
The form of a **verb** which gives extra information, e.g. about the time it happens:
*He **likes** football.*   (= present simple tense)
*He **liked** volleyball.*   (= past simple tense)
*He **was playing** very well.* (= past continuous tense)

verb
A word which describes what happens:
*I **watched** a film.*
*We **feel** sad.*

CD Tracklisting

Recording	CD1 track
Title information	1
1	2
2	3
3	4
4	5
5	6
6	7
7	8
8a	9
8b	10
9	11
10	12
11a	13
11b	14
12	15
13a	16
13b	17

Recording	CD2 track
14	1
15	2
16a	3
16b	4
17	5
18	6
19	7
20	8
21	9
22	10
23	11
24	12
25	13
26	14
27	15
28	16
29	17
30	18